Aging, Death, and Human Longevity

Aging, Death, and Human Longevity

A Philosophical Inquiry

Christine Overall

UNIVERSITY OF CALIFORNIA PRESS

Berkeley   Los Angeles   London

heal

0140738833

University of California Press
Berkeley and Los Angeles, California

University of California Press, Ltd.
London, England

Library of Congress Cataloging-in-Publication Data

Overall, Christine, 1949–
    Aging, death, and human longevity : a philosophical
inquiry / Christine Overall.
       p.   cm.
    Includes bibliographical references and index.
    ISBN 0-520-24487-7 (pbk: alk. paper)
      1. Aging.   2. Longevity.   3. Terminal care.
   I. Title.

RA564.8 .O95   2003
305.26—dc21   2002001861

Manufactured in the United States of America
12 11 10 09 08 07 06 05
10 9 8 7 6 5 4 3 2 1

The paper used in this publication is both acid-free
and totally chlorine-free (TCF). It meets the minimum
requirements of ANSI/NISO Z39.48-1992 (R 1997)
(*Permanence of Paper*).

For my "big sister,"
Kathy Silver

CONTENTS

ACKNOWLEDGMENTS

This has been an exciting book to write. I've been fortunate to have the opportunity of talking to wonderful people, both in formal academic contexts and in informal conversation, about human longevity issues. For their questions, comments, and suggestions I am grateful to the audiences at the Queen's University Department of Philosophy Colloquium Series (1999, 2000, and 2001), the Royal Society Kingston Seminar (Queen's University, 1999), the Annual Meeting of the Canadian Society for Women in Philosophy (McMaster University, 1999), the Champlain Society (Champlain College, Trent University, 1999), the Kingston Later Life Learning lecture series (1999), the conference "Feminist Utopias: Redefining Our Projects" (University of Toronto, 2000), the Applied Philosophy Lyceum Series, Middle Tennessee State University (2001), and the Annual Meeting of the Canadian Philosophical Association (Laval University, 2001), at all of which I presented sections of this book.

For the opportunity to discuss various aspects of these issues and for feedback on my ideas, I am grateful to Sylvat Aziz, David Bakhurst, Diane Ball, Samantha Brennan, Sylvia Burkinshaw, Jackie Davies, Nicholas Dixon, Leslie Elliott, Al Fell, Deborah Knight, Will Kymlicka, Henry Laycock, Steve Leighton, Alistair Macleod, Lisa McNee, Adèle Mercier, Ellen Merrin, Carlos Prado, Cindy Price, Millard Schumaker, Kathy

Silver, Jack Stevenson, Christine Sypnowich, Don White, Narnia Worth, and Ted Worth. Thanks to Samantha Brennan for believing in the value of this investigation and for alerting me to a number of sources that I might otherwise have missed and to Jennifer Parks for her encouragement and for providing several references. Special thanks to Sue Donaldson for nutritional guidance and for her wholehearted support for the subject of this book, her stimulating conversation, and her extraordinary insights into the issues.

Thank you to Maxine Wilson, Jackie Doherty, and all my colleagues in the Department of Philosophy, and to the dedicated, hard-working, and knowledgeable associate deans and staff in the office of the Faculty of Arts and Science, Queen's University. Dean of Arts and Science Bob Silverman is a model of courageous and witty leadership. Quietly and resourcefully, Diane Reid has transformed my working life and made it much easier to handle my administrative role. Steve Leighton, Carlos Prado, and Nancy Cutway patiently provided much-needed computer information and help. Jane Isaacs-Doyle was an effective and efficient research assistant, locating much of the necessary empirical information for this study. Jan Allen, of the Agnes Etherington Art Centre, kindly contributed to my quest for book-cover images.

At the University of California Press, Eric Smoodin, formerly the film, media, and philosophy editor, was supportive and encouraging from the start. I am fortunate that he shares my passion for this project. In the last stages of the book I was assisted by David Gill, project editor, and Kate Toll, acquisitions editor. The external reviewers, Anita Silvers, Department of Philosophy, San Francisco State University, and Rosemarie Tong, Department of Philosophy, University of North Carolina at Charlotte, provided incisive and insightful commentaries at key points in the development of the manuscript. Pamela Fischer is a superb copy editor who preserved and enhanced the spirit of the book while also reducing its unnecessary wordiness.

My generous friends Kathy Silver, Ruth Dubin, Beth Morris, Sue Hendler, Steve Leighton, Margaret Hagel, Tom Russell, Audrey Kobayashi, Roberta Hamilton, Bev Baines, Roberta Lamb, and Anna Kim, all of them attentive listeners and astute observers, have sustained me throughout my research and writing. Each in her own way, Diana Wyatt and Adriana Vanderhelm have been indispensable; my thanks to both of them. Lucy Haworth, my sculling partner, provided stability and direction during our doubles practices at the Kingston Rowing Club.

My deep love and gratitude go to my mother, Dorothy Edith Kathleen Bayes Overall, to my life partner, Ted Worth, and to my children, Devon Worth and Narnia Worth, who are the best possible reasons for me to want to live a very long life. Finally, I want to express my appreciation to my cousins, Don White and Melba White, my aunts, Mary Desson and Gwenyth Bayes, my parents-in-law, Catherine Worth and Arthur Worth, and, posthumously, my grandmothers, Hazel Irene Bayes and Daisy Emma Overall, and my grandfather Charles William Bayes, for their positive examples of aging happily. With their gusto for life all of them have shown me that we should make the very most of the only life we have.

ONE

Introduction

"Death Twitches My Ear"

Death twitches my ear. "Live," he says. "I am coming."
Virgil, Minor Poems,
quoted in Bartlett 1968, 119[1]

In its entry on the subject "death" *The Oxford Companion to Philosophy* states, "Apart from trying to avoid it for as long as possible the philosopher has two main problems about death: What is it? And why does it matter?" (Honderich 1995, 177). But this claim begs the question of why the philosopher—or anyone else, for that matter—should attempt to avoid death for as long as possible. Whether we should try to prolong our lives and postpone our deaths for as long we can is a genuine, difficult, and significant question. This book inquires into that issue, which goes to the heart of speculation about why we (ought to) value our lives and what gives human existence meaning.

Philosophers have not all agreed about whether it is beneficial to think about one's own impending mortality, the condition of being subject to death. As Mary Mothersill (1999, 10) points out (with only a little exaggeration), philosophical opinion appears to be divided between those who think that such contemplations will induce a requisite and laudable change in one's present behavior and values and those who believe such thoughts are a waste of time or, worse, an invitation to depression and lassitude and a second-rate substitute for more valuable activities.[2]

I believe it is neither immature nor irresponsible to dwell on human mortality. Indeed, it is contrary to the history and spirit of the philosophical enterprise to declare a topic off limits for philosophical thought—even, or maybe especially, if thinking about it causes negative emotions. In Muriel Spark's novel *Memento Mori*, the characters repeatedly receive anonymous phone messages, conveyed in different voices, saying, "Remember you must die." One character, Henry Mortimer, believes much can be learned from these unidentified callers. He remarks to the other characters:

> If I had my life over again I should form the habit of nightly
> composing myself to thoughts of death. I would practise, as it
> were, the remembrance of death. There is no other practise which
> so intensifies life. Death, when it approaches, ought not to take one
> by surprise. It should be part of the full expectancy of life. Without
> an ever-present sense of death life is insipid. You might as well live
> on the whites of eggs. . . . Now, one factor is constant in all your
> reports. The words, "Remember you must die." It is, you know,
> an excellent thing to remember this, for it is nothing more than
> the truth. To remember one's death is, in short, a way of life.
> (Spark 1959, 150–151)

To keep directly before one's mind the observation that human beings are mortal, that most obvious and banal fact of human existence, and to further remind oneself that one is included within that most dreadful generalization, is a stimulus to ongoing reflection about the nature and purpose of one's life. It is a reminder that, whatever apparent security medical science and technology may offer, our lives are fragile and our connection to a personal future only tenuous.

Although thoughts of death can at times produce depression and lassitude, such feelings are a signal of the significance of the topic and do not therefore show that it ought not to be contemplated. Moreover, if they are handled carefully, these feelings are not necessarily an impediment to creative inquiry. It seems unlikely that philosophical thinking about mortality is a waste of time, unless it should turn out that it is impossible to say anything of value on the subject—an outcome that I hope the succeeding chapters will obviate. Indeed, one theme of this book is that thinking about mortality and longevity may give new life to perennial philosophical questions about human purposes and values.

AUTOBIOGRAPHICAL REMARKS

> But, at my back, I always hear
> Time's winged chariot hurrying near
> *Marvell 1964, 243*

Part of what brought me to the study of philosophy was the desire to make some sense of my own and others' mortality. I write this book as a middle-aged woman, born in 1949. When I celebrated my fiftieth birthday I was compelled to acknowledge that I probably had less than half my life left. As May Sarton observes, "It is only past the meridian of fifty that one can believe that the universal sentence of death applies to oneself" (quoted in Heilbrun 1997, 75). This book is the result of my attempt to face death, both as a general fact and as a particular constraint of my own life and of the lives of everyone about whom I care. I seek to confront the reality of my own finite longevity and diminishing life duration and to examine the reasons for and against desiring to live longer.

Consciousness of my own mortality and that of those whom I love has been a theme of my cognitive life since I was quite young. When I first grasped the fact of death as a small child, I would lie awake many a night, seeking but never finding comfort for the fact that the lives of all the people whom I knew and most cared about would end. Because for years I implicitly felt, as perhaps many or most young people do, that I was immortal, I was kept awake, at that time, not so much by a fear of my own death. Instead, my horror and fear of death were exacerbated by what seemed to me to be its injustice.

Now, it could be argued that my youthful feelings were founded on a category mistake. A so-called natural death—that is, a death that is not inflicted by the deliberate action of human beings—is not and cannot be a matter of either justice or injustice. Within a secular world-view there is no divine lawgiver who metes out death as a punishment to wrongdoers. Death just *is;* it is a defining condition of being a human being, and it is not only fruitless but also irrational to protest against death on moral grounds.

I agree that as far as we can discern, there is neither any cosmic system of justice nor any heavenly lawmakers or law enforcers who mete out death to human beings. I adopt a secular standpoint in this book, making no assumptions about the supposed truth of religion-based perspectives. It is indeed an error to suppose that death can be called unjust by reference to any divine system of justice, for there is no such system. But as a small child I had something more modest in mind: from the perspective of individual human beings, their projects and plans and their network of loved ones, death appears to be an inappropriate and disproportionate outcome for a lifetime that is often composed of hardship and struggle. An anonymous message circulating in 1999 on the Internet expresses this sentiment exactly: "The most unfair thing about life is the way it ends. I mean, life is tough. It takes up a lot of your time. What do you get at the end of it? A death. What's that, a bonus?" More poetically, Martha Nussbaum (1994, 209, 210) remarks:

> Death, when it comes, does not only frustrate projects and desires that just happen to be there. It intrudes upon the value and beauty of temporally evolving activities and relations. [Moreover,] at the deepest level, there is, when death arrives, the interruption of every one of [the] patterns of life—of work, of love, of citizenship, of play and enjoyment: the interruption, then, of a project that lies, however vaguely and implicitly, behind them all: the project of living a complete human life.[3]

Because, as I shall assume in this book, death is nonexistence, I am not arguing that death itself should be feared,[4] although a pain-ridden process of dying is a fearsome prospect. Being dead is not a dreadful state for by definition it is not a state (of a person) at all. Rather, it is the ending of life that I find dreadful. To die—not only to die in great pain or with great debility, but to die under any circumstances—appears to be an ignominious and senseless culmination of any life. In general, I say that human beings do not deserve to die.[5] And what I mean is that, within the context of the individual human life, people have almost always not done anything that in any way appears to make death a fitting outcome of their goals, hopes, strivings, and achievements.

My grandmother, Hazel Irene Bayes, died in 1994, when she was almost ninety-three years old. When I grieved her death, people attempted to comfort me by reminding me that she had had a long life. She had enjoyed many years of activities, experiences, and relationships. Like Sherwin Nuland, my would-be comforters believed that "old age is the preparation for departure, the gradual easing out of life that makes its ending more palatable not only for those who are elderly but for those also to whom they leave the world in trust" (Nuland 1994, 87). Was her long life a genuine compensation—or even just a suitable preparation—for her death, whether from her point of view or from the point of view of those who mourned her? At the time of her death I thought that although it is indeed better to live to 92 than just to 42, that comparative judgment does not mean that it would not be even better to live to 192, if that were possible. The greater length of some people's existence does not make their death any less senseless or disrespectful of their life projects. For an individual with my grandmother's exuberant love of life, an even more extended life span, if it could have been lived in reasonably good health, would have been better than the almost ninety-three years she enjoyed.

But perhaps, in my situation, I ought not to make such a judgment. As a feminist philosopher I acknowledge and try to adhere to feminist methodology, according to which it is essential, in any scholarly project, to be respectful of the beliefs and experiences of those who most closely live with and are affected by the topic or condition being researched. As a woman in midlife, I have wondered whether, in writing about aging, death, and the potential prolongation of human life, I am inappropriately encroaching on matters that most directly affect older people and about most of which they have much more direct experiential knowledge.

In this book I have certainly endeavored to be sensitive to and inclusive of the views of older individuals. Nonetheless, I believe, for three reasons, that it cannot be inappropriate for younger people such as I to explore and evaluate issues of human longevity. First, because mortality is a fact, perhaps *the* fact, of human life, any of us can die at any age. For that reason each of us should heed the advice "Remember you must die," and we are justified in being concerned about death and life-duration issues long before we reach old age. Second, age identity is one of the few biologically based identity categories through which people are fundamentally mobile. While middle-aged now, I shall one day, I believe and hope, join the cohort of elderly persons, and it is appropriate for me to think critically about a life condition in which I will eventually find myself, later if not sooner. Third, although I have a self-interested reason for being concerned about death and mortality, I also have grounds of solidarity and alliance for my concern. I am a relative of a number of old people and a friend of some others, and I am deeply concerned about their future prospects as well as my own. For all these reasons, then, I do not regard aging, impending death, and human longevity as the domain solely of those who are elderly. In writing this book, I have sought to understand an issue that I regard as intimately my own.

LIFE EXPECTANCY
AND MAXIMUM LONGEVITY

According to Psalm 90, verse 10, "The days of our years are threescore years and ten; and if by reason of strength they be fourscore years, yet is their strength labor and sorrow; for it is soon cut off, and we fly away."

In response to this venerable statement, feminist literary critic Carolyn Heilbrun (1997, 7) says:

> [I had] always considered this biblical life span to be a highly reasonable one. Having reached my seventieth year, I did not at once search for reasons to question its veracity. True, my life was good. But is it not better to leave at the height of well-being rather than contemplate the inevitable decline and the burden one becomes upon others? . . . Now, turning seventy, I recalled a snatch of conversation from an Ivy Compton-Burnett novel. One of the characters says: "Cassius was not of an age to die." "What is the age?" her sister asks. "About seventy," a brother answers, "when we have had our span, and people have not begun to think the less of us." Well, I thought, that's where I am.

But I wonder whether we should accept Heilbrun's judgment. In the present time, the early twenty-first century, is a life of threescore years and ten "highly reasonable," as she claims? Or is it instead both reasonable and beneficial to hope and strive for a life that is longer than the biblical norm? In order to decide, we need first to distinguish between life expectancy, the average age at death of a specific cohort of people, and maximum life span, which is the outer limit of human longevity, "the age beyond which virtually no one, however far he may be above the average, can expect to live" (Gruman 1977, 7).

In the industrialized nations life expectancy is growing. As life expectancy increases, there will be more and more older people in better and better health. According to Thomas Perls and Margery Hutter Silver (1999, xii), in 1999 one out of ten people on this planet was age sixty or older, and by the year 2050 the statistic will be one in three. In Canada, for example, the increases in life expectancy are especially large for people over sixty-five; the number of individuals over sixty-five years of age more than doubled in the twenty-five years before 1997 (Moore and Rosenberg 1997, 12). According to the census, in 1996, 787,700 people were eighty years or over in Canada, which was a 19.3 percent increase from

1991 and over twice the number of people eighty years or older eighty years previously; two-thirds of individuals eighty years and over were women (Statistics Canada 1997). By 1997, the latest year for which figures are available, the life expectancy of Canadian men had reached 75.8, and that of women, 81.4 (Statistics Canada 1997). Moreover, the number of years of "dependence-free life" in Canada is increasing, so that men are living 93 percent of their lives and women 88 percent of their lives in good health. "Dependence-freedom" is defined as the absence of physical dependence on others, except for help with heavy housework (Beauchesne 1999, 12).

In the United States, mean life expectancy increased by more than twenty-five years in the previous century. Over the previous two centuries, the increase was forty years, with more than a doubling of the mean life expectancy at birth since 1800 (Smith 1993, 113). In 1997 the life expectancy at birth for Americans was 76.5 years, an increase of 0.4 years from their 1996 life expectancy (Anderson 1999, 1). Life expectancy in 1997 for women was 79.4; for men, it was 73.6 (Anderson 1999, 3). Race strongly affects life expectancy in the United States: in 1997 the life expectancy for whites was 77.1, but the life expectancy for blacks was 71.2 (U.S. Bureau of the Census 1999). "Although the white-black difference in life expectancy narrowed from 15.8 years in 1900 to 5.7 years in 1982, it increased to 7.1 years in 1993 before declining from 1994 . . . to 1997. . . . The increase in the gap from 1983 to 1993 was largely the result of increases in mortality among the black male population due to HIV infection and homicide" (Anderson 1999, 3). This race-based disadvantage in life expectancy for black people is evident in statistics dating back to 1900, and projections until 2010 foresee the continuation of this liability, albeit to a diminished extent (Anderson 1999, 3). About one-third of the U.S. population survives beyond the age of eighty-five (Anderson 1999, 1). However, in terms of what the World Health Organization (2000) calls "Disability Adjusted Life Expectancy," or the number of years lived in full health, the United States ranks only twenty-fourth in the world, well behind nations such as Japan, Australia, France, Sweden, Spain, and Italy.

In general, women live longer than men, a pattern that may be centuries old. Indeed, in the United States the difference in life expectancy between women and men increased from 2.8 years to 7.8 years from 1900 to 1975, although after 1979 it narrowed again to 5.8 years (Anderson 1999, 3). "In all developed countries and most developing ones, women have greater life expectancy than men, sometimes by a margin of as much as ten years" (Perls and Silver 1999, 88). In nations such as India, Pakistan, and Bangladesh, where men's life expectancy is greater than that of women, the reason for this departure from the norm is at least partly discrimination against women, through practices such as female infanticide and bride burning (Perls and Silver 1999, 87–88).

A small but increasing number of people attain the age of one hundred, and throughout the world nine times more women than men are aged one hundred or more. The probability that people in the West will live to one hundred has been doubling approximately every ten years, "with the chances for women being about four times those for men" (Smith 1993, 122). In 1900, 0.03 percent of all Americans lived to one hundred; by 1997 the figure was 1.5 percent (Anderson 1999, 3). Perls and Silver (1999, 10, 11) suggest that about one in every 8,000–10,000 Americans is a centenarian, and they estimate that there could be nearly a million centenarians in the United States by 2050. Perls and Silver's New England Centenarian Study, an investigation of women and men aged one hundred and over, demonstrates, the researchers say, that "long life can mean a healthy, enjoyable life, a life with friends and loved ones close by, a life of satisfaction" (Perls and Silver 1999, xiii).

Demographer David Smith points out that the human species is the most long-lived of all warm-blooded animals.

> Our maximum species life span exceeds the minimum for species survival by a factor of three or four. . . . Human life expectancy

continues to increase, and there are sound reasons to expect this
increase to continue for many more years. A consequence is that
ever more people will reach advanced ages. The maximum human
life span as it is established today will be tested as it is approached
by greater numbers of individuals. There will be more outlyers as 1.5
percent of those born live to 100 years and beyond. (Smith 1993, 19)

Smith (1993, 124) predicts that the existing documented record of 120
years will in future be exceeded "at least marginally within the limits of
an unchanged potential maximum human life span."

Thus, although average life expectancy has increased enormously in
North America, the maximum life span has remained more or less fixed
at about 120. At this point, the longest-living human being whose life
span has been verified is French citizen Jeanne Calment, who was born
in 1875 and died in 1997 (Gendron 1999, 31). The empirical evidence
so far suggests that although human life expectancy probably can and will
continue to increase, the maximum life span may be much harder to
change. Some scientists, such as Nuland, acknowledge that life expectancy has increased well beyond the scriptural dictum but describe
the prospects for further extending the maximum human life span in pessimistic terms:

Whether the result of wear, tear, and exhaustion of resources or
whether genetically programmed, all life has a finite span and each
species has its own particular longevity. For human beings, this
would appear to be approximately 100 to 110 years. This means
that even were it possible to prevent or cure every disease that
carries people off before the ravages of senescence do, virtually
no one would live beyond a century or a bit more. . . .

Though biomedical science has vastly increased mankind's *average*
life expectancy, the *maximum* has not changed in verifiable recorded
history. In developed countries, only one in ten thousand people
lives beyond the age of one hundred. Whenever it has been possible
to examine critically the claims of supposed record-breakers, they
have not been substantiated. (Nuland 1994, 84–85, his emphasis)

In order to assess the potential prospects for increasing life expectancy and maximum life span and the possible value of improved longevity, we need to consider the conditions that may promote it. As Aristotle remarked many centuries ago, "The reasons for some animals being long-lived and others short-lived, and, in a word, the causes of the length and brevity of life call for investigation" (1984, 742).

The remarkable increases in life expectancy in North America over the past century are mainly the result of improvements in nutrition and water purity and developments in medicine and public health. These advances have produced reductions in infant mortality and in deaths due to infectious diseases (Moore and Rosenberg 1997, 11). For example, partly because of more hygienic feeding practices, infant mortality has declined dramatically. Whereas, in 1900, 87.6 percent of all babies born in the United States survived the first year of life, by 1997, 99.3 percent of all babies survived (Anderson 1999, 3). Care during pregnancy and delivery has also contributed to a sharp decline in maternal mortality. In addition, through the use of vaccinations against disease and the development of antibiotics, many of the causes of death in infants and young people have been limited or even eliminated (Smith 1993, 41). These diseases include smallpox, cholera, tuberculosis, measles, pneumonia, influenza, whooping cough, syphilis, poliomyelitis, typhoid, and diphtheria (Dychtwald and Flower 1989, 5).[6] Public health campaigns have contributed to a decline in the rate of smoking, with a concomitant drop in lung-cancer rates. Successful treatments of diseases such as heart disease, pneumonia, diabetes, and cancer have also extended life expectancy (Perls and Silver 1999, 9).

Within this context of increasing life expectancy, prospects are good for using new scientific techniques and improving public health practices to deliberately increase the average length of human life even further. Possible approaches to extending human longevity include the following:

- prevention of and cures for age-old deadly diseases, such as cancer, heart disease, and Alzheimer's, and for newer diseases, such as Acquired Immune-Deficiency Syndrome

- nutritional regimens, including calorie restriction and the consumption of antioxidant supplements (Yu 1999, 76–81)
- the use of hormones, including estrogen and testosterone, growth hormone, dehydroepiandrosterone, and melatonin (Yu 1999, 81–84)
- interventions in or modifications of the human genome to enable people to age more slowly and to resist diseases of aging (Smith 1993, 131; Hall 1999, D8; Perls and Silver 1999, 123)[7]
- therapies for regenerating or replacing damaged body parts (Momeyer 1988, 30)—for example, through the development of human embryonic stem cells
- the cloning of body parts, which would not be subject to rejection by the recipient's immune system[8]

Most important for the purposes of this book, altering "public attitudes concerning the desirability of prolonging the lives of very old people . . . and concerning laws and policies about the 'right to die'" (Smith 1993, 128) could have a genuine impact on how long people live. Our moral values and social policies with respect to human longevity and mortality create a context in which the probability of living longer may be increased or decreased. A cultural environment in which postponing mortality and increasing the length of the life span lived in health are valued could have a positive effect on human longevity.

THE PHILOSOPHICAL ISSUES

In light of this potential, it is important to examine the normative question of whether prolonged life should be sought. Biblical strictures notwithstanding, it seems better, *ceteris paribus*, that most human beings in the Western world now live longer than they did a century ago. To die at seventy or eighty or ninety seems better than dying at thirty or forty or fifty. If so, could it be even better to die at 100, 110, or 120? The complexity of this question and contemporary ambivalence about its answer are hinted at in a "Wizard of Id" comic strip. A physician says to the Spook, "The good news is you're going to live to be a hundred." The Spook asks, "What's the bad news?" The physician replies, "You're going to live to be a hundred" (Parker and Hart 1999).

Exploration of this issue raises central questions about the nature, value, and meaning of human life itself and its social and cultural context. What sorts of persons should we human beings seek to become? What kinds of lives should we live, and how, if at all, is the length of our lives related to what is possible and what is desirable for us? What, if any, are the implications of our increasing longevity with respect to our obligations to other persons and society as a whole? What are the potential social-policy outcomes of the assumptions we make about the desirable length of human life?

In this book I discuss the normative questions of whether increases in the length of human life are good or bad and whether they should be taken as a goal either individually or as a matter of social policy (or both). Hence, broadly speaking, my discussion has both theoretical and practical parts. On the level of the individual, the question is whether it is in the individual's interest to seek a longer life. Is wanting to live longer a rational desire? I argue that, other things being equal, it is. The social-policy question is whether the extension of human longevity would be good for and in the interests of the greater community, indeed for the collectivity of human beings. Would it be rational for a society to devote resources to scientific investigation, welfare and social assistance, and the development of health care in order to increase the average life expectancy or to extend the maximum life span? The answers here are less clear, and I shall identify some important strictures on the steps that I think societies should take, but I answer affirmatively, at least with respect to life expectancy.

In my discussion of the normative aspects of human longevity, I assume that, given the evidence (or, rather, the lack of evidence), human beings are not—at least at present!—in any way immortal and, in particular, that any form of survival of death is highly unlikely.[9] We do not know of any existence beyond death; this life on earth is the only one of which we can be assured. Hence issues of human longevity must be considered within that context: we are dealing with the only life we know that we have. For the sake of this discussion, I therefore adopt a skeptical outlook on religious promises of everlasting life after death.

However, the immortality that is promised by, for example, the Christian religion, and also by other religions that endorse concepts of reincarnation, and the widespread willingness to believe in this prospect show that many people are not ready to contemplate the end of their own conscious lives. These beliefs are de facto evidence of the widespread human desire to live as long as possible. Yet, despite the tendency of many religious adherents to believe in the indefinite prolongation of life after death, there need be no inevitable relationship between one's spiritual beliefs and one's attitude toward longevity here on earth. Belief in an afterlife does not obviate questions about the value of a longer life before death, and disbelief in an afterlife does not, of itself, make a longer earthly life automatically desirable. The case for increased longevity must be considered for its own sake.

This is not a book about the standard ethical, end-of-life issues, such as suicide and the so-called right to die, assisted suicide, and active and passive euthanasia, topics that are the usual focus for biomedical ethicists. These issues are undoubtedly important. There are complex debates, for example, about the wisdom of deliberately prolonging the life of someone who is in a persistent vegetative state or who is in constant and unrelieved pain or who is suffering from a fatal, degenerative disease. The general question that underlies these debates is what degree of pain, illness, or debility (or some combination of these) makes life no longer worth living. Such ground is well traveled, and it is not my aim to explore it here. Instead, I hope to contribute to philosophical debates about end-of-life issues by untangling and assessing the arguments for and against increasing the length of human lives. Indeed, exploring general questions about whether increases in the length of human life are desirable may have implications for how society handles policies specifically connected with euthanasia, living wills, suicide, assisted suicide, and the care of elderly people. All these policies are founded, at least in part, on sometimes only implicit notions of how long a good life is, how long people are entitled to live, and how long people ought to be helped to live.

In this book I am concerned primarily with a different set of questions: whether it is wise to deliberately extend the lives of people who enjoy reasonable health and want to live longer, and whether encouraging and enabling old people to get even older is a beneficial social practice. In considering the possibility of extending human life, I am not referring to mere biological survival; I am speaking of the continuation of life with the human capacities for emotion, perception, thought, and action intact to at least some minimal degree. (Just what is the minimum level of capacity that makes continued human life worthwhile is a difficult and highly significant question and is open to debate, but I shall not pursue this issue here.) The answer to the question about the justification of the prolongation of healthy life will also have practical implications both with respect to the roles of scientists and health-care providers and with respect to social policies governing health care, the directions of scientific research, and resource allocation throughout the life course.

Although several of the ancient philosophers, including Epicurus and Lucretius, were fascinated by questions pertaining to the length of human life, relatively little contemporary philosophical work takes as its specific focus the exploration of normative aspects of human longevity. Thus, for example, a computer search of *The Philosopher's Index* (1940–2001) reveals that only a handful of articles exploring questions about the possible value of human longevity were published during the period covered by the *Index*. Indeed, Gerald Gruman (1977, 6) is not exaggerating when he remarks that the subject of prolonging human life has been "relegated to a limbo reserved for impractical projects or eccentric whims not quite worthy of serious scientific or philosophical consideration." Moreover, as I shall show in the next three chapters, most of the modern philosophical discussion—what there is of it—along with a great deal of less formal extra-academic cultural commentary, seems weighted against the prolongation of human life. As philosopher Felicia Ackerman (1999, 7) pointedly remarks, "As a future old person, I already feel at odds with the social climate, which encourages disparagement of those who want to live too long."

Two different perspectives on deliberate efforts to prolong human life can be found in Western thought. Following Gruman, I shall call these perspectives apologism (or quietism) and prolongevitism (or meliorism). In general apologism accepts the earthly conditions that are humanity's lot and condemns efforts to change them (Gruman 1977, 10). Specifically in regard to the duration of human life, apologism is "the belief that the prolongation of life is neither possible nor desirable." Apologism accepts old age and death as inevitable occurrences and, while not attempting to change them, tries to provide satisfactory explanations for them (Gruman 1977, 6, 10). The work of American bioethicist Daniel Callahan is a clear and unambiguous example of apologism. He writes, "It should be the aim of medicine to assist people in successfully passing through the different stages of life, from birth to maturity to old age. . . . There is *no good reason* why this cycle need be any longer, on average, than it now is in the developed nations: namely, seventy-five to eighty-two years" (Callahan 1998, 130, my emphasis). He adds, "Any future increases in average life expectancy (which surely there will be) should be encouraged to come about *only* as the natural by-product of healthier lifestyles and the consequent reduction of illness in old age, not as the result of deliberate efforts" (253, his emphasis).

Meliorism, by contrast, is defined by Gruman (1977, 10) as the belief that "human effort can and should be applied to improving the world"; such efforts include attempts to increase life expectancy and lengthen the usual human life span. Gruman (1977, 8) uses the label *prolongevist* to describe "anyone foreseeing [and striving for] an extension of life much beyond [the age of 110]," but I shall use the term to describe any individuals or theories that advocate the extension of the human life span significantly beyond its current typical length. The prolongevist seeks "not merely an increase in time *per se* but an extension of the healthy and productive period of life" (Gruman 1977, 8).

Papers by Thomas Nagel and Bernard Williams provide examples of prolongevitism. Writing in the seventies, Nagel advocates prolongevitism when he claims that more life is better: "like most goods, this [life] can be multiplied by time: more is better than less." He adds, "The fact that it is worse to die at 24 than at 82 does not imply that it is not a terrible thing to die at 82, or even at 806" (Nagel 1975, 402, 408). Williams (1975, 413) says, "Surely getting to the point of possessing them [the good things in life] is better than not getting to that point, longer enjoyment of them is better than shorter, and more of them, other things being equal, is better than less of them."

Prolongevists have disagreed as to whether old age itself can be a happy phase of life well worth prolonging or whether a fulfilling form of prolonged life requires rejuvenation and the extension of youthful life phases (Gruman 1977, 69). This disagreement reflects the fact that a prolonged life might take two different forms. The prolongation of human life might involve the extension of existence during old age. Instead of dying at 70 or 80, persons would live until 90, 100, or 110, and their years as healthy old people would be extended. The other way of prolonging human life would be through the extension of each stage of life.[10] So, childhood might last until the age of twenty, puberty might extend from twenty to thirty, adolescence throughout the thirties, and so on.

Both sorts of prolongation of human life have occurred within the last century and are still occurring. Elderly people are living longer and more healthy and vigorous lives. In addition, the earlier stages of people's lives are also being extended, primarily by means of new social (rather than biological) conditions that allow the redefinition and reconstruction of life stages. For example, acquiring the education necessary for functioning in a complex world demands the prolongation of the period of relative immaturity that we think of as childhood. Preparing for employment and the accumulation of large debts during the period of higher education may create a prolonged period of material dependence, a situation that postpones many young people's arrival at adulthood. Establishing a career often pushes mate selection, procreation, and child rearing past the ages at which these activities used to be embarked on.[11] Ironically, in the West the initial period of social dependence and absence of or reduction in material and social responsibilities is being extended at the same time that some of the biological markers of maturity are arriving earlier. Consider, for example, the fact that puberty in girls now occurs around age twelve or even eleven, rather than at fourteen, fifteen, or even sixteen, as it did in the past. Hence, the prolongation of childhood, adolescence, and young adulthood is not being produced by unmediated biological developments or by increases in life expectancy per se. Instead, the social and medical changes that enable people to live longer also create an environment in which standard life milestones and expectations are being redefined and hence are arriving later in life than they did in the nineteenth and early twentieth centuries.

In my discussion in this book of the debate between apologism and prolongevitism and of their social-policy implications, I am concerned primarily with the implications of each of the two perspectives with respect to the extension of life during old age rather than with its expansion during earlier phases of life. I have three reasons for this focus. First, on a theoretical level, most of the historical and contemporary arguments about human longevity are directed at the advantages and liabilities of prolonging the last stages of life: philosophers and cultural commentators have been most interested in the positive and negative implications of extending old age, not childhood or adolescence.

Second, by focusing on the arguments for and against prolonging the last stages of life, we can see clearly the equity issues that are raised when the extension of human life is contemplated. The prospect of extending the lives of elderly persons generates special concerns about fairness and the distribution of scarce resources. Moreover, as I show in the next two chapters, in the debate about the practical applications of prolongevitism for elderly people biases such as ageism, ableism, sexism, and classism pervade many of the arguments.

Third, in pragmatic terms many of the measures that, when implemented over the course of a human life, serve to prolong the last stages of existence—measures such as good nutrition, preventative health care, reproductive autonomy and safety, and improved hygiene and sanitation—also enable human beings to devote more of their time to extending and enjoying the earlier stages of human life. Indeed, the dramatic increases in life expectancy in the twentieth century have already had an impact on earlier stages. For example, with respect to education, not only are individuals able to devote a growing number of years to training and education, but they are also likely to return for formal education at stages of their lives beyond the first two decades. To take another obvious example, if, as is possible in the West, a woman knows she is likely to live well past the age of sixty-five, at least partly because pregnancy and childbirth have become much safer, then she has at least one fewer reason for worrying about having children relatively late in her reproductive years. She knows that she can give birth to her children in her late thirties or early forties and still be alive long enough to raise them to adulthood.[12]

So, practically speaking, the extension of the last stages of life also helps to extend earlier stages, and a discussion of the wisdom of prolonging old age has implications for the wisdom of prolonging earlier life stages. But even though the extension of the period of old age may contribute, indirectly, to the socially constructed extension of earlier stages in human life, prolonging old age would not, by itself, be a substitute for direct interventions to manipulate the duration of earlier biological life stages if they should be considered desirable. Moreover, steps directed at extending the last stages of human life do not always help to expand earlier stages. So-called heroic measures to keep very elderly persons alive in their last months or years, when they may be suffering from advanced cases of cancer, Alzheimer's, or heart disease, cannot have a retrospective effect on the earlier stages of individuals' lives, and the science on which such measures are based may have no general repercussions for the medical care of younger people. So the ethical questions about the value of some forms of prolongevist medical care for elderly persons are unique to individuals at that stage of life and cannot be generalized. Nonetheless, for the three reasons I have just given my discussion in this book focuses on the applications of apologism and prolongevitism to the last stages of human life.

By "the last stages of life" I have in mind the years from age sixty-five onward, and I shall use the adjectives *aging, elderly,*[13] or *old* to refer to individuals in this group, eschewing the sanitized term *senior citizens.*[14] It might be objected that age sixty-five is too early to be used as a marker of the last stages of life. In light of the current increasing life expectancies of women and men in North America, the average sixty-five-year-old can look forward to more than a decade of additional life, and many will live even longer, often in good health and without serious disabilities. Ken Dychtwald and Joe Flower, for example, argue that it is now anachronistic to use the attainment of age sixty-five as a sign of oldness; they regard eighty or eighty-five as a more appropriate marker of old age. According to them, "middle adulthood" is the period from fifty to sixty-four, sixty-five to seventy-nine is "late adulthood," and eighty and older is "old age" (Dychtwald and Flower 1989, 33, 273).

Nonetheless, I contend that sixty-five should be treated as an important marker of old age. As we have already seen, apologists like Callahan regard seventy-five to eighty-two as the outer limits of the desirable length of human life. Within that perspective, sixty-five is clearly the start of the last stage of life, and although I argue against apologism, it is important to acknowledge and analyze the time frame that apologism places at issue. The biblical concept of "threescore years and ten," along with other cultural stereotypes about the length of human life, reinforces the idea that sixty-five is at least the beginning of the end. In addition, the cultural standard for the age of retirement, with or without legislation to make it compulsory, has remained constant at sixty-five years. At that point in life many people begin, or are expected to begin, a new life phase distinct from their earlier working lives. In North America, the life phase after retirement from paid employment is regarded as the last part of life.[15] When I use the terms *old* or *elderly*, I shall therefore mean, unless otherwise indicated, the period of life from sixty-five onward.

LOOKING AHEAD

In the next chapter I begin the investigation of the two main philosophical and cultural perspectives on human longevity. Chapter 2 is devoted to evaluating apologism, the view that the prolongation of life is neither possible nor desirable. I argue against the primarily apologistic philosophical mainstream as it has been exemplified in a variety of writings, from those of Epicurus and Lucretius in the third and first centuries BCE to those of Daniel Callahan and Norman Daniels in the twentieth century. In Chapter 3 I present a close analysis of the so-called duty to die, a notion promulgated by philosophers such as John Hardwig and Margaret Pabst Battin, which is used to support the idea that human life ought not to be prolonged and that individuals should recognize their moral obligation to die. In evaluating the strengths and weaknesses of apologism, I attempt to reveal the ageist, ableist, sexist, and classist assumptions that animate the debate about human longevity.

In Chapter 4 I examine arguments in favor of prolongevitism, the view that the extension of life is both possible and desirable. I argue that although it is rational to desire a longer life and to take measures to secure it, not all the standard arguments in favor of prolongevitism are successful. If more life is better, how much life is enough? In Chapter 5 I turn to the idea of immortality. My focus is not the usual philosophical question of whether immortality is possible but the far less often examined issue of whether a life without death is desirable. Assessing the ostensible value of immortality requires, in Chapter 6, a deeper exploration of the nature of selfhood and of the possible meanings of human lives within a context of much longer existence.

In Chapter 7 I conclude the book with a discussion of the general social-policy implications of the implementation of a qualified version of prolongevitism. I advocate a stance that I call affirmative prolongevitism, which takes a life-course approach to the social support of elderly people and entails the adoption of social policies directed toward increasing average life expectancy and compressing morbidity, particularly for those groups, such as native people, black people, and poor people, who have not so far benefited, or benefited enough, from the sort of increased longevity enjoyed by members of more privileged white cohorts.

At a funeral I attended, the minister stated that life is like a play. What is significant, he said, is not how long the play lasts but, rather, the excellence of the actors' performances. I agree that the excellence of our lives is of enormous personal, ethical, and social importance. Still, this book is dedicated to exploring the idea that the length of the play in which each of us finds ourselves does matter and, indeed, that its duration can make a significant difference to the quality and value of our lives.

TWO

"Remember You Must Die"

Arguments against
Prolonging Human Life

In this chapter I discuss four main historically dominant groups of arguments for apologism—that is, arguments against the prolongation of human life. I call these groups "why death should not be dreaded," "why death is a natural part of the 'rhythm of life,'" "why the human life span is long enough," and "why the social costs of prolonging human life are too high." Despite the intellectual predominance of apologism, all these arguments are inadequate to support the case against prolonging the length of human life.

WHY DEATH SHOULD NOT BE DREADED

In discussing the effects of the fear of death on human happiness, Fred Feldman (1992, 141) remarks, "If the fear of death makes your life worse for you than it would have been if you had not feared death, then the fear of death is also bad for you. You would be better off if you did not fear death. I would recommend, then, that if possible, you stop fearing death. No matter how bad death may be for you, you will be better off if you don't fear it." But we might wonder whether it is rational both to believe that X is very bad for you and yet not to fear X, or indeed whether it makes sense to believe that X is very bad for you and yet to seek a psychological method of ceasing to fear X. Some philosophers have sought instead to show that death is not bad; hence it is entirely irrational to fear it or even to postpone it.

Such an approach to the justification of apologism dates back at least as far as the Roman philosopher Lucretius (99/94–55/51 BCE), whose work was strongly influenced by Epicurus (341–270 BCE). Lucretius believes that people attempt to prolong their lives mainly because they have a mistaken horror of being dead. In his long philosophical poem *On the Nature of Things*, Lucretius writes, "We may be assured that in death there is nothing to be dreaded by us; that he who does not exist, cannot become miserable; and that it makes not the least difference to a man, when immortal death has ended his mortal life, that he was ever born at all" (1997, 137).

If indeed there is no more life after our earthly death, Lucretius is surely correct to say that there is and can be nothing horrible to the dead person about being dead. Once dead, we feel and know absolutely nothing. To be dead is no longer to be, or to have the possibility of being, the subject of any experiences of any sort whatsoever (Rosenberg 1983, 192). So it is a mistake, as Lucretius rightly points out, to worry now about a supposed future lying cold and alone and regretful in the grave. If dread of the state of being dead were its only basis, then prolongevitism would have no legitimate foundation.

However, I believe that Lucretius is mistaken in his emphasis. Prolongevists wish to prolong human life not because they dread the state of being dead but because they value the state of being alive (Nagel 1975, 403). This mistaken emphasis is revealed in another of Lucretius's arguments. He says that because we feel no regrets about the time that elapsed before we were born, we should likewise feel no regrets about the time that will elapse after we cease to exist: "Consider, also, how utterly unimportant to us was the past antiquity of infinite time, that elapsed before we were born. This, then, nature exhibits to us as a specimen of the time which will be again after our death. For what does there appear terrible in it?" (Lucretius 1997, 140). His point seems to be that the state of nonexistence is not to be dreaded, whether it occurs before our birth (or conception, if fetuses can be conscious) or after our death.[1]

I'm not completely convinced that people feel no regrets about their nonexistence during the time that elapsed before they were born. Although people do not fear or dread their nonexistence before their birth, as they may their nonexistence after death, and probably most people do not lament "the past antiquity of infinite time," some people occasionally feel regrets about the years, decades, or even centuries before their birth. At the level of pop culture, in some songs and stories the narrator expresses sadness about being born too late to love someone who is much older. We could say that the narrator wishes she had been born some years earlier for the instrumental reason that being born, say, ten years earlier, would have enabled her (she thinks) to enter into a relationship with the object of her love. I have also heard some people express regret that they were not born to live in an earlier time that was, in their view, simpler, more natural, less polluted, less rushed and harried, less imbued with technology. Their nostalgia about earlier eras may be mistaken, but there can be no doubt that they wish that their birth had been earlier, perhaps considerably earlier, than it was.

Yet the existence of this sort of melancholia does not constitute a refutation of the Lucretian argument. Individuals who experience it do not seem to be wishing for an earlier birth for its own sake or feeling horror about the eons of time that elapsed before their conception. Nor are they expressing regret for the shortness of their life or a desire for greater longevity of life achieved through an earlier birth. They regret only the temporal placement of their birth.

Still, one might also want to have been born earlier than one's actual year of birth in order to gain a longer, and potentially fuller, set of life experiences. As F. M. Kamm (1993, 27) points out, people might have "commitments or plans for the future whose fulfillment requires [their] having been born earlier; a plan for [their] immediate future might be frustrated because [they] did not begin life earlier." If one imagines a hypothetical external view of one's possible life course, then other things being equal (that is, setting aside the dangers of suffering in wars, famines, and other events with devastating consequences to human existence) one should prefer lifetime X, lived from 1930 to 2010, over lifetime Y, lived from 1960 to 2020, simply because X is longer and provides more opportunities for the development and expression of life plans, experiences, and activities. The fact that lifetime Y extends farther into the future than X gives it no advantage over X, when the two are contemplated from a position outside both lives. From a God's-eye point of view it could well be rational to choose the life begun earlier in time, provided that it is longer. In such an imaginary case, the years within a hypothetical lifetime that extend before one's actual birth would indeed be of great import. And if God were to saddle me with lifetime Y, after I became aware of the option of lifetime X, then I would have reason to regret at least some of the time that elapsed before I was born.[2]

However, from the real-time perspective of now, at the beginning of the twenty-first century, were I somehow to be given the choice of these two lifetimes, it would be rational for me to choose Y over X. Although X gives me more years in total, most of those years are in the past, and I would have relatively few left. Y, while shorter, would give me more years yet to live, hence more time to explore future opportunities. We assess the prospect of more life from our perspective now, as living beings immersed in the present. Because the past is over, most of us are unlikely to waste time regretting that we were not born earlier.

To that extent, Lucretius is correct in his premise that during our actual real lives we do not normally look back to the years before our birth and covet them as a lost opportunity to be alive and to engage in experiences for their own sake. However, he is wrong in alleging that the time before my birth (or conception) and the time after my death are analogous. Most people's intuitive reaction is that, contrary to Lucretius, there is an asymmetry between the time before conception and the time after death. The reason lies partly in the capacity for experience, which does not exist before conception, before the individual has come into existence, but is the central feature of life and is interrupted by death. We legitimately feel concern about being able to extend our living time farther into the future. As Anthony Brueckner and John Martin Fischer (1998, 114, n. 12) remark in connection with Lucretius's argument, "All other things being equal, one has a rational preference for pleasure in the future over pleasure in the past." The not-yet-born (or not-yet-conceived) do not have projects and plans; living human beings do (Nussbaum 1994, 208). Death deprives us not only of what we might have but also of what we already have—relationships, activities, interests, work, and pleasures. It destroys the "project of living a complete human life" (Nussbaum 1994, 210). "By contrast, prenatal nonexistence does not deprive us of what was ours already" (Kamm 1993, 40). Moreover, "for every person who ever exists, the absence of goods (and nothingness) prior to his birth comes to an end, but the absence of goods and nothingness caused by death is permanent" (42). Finally, whereas prenatal nonexistence is followed by existence, death is the permanent end to all possibility of life (64).

Another important reason for the asymmetry between preconception existence and postdeath existence is that before I was conceived there was no me and no possibility of there being a me. Some philosophers have claimed that my genetic material might have come into being earlier than it did.[3] But even if this is empirically possible, the me that exists now is the product of the whole complex of experiences that have occurred since my birth or even since my conception. If my genetic material had come into existence ten years earlier, the individual comprised of that material would be different from me as I am now, by virtue of the experiences from birth to age ten. As Frederik Kaufman (1996, 309) puts it, "It is not possible for a person in the psychological sense to exist earlier than in fact he or she did because a psychological continuum which, by hypothesis, starts earlier, would be a sufficiently different set of memories and experiences, and hence be a different psychological self." So a desire on my part to have been born earlier than I was would have to be—could only be—a desire to be someone different from who I am now. It would be a person with different experiences, problems, and achievements, and I may very well be justifiably attached to the experiences, problems, and achievements I have had in this life (Kamm 1993, 37). Moreover, it is unlikely that that someone could be someone whom I could rationally aspire to become, to make myself into through my own choices and actions. I would have to desire to be different, but in ways that would have no particular continuity with my desires and personality as they are now because they would be in no causal relationship with my existing personhood.

My death, however, cuts short the survival and life experience of a me that already exists and whose termination will only be a matter of contingent fact. I had no possible potential for experience and activity before my conception, but my death deprives me of the potential for further living that I would have had if my death could have been postponed. Whereas to want to have been born earlier is to want an identity different from and unrelated to the one I have now, to want to live longer is to want to go on existing as a version of myself that is at least related, by aspiration, decision, and action, to the me that exists in the present (Kaufman 1996, 310). For that reason, Lucretius's argument implying that the time before our birth is completely analogous to the time after our death is unsuccessful. Although it is possible to be deprived, by premature death, of the time we would have enjoyed in the future, the person that I am now cannot be likewise deprived of time prior to my birth because there was no such person.

Lucretius also suggests that in prolonging life we do not diminish in the slightest the infinity of time that will elapse after our death: "Nor, by protracting life, do we deduct a single moment from the duration of death;

we cannot diminish aught from its reign, or cause that we may be for a less period sunk in non-existence. How many generations soever, therefore, we may pass in life, nevertheless that same eternal death will still await us" (1997, 144). In a related argument, Marcus Aurelius states that the length of one's life is in fact a matter of no significance because death is a fate that occurs to everyone: "Though thou shouldst be going to live three thousand years, and as many times ten thousand years, still remember that no man loses any other life than this which he now lives. . . . The longest and shortest are thus brought to the same" (quoted in Gruman 1977, 15). According to this perspective, like all human beings I have to die some day, and whether the amount of time that I'm dead starts in 2004 or in 2040 makes not the slightest difference to the infinity of time that will stretch out after my demise. So nothing significant is to be gained from prolonging my life.

But this argument is flawed. Once again, the prolongevist wishes to postpone death and prolong life not out of some mistaken belief that the state of being dead is bad in itself or that the length of the state of being dead should be shortened but rather because death is the surcease of all potential for the activities and experiences that life permits.[4] As Nagel expresses it, "The time after [a person's] death is time of which his death deprives him. It is time in which, had he not died then, he would be alive. Therefore any death entails the loss of *some* life that its victim would have led had he not died at that or any earlier point" (1975, 407, his emphasis; cf. Feldman 1992, 138–139).

In sum, I agree that the state of death itself ought not to be feared or dreaded, that the time after we are dead may well be infinite (just as the time before we were born may have been infinite), and that death is the final end of every human life no matter how long it may be. Nevertheless, none of these facts gives us any reason not to resist our death and to want to prolong the brief lives that we do have. The time before our existence and the time after our death are not analogous from the point of view of an individual living her life.

WHY DEATH IS A NATURAL PART OF THE "RHYTHM OF LIFE"

To every thing there is a season, and a time to every
purpose under the heaven.
A time to be born, and a time to die; a time to plant,
and a time to pluck up that which is planted.

Ecclesiastes 3:1–2

Apologists seek to remind us that death is normal and natural. "Even if the soul were not immortal, [Cicero said,] it is desirable that the duration of life be limited just as a play is limited in length" (Gruman 1997, 14–15). This set of arguments against the prolongation of human life rests on the alleged value of what I shall call the "rhythm of life." As Lucretius puts it, "A certain bound of life is fixed to mortals; nor can death be avoided, [n]or can we exempt ourselves from undergoing it" (1997, 143). And Callahan (1998, 116) writes, "A life marked by a rise in possibilities, followed by a destructive decline—the movement from youth to old age—is surely in one respect fearful and intolerable. Who wants that? Yet at the same time, it is the fate that nature has given us." Apologists believe not only that our current life limits have a basis in biology but also, just as important, that they have moral significance. Callahan says that the existing human life cycle in the Western world serves as "a foundation for living within the boundaries of nature" and a foundation for a sustainable medicine (130).[5] Therefore, he concludes, a certain degree of fatalism about human life is both realistic and desirable: "A steady-state medicine will work to convince people—through persuasion if possible, and through their pocketbook if necessary—that they must accept the finitude of the body, the fragility of the mind, and the fleeting nature of health. A little fatalism, a little loosening up in the search for health, a little acceptance even of that nature red in tooth and claw seem necessary here" (248).

Contemporary apologists generally disparage what they take to be the contemporary attitude that death is incidental or merely accidental

(Callahan 1998, 143). They criticize our modern resistance to death, a resistance that is claimed to be quite different from the predominant attitude during the Middle Ages (Ariès 1974), when people were more accepting of the rhythm of life. Indeed, it has become a convention for many scholars to decry death avoidance, in both its personal and its medical manifestations, as constituting an effete decline from the more robust attitudes predominant in the early Middle Ages.[6] At that time, according to Philippe Ariès (1974, 28), "In death man encountered one of the great laws of the species, and he had no thought of escaping it or glorifying it." Supposedly, medieval human beings did not dread death or attempt to avoid it. The "passionate love for things and persons," which is arguably part of the source of our contemporary horror of death, was regarded, until the sixteenth century, as a type of temptation that could operate, for a person on his deathbed, as a ticket to hell (Ariès 1974, 37).

According to Ariès (1974, 40), only during the waning of the Middle Ages did the "horror of death" develop as a sign of human beings' inordinate "love of life." Ariès regards this horror of death and the concomitant drive to prolong life as a psychological and spiritual failure. He says that the thirteenth to fifteenth centuries saw the development of "a more personal, more inner feeling about death, about the death of the self, [which] betrayed the violent attachment to the things of life but likewise . . . it betrayed the bitter feeling of failure, mingled with mortality: *a passion for being, an anxiety at not sufficiently being*" (Ariès 1974, 105, his emphasis).

Thus, apologists regard modern prolongevitism as a manifestation of hatred of the body, love of the self, and denial of reality. The fight against death is said to cause the vilification of old age (Bell 1992, 84). Callahan writes:

> By its tacit implication that in the quest for health lies, perhaps,
> the secret of the meaning of life, modern medicine has misled
> people into thinking that the ills of the flesh, and mortality itself,

are not to be understood and integrated into a balanced view of life
but simply to be fought and resisted. It is as if the medical struggle
against illness, aging, and death is itself the source of (or at least
a source of) human meaning. (Callahan 1998, 31, his emphasis)

According to apologists it is a psychological, moral, and spiritual weakness of modern humanity that, limited by our feelings of inadequacy and
our too-strong attachments to the things of this world, we are no longer
able simply to acquiesce in the rhythm of life and its inevitable destiny,
death. Indeed, "modern medicine's response to death has been to say, in
effect, that the problem is not to find the meaning of death but to overcome it. Death is not to be understood: it is to be *fought*" (Callahan 1998,
144, his emphasis). On the contrary, Callahan (1998, 21) claims, accepting our deaths is a mark of our humanity: "Death is an inescapable reality of human life and always will be. Medicine must build that understanding into its mission, not seek to overcome it. Our humanity is, in
great part, defined by our willingness to accept and live with death." Similarly, philosopher John Hardwig (2000, 160) writes, "We are mortal beings, and death is not only the end result of life, but its telos—the aim
or purpose for which we are headed biologically. . . . Our natural rhythms
are cyclical; we are structured to live and then to die. The question is not
if, but when and how."

But I suggest that medieval European attitudes toward death do not
provide a model for our own era. Although attaining happiness was not
impossible, many aspects of life in medieval times were likely onerous and
miserable for the vast majority of laborers and peasants. If we set aside
undue romanticism about our simpler ancestors, we see that the reality of
life included heavy labor, material scarcity, intense superstition, virtually
no formal education, high maternal, infant, and childhood mortality, and
illnesses, epidemics, and disabilities, both physical and mental, that had
to be accepted because they could not be cured. Human culture offered
no reliable means of healing and prolonging human lives. Moreover, as
good Christians, the vast majority believed that if they attained sufficient

spiritual purity, they had prospects for an afterlife in heaven. Indeed, in early medieval times, as Ariès (1974, 104) himself points out, people "did not make as great a distinction as we today make between the time before and the time after, the life and the afterlife." For these reasons, then, medieval people probably had little basis for clinging to life here on earth and every reason to regard death as a relief and a release.

Although Ariès (1974, 93–94) claims that "the [contemporary] need for happiness—the moral duty and the social obligation to contribute to the collective happiness by avoiding any cause for sadness or boredom, by appearing to be always happy, even if in the depths of despair"— produces the interdiction on anything in modern life that is connected with death, I believe that this interdiction has developed because people now recognize only too clearly (even if they did not, in medieval times) that death is the end of any possibility of personal happiness and that the death of other persons can severely compromise one's own happiness.

Certainly the idea of nature's supposed limits on our lives is not, in phenomenological terms, compelling. Nagel writes:

> Observed from without, human beings obviously have a natural lifespan and cannot live much longer than a hundred years. A man's sense of his own experience, on the other hand, does not embody this idea of a natural limit. His existence defines for him an essentially open-ended possible future, containing the usual mixture of goods and evils that he has found so tolerable in the past. Having been gratuitously introduced to the world by a collection of natural, historical, and social accidents, he finds himself the subject of a *life*, with an indeterminate and not essentially limited future. Viewed in this way, death, no matter how inevitable, is an abrupt cancellation of indefinitely extensive positive goods. Normality seems to have nothing to do with it, for the fact that we will all inevitably die in a few score years cannot by itself imply that it would not be good to live longer. (Nagel 1975, 409, his emphasis)

Nor does it follow that it is either unreasonable or immoral to seek a longer life. Apologists are misleading at best when they criticize prolongevitism by equating it with a desire to avoid or deny death altogether. Pro-longevitism need not be committed to an irrational denial of the reality and inevitability of death; it is committed only to the promotion of the postponement of death. I think that one could consistently both seek the "meaning" of death, as Callahan advocates, and also resist it. To resist death does not require that one believe that it will not eventually occur.

It is indeed true that death is, and probably always will be, inevitable for human beings, and because it is inevitable, we must recognize and ac-knowledge it. However, I do not think it follows that we must like this aspect of being human. As Richard Momeyer (1988, 10) puts it, "The mystique of death acceptance advocates an essentially passive and com-placent view toward the status quo," a view easily open to exploitation by politicians, military leaders, and corporate executives whose goals would be facilitated by a populace that is accepting of death. Focusing on ac-ceptance as the uniquely moral and psychologically healthy response to one's inevitable death runs the risk of making lack of acceptance of death a greater problem than death itself (Momeyer 1988, 8). Momeyer strongly advocates resistance to death, or what he calls "rebellion," in order to "as-sert our humanity, preserve our integrity, and affirm our dignity even in the face of the absurd assault upon them that death presents" (13).

Nor is there any moral obligation to be preoccupied with the fact of death and its inevitability. Although, as I suggested in Chapter 1, we should "remember that we must die," I see no greater a priori value in focusing on death, especially in old age, than, say, in devoting oneself to the arts, travel, relationships, or work. When old age is prolonged, the advantage, according to some prolongevists, is that death is, eventually, not unexpected (Gruman 1977, 70); it arrives, as anticipated, in extreme old age, after many years of worthwhile experience and activity. Nor do I see either truth or value in regarding death, as Hardwig urges, as the "purpose" for which we are headed. To the extent that it makes any sense at all to speak of the purpose of human life in biological terms, that pur-pose is likely to lie in the reproduction of our kind, not in dying.

Moreover, the assumption that current biological restrictions on the human life span have, in themselves, a normative force for personal decision making and social-policy formation is unjustified. Indeed, it may be immoral even to accept as a given the "natural" course of many life events. In scientific research, social-policy formation, and individual decision making, human beings have shown that we need not and do not accept existing biological limits in areas such as reproduction, disease management, and infant and maternal mortality. Instead, through disease prevention, health promotion, and extensive medical care, we seek to modify nature's dictates in order to limit the numbers who are born, reduce illnesses, enhance the quality of our lives, and eliminate premature death. The appeal to nature, to "monolithic 'species' prototypes," is incompatible with an appreciation of and support for the diverse forms that human life can take (Dixon 1994, 618).[7] We are fortunate that medical scientists in the previous two centuries were not persuaded by the supposed normative force of earlier human life-span limits. What is now normal and natural for the human life span does not, of itself, necessarily imply anything about the desirability of or justification for prolonging human life, either for individuals or as a matter of policy.

In her fascinating book, *Declining to Decline: Cultural Combat and the Politics of the Midlife*, Margaret Morganroth Gullette (1997a, 14) issues a challenge to "mainstream connotations of 'aging' as a natural, biological, prenarrativized, ahistorical, universal decline." Her primary target is the social construction of so-called midlife, but the strength of her underlying arguments for skepticism about the inevitability and naturalness of midlife as a stage are easily transferable to the category of old age. She argues that all of us, everywhere, are "aged by culture" through a system of "age ideology" (3) that is "popularly disseminated, semiconscious, so familiar and acceptable that it can be told automatically" (161). Different human ages are accepted as both real and universal, separable from each other and also from ongoing life processes, and they thereby acquire ontological status (4).

In contemporary Western culture, human aging is structured by a biologized, asocial concept of decline, which "replaces all other sources—

accident, history, economics, politics—with a body-based narrative that permits only one meaning: personal declineoldageanddeath [*sic*]." According to the decline narrative, "'age' equals 'aging' equals 'old age' equals 'sickness' equals 'death'" (Gullette 1997a, 8, 12). We tell each other and ourselves the decline narrative even when we are materially well off, healthy, accomplished, and likely to live long lives. This decline narrative, along with the other forms that ageism takes, acts as "a stressor, a depressant . . . a psychocultural illness" that affects almost every one of us (Gullette 1997a, 116). Hence, given the degree and extent of negative social interpretations of aging, we do not yet fully comprehend what is possible from those who are enabled to live healthy longer lives. Nor do we know what human lives would be like if they were not inevitably structured by "stages" replete with an ideology of expected decline. But longer lives, freed of the fetters of ageism and supported by medical research to sustain the quality of life, would open up the potential for activity and accomplishment by those whom we now regard as old.

Callahan has an interesting response to this argument. He writes that it risks two errors:

> The first is to think that what was appropriate in the past remains equally appropriate in the present. Precisely because we made those past advances, we can now afford to think about changing our priorities; we are now far better off. The second error is to believe that the future must always repeat the past, that because we were successful earlier with one group of diseases, we will be equally successful with another. . . . We have now, in general . . . entered the era of chronic disease and illness as well as conditions associated with advanced old age, and they are proving far more resistant to conquest. (Callahan 1990, 121)

The response to Callahan's first alleged error is that an adequate case must be made for the changing of priorities. Within the limits of this book, it is not possible to evaluate all the alternative priorities that a society might adopt, and social needs and goals could justifiably vary from nation to nation. But it is also not obvious that we must assume, a priori, that various priorities must necessarily be incompatible with each other. Moreover, if priorities are to be changed, part of the case for doing so must be that the old priorities are no longer (as) important. As this chapter and the following one show, the arguments in favor of an apologist perspective on human life are not adequate; that inadequacy itself is a reason to be cautious about changing our medical priorities if such change means redirecting resources away from researching and creating methods and means that will prolong human life.

The response to Callahan's second alleged error is just that we cannot know, now, that the scientific future will not be like the past and that researchers will no longer be successful in combating chronic diseases and illnesses associated with old age. This is, of course, an empirical matter. If in the future it turns out that scientific successes are greatly diminished, then, and only then, would Callahan's second "error," the assumption about the prospects for scientific progress in curing disease, be genuine. In the meantime, successes have been sufficiently frequent and large to justify some optimism. In short, an appeal to a supposedly natural "rhythm of life" does not justify apologism.

WHY THE PRESENT LENGTH
OF HUMAN LIFE IS LONG ENOUGH

Another standard reason for not seeking a longer life is that the present human life is long enough: human beings will run out of worthwhile things to do. This claim is related to the biblical aphorism that there is nothing new under the sun (Ecclesiastes 1:9); hence a lengthened life would be a wearying round of the same experiences (Gruman 1977, 75). Thus Lucretius says, quite explicitly, "We are continually engaged and fixed in the same occupations; nor, by the prolongation of life, is any new pleasure discovered" (1997, 143). According to this view, life's enjoyments and gratifications are fixed and limited; if we live too long, we will have no choice but to simply repeat what we have already done, and such repetition would be boring and futile. As Gruman (1977, 14) explains, in the era of ancient philosophers such as Epicurus and Lucretius there was no concept of progress comparable to our own; therefore the Epicureans could reason that there is no justification for living to see what the future might bring.

Epicurus taught that "one could be just as happy in a short life as in a long one, and, therefore, the prolongation of life was not an important matter" (Gruman 1977, 14). Lucretius provides a developed form of this argument. He imagines that what he calls Universal Nature speaks as follows to a man who fears dying:

> Why do you groan and weep, at the thought of death? For if your past and former life has been an object of gratification to you, and all your blessings have not, as if poured into a leaky vessel, flowed away and been lost without pleasure, why do you not, O unreasonable man, retire like a guest satisfied with life, and take your undisturbed rest with resignation? But if those things, of which you have had the use, have been wasted and lost, and life is offensive to you, why do you seek to incur further trouble, which may all again pass away and end in dissatisfaction? Why do you not rather put an end to life and anxiety? For there is nothing further, which I can contrive and discover to please you; everything is always the same. If your body is not yet withered with years, and your limbs are not worn out and grown feeble, yet all things remain the same, even if you should go on to outlast all ages in living; and still more would you see them the same, if you should never come to die. (Lucretius 1997, 139)

Given this assumption about the narrow limits of our pleasures, interests, and diversions, Lucretius reasons that whether individuals have had a fulfilling life or an unfulfilling life they have no good reason for wanting to prolong their existence and postpone death.

This view finds a modern-day equivalent in the work of Ariès (1974, 106), who suggests, rather plaintively, that the contemporary denial of death, with its accompanying feeling that "we are non-mortals," does not in any way gladden our lives. Callahan (1998, 253) argues that the average life expectancy now achieved in developed nations is sufficient to constitute a full life. The life-span framework that is now provided by "nature," he says, is "perfectly adequate for human life, both collectively and individually" (134). He suggests that some people might want to "have eternal youth, to see the clock of the life cycle stopped at a particular point." But the gratification of such a wish would not be good for us as individuals, says Callahan, for "a life perpetually stuck at one stage" would "soon come to boredom and ennui, with the possibility of significant change arrested and frozen." He adds that if, as is possible, one's life did not go well at the particular stage at which one had chosen to arrest it, then the supposed benefit "would soon turn into a straitjacket. Given that prospect, time and change do not appear such terrible alternative fates" (131–132).

According to Callahan:

> The average person in good health in the developed countries
> of the world (and living in a reasonably safe environment), *already*
> lives long enough to accomplish most reasonable human ends. . . .
> Neither the human species as a whole, nor most individuals, need
> more than the present average life expectancy in the developed
> countries (the mid-seventies to low eighties) for a perfectly satis-
> factory life. This idea of a steady-state life expectancy at its present
> level would establish, happily, a finite and attainable goal: "Enough,
> already." (Callahan 1998, 82, his emphasis)

Callahan (1996, 442) refers to the late seventies or early eighties as constituting a "natural life span." He concludes that society should not use its common resources to extend life, for "the present average life expectancy in the developed countries has proved perfectly adequate for most people to live a full life and for those countries to flourish economically and intellectually" (Callahan 1998, 133). An increase in average life expectancy from the low- to the mid-eighties would not "lead to a better family life, greater economic productivity, a richer cultural and scientific life, or a generally higher standard of collective happiness and sense of well-being." "More life beyond a certain point seems to offer no proportionate gains" (134). Indeed, he even complains that such progress as has been achieved in extending human life has not resulted in increased appreciation of or respect for elderly people. Instead, society's ambivalence about whether old age is to be rejected and resisted has robbed old age of "any substantive meaning it might have once had as an honored stage in an inevitable life cycle. Apart from ideological commitments, no one really knows now what to make of old age" (Callahan 1995, 25).

There are, however, many flaws in this set of arguments claiming that the present human life is long enough. Fears of futile repetition may be justified if we imagine that a prolonged life must necessarily be spent in mindless drudgery or be severely limited by lack of health, education, resources, and opportunities. But there is no reason to assume that a prolonged life must be marred by such constraints. In evaluating the benefits and liabilities of a prolonged life, one errs in taking as one's standard the lives of the poorest, most diseased, or most miserable and deprived human beings. In raising questions about prolongevitism, we need to engage in thought experiments about the genuine possibilities for human beings. The debate about prolongevitism and apologism should motivate us to rethink social arrangements and the limits now placed on the development of human potential.

Apologists would claim that these remarks are based on unjustifiable optimism about the prospective quality of prolonged life. Certainly, some people prefer not to prolong their lives because they fear that great old age inevitably brings misery. As Gruman (1977, 12–13) puts it, "What is the use of living long, if one extends, thereby, the hardships and infirmities of old age?" People dread a time when their capacities may decline, when they could be sick, and when disabilities may multiply.

In discussing the desirability of longevity I've sometimes encountered a type of *ad hominem* argument that claims that only young or middle-aged people are prolongevists, while older individuals, with the greater wisdom of age, are able to accept death. The implication is that pro-longevitism is a state of mind that one eventually outgrows. But even if there were a correlation between one's age and one's tendency to accept apologism (and there is no evidence that there is), such a correlation would not necessarily demonstrate the correctness of apologism. The question remains whether the experience of getting older itself provides reliable evidence that greatly prolonged life is not desirable; whether illness, poverty, or a lack of good care in old age makes people less inclined to go on living; or even, more insidiously, whether apologist cultural tendencies eventually achieve their desired outcome by convincing elderly people they ought not expect to live longer.[8] As I shall argue, the experience of getting older does not necessarily provide reliable evidence that a longer life is not desirable—or at least the aspects of the experience of aging that appear to make an increased length of life undesirable are in no way intrinsic to aging itself.

If the available medical, social, and material resources are so limited that one's extra stretch of time is lived in misery, then that is a problem, and no prolongevist advocates the extension of human life if it can be lived only in poverty, pain, and ill health. As the antiageism activist Baba Copper quite reasonably points out, "Just staying alive is a false goal. . . . It is the *quality* of that extra time that is important" (1988, 74, her emphasis). But the actual likelihood of being impoverished, in pain, or ill in old age is an empirical question. It is likewise an empirical question—as well as a matter of social policy—whether these conditions can be ameliorated. There is no reason to assume, a priori, that a long life must necessarily be a life of physical pain, illness, and disability. Undoubtedly, some old people—maybe especially those who have not received adequate medical and psychological care and support—are miserable, just as some ill-treated, deprived, and oppressed young people are miserable—that is, the quality of one's life is not inevitably related, whether positively or negatively, to the length of one's life. The error is to let one's views of long life be biased by the notion that being old necessarily involves misery.

This error is generated by ageism, which I define as unjustified bias, stereotyping, and discrimination on grounds of age, usually (although not always) on grounds of old age.[9] Ageism may be generated by a fear of aging. But antiageism writer Barbara Macdonald (1991, 152) points out that although nondisabled people may have a horror of "living in a wheelchair, being paralyzed from a stroke, unable to hear or see, or being unable to speak," these conditions are not "inherent risks of old age—they are inherent risks of life, which any of us may face at any age, any day of our lives." Dychtwald and Flower (1989, 34) challenge the mistaken beliefs that aging and disease inevitably go together and that most older people are in poor health. They insist that although older people acquire more chronic health problems, most are not bothered or limited by them. Perls and Silver cite evidence suggesting that although health-care costs rise as people grow older, in the United States the proportionate expenses level out when people are around seventy-five, and from that point their proportionate health-care costs fall. Perls and Silver speculate that part of the reason may be that elderly people (that is, those over eighty) are less likely to demand intensive and costly medical care than are those under eighty.[10] A second possibility is that those who are very elderly need less intensive testing because their ailments have already been diagnosed. And a third possibility, which Perls and Silver stress, is that the "oldest old" are just not as sick as those who are younger:

> If a person has not developed certain diseases such as life-threatening cancer, diabetes, heart disease, stroke, and Alzheimer's disease, at the time when most others are prone to developing them, it becomes less likely with advancing age that the person will come down with these and other conditions. The oldest old are a select group of individuals who "get over the hump" because they are able to delay illness to a short period at the end of their lives—to compress morbidity. (Perls and Silver 1999, 149)

It is especially ironic that bioethicists such as Callahan seek to treat the maximum desirable length of human life as seventy-five or eighty, which is just around the age at which the cohort of individuals who live that long may begin to anticipate fewer health problems than those in slightly younger cohorts. Callahan's notion of a "natural life span" is biased against anyone with the inherent capacity to live longer.

Part of the ageist ideology is the idea that decline is inevitable and sets in early, that "Time" ensures "losses to prior achieved identity" (Gullette 1997a, 197). Yet people start out from varying levels of capability and they age at different rates, so it is erroneous to assume that everyone of a particular age experiences the same level of debility (Posner 1995, 20). Sara Ruddick points out that supposed symptoms of aging such as memory loss are present in people of all ages, and older people vary greatly in cognitive capacities. "Moreover, loss of memory is culturally diagnosed. What would have passed as momentary forgetting for someone in midlife is taken as a portentous 'senior moment' for someone over 65." Illness and death occur in old age but are not confined to old age, and rates of illness and death may be affected by many social factors in addition to age (Ruddick 1999, 48). Given the right forms of health care and social opportunities and support—entitlements that I believe belong to people of any age—old age need not be miserable, and the misery that some elderly people experience is not unique to old age.

Furthermore, the view that "I'd rather be dead than a disabled old person" reflects tremendous ignorance about disability. Even if old age often does bring a diminution in some capacities, it is usually not excessive. Statistics Canada (1991) reports, for example, that men aged sixty-five can anticipate 11 more years of living in a condition free of severe or moderate disability; for women the figure is 12.1. Disability in elderly persons is declining too. The U.S. Bureau of the Census (1999) reports that in 1996 those over sixty-five had an average of 30.5 "restricted activity" days due to illness or injury, down from 39.2 in 1980, and an average of 5.9 "bed disability" days (defined as staying in bed because of illness or injury for at least half the day), down from 7 in 1980. More important, it is false, as antiableism activists and writers insist, to suppose that a life lived with disabilities is a life not worth living or that it is less worth living than the lives of nondisabled persons (Wendell 1996).

Peter Singer argues that extending human life significantly—for example, by seventy or eighty years—will inevitably lead to a lower average quality of life because "individuals will enjoy the freshness of youth for a comparatively small portion" of their total life span and because their average level of health will be not quite as good as the average level of health of those leading shorter lives. Moreover, the requirements of population control in the face of diminishing resources would demand that many fewer people be conceived and born. The result, he says, is that fewer individuals living worthwhile lives would come into existence; so if we are governed by the goal of generating as much happiness as possible, we should not seek to extend the length of human lives (Singer 1991, 139–140). Within the bounds of Singer's utilitarian calculus, and even granting his two (questionable) assumptions about the freshness of youth and the level of health of very old people, I suggest that his argument fails to take into account the potentially large quantitative gain in total happiness as a result of the sheer increase in years lived by people who genuinely want to live longer. In addition, the utilitarian calculus itself implies that one would aim for a balance of human lives and supportive environmental conditions so that happiness could be optimized.

Apologists and prolongevists are, I believe, in agreement about the importance for end-of-life issues of quality of life. Proponents of both sides support the maintenance of as high a quality of life as possible for aging persons. Prolongevists insist that when they argue for the prolongation of human life, it is a life as healthy and as highly functioning as possible. Apologists, however, are worried about the possibly lower quality of life that very elderly people may experience. One crucial point where the two sides depart is with respect to the possibility and attainability of high-quality living near the end of life. We could say that, with respect to this issue, apologists are pessimists,[11] whereas prolongevists are optimists. I am suggesting that the apologists' pessimism is founded, at least in part, on implicit ageism.

If we reject unwarranted assumptions about the quality of prolonged life and the nature of elderly persons' existence, then there are good reasons for repudiating the Epicurean and Lucretian pessimism about the absence of novelty in individual lives. Just consider all the areas of the world you have not yet explored; the people whom you have not yet encountered; the capacities, talents, and interests you have not yet developed; the hours you have not yet passed with your parents, siblings, children, or grandchildren, your lovers and your friends; the music and art you have not yet created or experienced; the books you have not yet read; the films or plays you have not yet seen; the sports, games, hobbies, and leisure activities you have not yet indulged in; and the new projects you have not yet undertaken. This is a general list, abstracted from any particular individual, but it can be made more vivid and compelling if we consider the particular motives, interests, values, and penchants of specific individuals. Many elderly people with whom I have discussed the longevity issue emphasize that one of the extraordinary gifts of their years after retirement is the opportunity to learn a variety of new things and to pursue further education, both formal and informal. My point is that everything you have not yet done provides good reasons indeed for you to want a longer life. "Becoming more than we've ever been before is the point of extended life" (Dychtwald and Flower 1989, 342).

Thus, unlike Callahan, I do not see our lack of understanding about "what to make of old age" as a problem. If we cannot, or can no longer, make generalizations about *the* meaning of the last stages of life, it is a sign of the openness of the last stages of life to reconstruction and reorientation by aging people themselves. If, as I insist, old people are individuals with as many variations as the members of any other age cohort, then we must reject attempts to generalize about what the ends of their lives must mean either to them or to other members of society. And, in the absence of any empirical evidence, there is no reason to believe, as Callahan claims, that extending human life has destroyed respect for elderly people. *Post hoc, ergo propter hoc* remains a fallacy, and if a former era of respect for elderly people is more than a quaint myth, its demise was probably not occasioned by making people's lives longer and healthier.

Even if, as Callahan claims, one has "had ample time to know the pleasures" of the activities I've listed above (Callahan 1987, 67, quoted in Bell 1992, 83), their attraction, enjoyment, and benefit in the future are not necessarily thereby reduced. And although my list does not show that the potential enjoyment of and opportunities for learning and personal development are infinite, or even indefinitely numerous, it does strongly suggest that, for any finite individual, so much is potentially new under the sun that a longer life than is now considered "normal" could easily be filled, and filled happily and fruitfully, in exploring what the world offers.

Some people have interpreted this argument to suggest that I am saying that the true meaning of life is simply the consumption of experiences.[12] That conclusion is not what I intend. I am trying to respond primarily to the Epicurean and Lucretian pessimism about the lack of novelty in human experiences by arguing that the prospects for freshness in human experience are indefinitely large. Moreover, the desire for new endeavors or projects is not merely a wish to "consume" experiences. Such a description is inappropriate, for not just any experiences will do, and not all experiences are equal. (The issue of what experiences human beings should seek is a normative question, which I shall discuss further in subsequent chapters.)

In addition, although I am not saying that the sole meaning of life is the accrual of experiences, I do think that such experiences contribute to a meaningful life. An investigation of issues of human longevity inevitably raises issues about the meaning of human life—or, perhaps more accurately, the multiple meanings of human lives, and those meanings are connected to human projects, interests, and endeavors. To urge the value of greater longevity is not necessarily to assume that more of any sort of experience is always better or that everyone's life choices and projects must be uncritically endorsed. Some people make poor or even immoral uses of their allotted time; others vainly seek fulfillment in the mindless duplication of empty activities. Questions about the value of actual life experiences and goals still must be asked and their varying answers evaluated. Nevertheless, as the prospects for longer life become more realistic, we will have to recognize that conventional conceptions of the duties, responsibilities, projects, and goals associated with the traditional length of life will become outmoded. Apologists cannot argue that a certain life is "long enough" on the grounds that the individual who has lived it has accomplished and experienced all that could reasonably be expected within the length of human life as it has traditionally been conceived. As the span of life changes, what can reasonably and appropriately be considered to be people's legitimate aspirations and moral obligations will also change (Van Tongeren 1995, 32–33).

Callahan (1998, 82) claims that the average healthy person living in a developed nation already lives long enough to achieve most human goals and that neither individuals nor the species as a whole needs more than the current average life expectancy for a satisfactory life. He clearly has a one-size-fits-all concept of the meaning of human existence and the place of aging within human life (Callahan 1995). But his claim begs the question. It may well be that human beings have adjusted, and continue to try to adjust, their life strategies and goals to fit within the life span that they can reasonably expect. Our lives are satisfactory because, of necessity, we circumscribe them to fit the limits set by the current average life span. But this fact, if it is a fact, tells us nothing about what human beings might aspire to and might legitimately hope to experience, enjoy, and achieve if they were to have the opportunity of living longer. Looking back over the past two centuries, we can see that individuals' life choices have already been gradually changing with and accommodating to continued increases in human life expectancy. Consider the tendency to prolong schooling or to return to formal education at various points in adult life; the trend toward having multiple careers; women's increasing prospects for living an active life in the postmenopausal years; and even the choice by some people to raise a second family, with a new partner, after the end of an earlier relationship. The prospect of an even longer average life expectancy than we have today implies the need for re-assessing life plans and anticipating fulfilling new and more ambitious life goals, rather than merely regarding as adequate and unquestionable the present expectations for what one might get out of life.

The Epicurean belief that one can be just as happy in a short life as in a long one and the Lucretian claim that whether one's life is happy or unhappy one should be equally equanimous about the end of one's life can be turned on their heads. If one's (short) life is happy and fulfilled, why on earth would one not want more of it? Or, if one's life is unhappy, wouldn't one want the opportunities that a longer life could provide in order to improve one's situation, develop better relationships, have more rewarding experiences, learn more, and realize more of one's potential? Thus, contra Lucretius, both the happiness of a short life and the un-happiness of a short life constitute plausible reasons for seeking a longer life, in order in the one case to continue the happiness and in the other to seek and find it.

The badness of death is, in part, proportional to the degree to which human potential is left unfulfilled. For this reason, the death of a twenty-year-old is usually seen as more of a tragedy than the death of a seventy-year-old. Feldman (1992, 226) writes, "A person's death is bad to the extent that it deprives him or her of goods. This helps to explain our sense [that] the death of a young person is generally worse than the death of a very old person who has already enjoyed a full, rich life. The loss suffered by the young person is greater than that suffered by the old person." But a person of forty or fifty might well have enjoyed a life as full and rich as many persons of seventy or more. Does the enriched nature of the younger person's life thereby make her death in middle age more ac-ceptable, less regrettable? Is the early death of individuals who are for-tunate to have had interesting, varied, and versatile lives less sad than the later death of older people whose lives were dull and boring? I think not. The mere degree to which an individual's life has or has not already been filled with interesting experiences does not by itself determine the badness or otherwise of her death. Rather, present prospects and the potential for the future are most significant. On the one hand, the present and future prospects of enjoying a high quality of life are a good reason to want to prolong one's life and are a justification for taking steps to promote the extension of that life. On the other hand, having already enjoyed a high quality in the past does not make one less entitled to a longer life.[13] We should rethink the notion that the death of a more elderly person is necessarily less problematic than the death of a younger one. We should not make the assumption either that the prospects for future happiness of a person of seventy are nonexistent or that her potential has been entirely fulfilled, either because of the number and fullness of her talents, abilities, and capacities for experience or because of her lack of opportunities or both (cf. Nagel 1975, 406).

Theorists who are relatively complacent about a person's dying at seventy or seventy-five unjustifiably assume that lives beyond the age of so-called retirement, unlike lives in other stages, are all the same and undifferentiated, repetitive, and not interesting or fulfilling. Yet so much of most human lives is spent in productive and reproductive work (except perhaps in the case of those who are extraordinarily wealthy and privileged) that many people have little time and opportunity for experiencing a range of other human goods. In failing to recognize that possibility and its importance, apologism may well be classist as well as ageist.

Norah Kizer Bell suggests that a gender bias is also involved: "The argument in favor of believing that there is an appropriate time in a person's biography for claiming that her life could be considered full strikes me as advancing recognized forms of male bias: both a gender *devaluation of women's concerns* and *an indifference to a woman's 'life possibilities' apart from her abasement into more servile positions*" (1992, 85, her emphasis).[14] The existence of gendered expectations about women's biological and cultural roles makes it less likely that women will have had as full a human life as men may have had and more likely that the quality of their lives may be lower than that of men (Bell 1992, 86). But, with sufficient resources, a longer life gives individuals of both sexes a chance to extend and expand their sense of what is worth experiencing and doing, so that not all our lives need be spent in survival activities.

Callahan's version of the argument that the present human life is long enough is an excessively and unjustifiably biologistic view of the nature of human existence. He imagines, you will recall, that people acting on prolongevist principles would seek to arrest their development at some point in life, probably a youthful stage, and that such an arrested life would become boring because of its lack of development. I grant that if the prolongation of human life required being stuck at some point in physical, psychological, or mental development, so that one never got to experience sexual maturity, let's say, or reproductive capacity or the opportunity to nurture or the emotional and cognitive capacities of various stages of adulthood, such an arrested development would indeed be limited. But I fail to see why the prolongation of human life must take that form. Certainly, if their life were prolonged, people would legitimately prefer, as I've already acknowledged, to live it in a state of health and reasonable comfort. This preference is, I believe, the motivation behind traditional searches for the mythical "fountain of youth" or "elixir of youth." It is not that people literally want to be fixated at an immature stage of life but rather that they associate youth with health, capacity, and vigor, while they associate old age with inevitable illness, disability, and weakness. But if we envision a prolonged life that is healthy, spirited, and vital, we do not need to imagine it as being fixed in some specific stage of biological immaturity or youthfulness.

Moreover, it is false that all changes in life arise from biological events. Thus, even if the lengthening of life necessarily involved a prolongation of one early biological stage of human development (although I do not believe it does), it is a mistake to suppose that such a life would necessarily be filled with ennui and boredom. At almost any stage of life, if one is healthy, one has the potential for learning, developing relationships, trying new experiences, traveling, gaining moral and spiritual insight, creating art and artifacts, and engaging in physical activities. I fail to see anything problematic or dull in a life devoted to doing these things. But, in any case, the issue in the prolongation of human life is not the possibility of being arrested at some stage of immaturity but, rather, the possibility of maintaining and retaining a condition of health and well-being such as would permit the kinds of activities I have mentioned.

Finally, Callahan's claim that an increase in the average life span from the low- to the mid-eighties would not "lead to a better family life, greater economic productivity, a richer cultural and scientific life, or a generally higher standard of collective happiness and sense of well-being" (1998, 134) is unjustifiably ageist. He gives no evidence to support his claim that an increase in life span would fail to have these effects, and he makes empirically ungrounded assumptions about the supposed lack of power and potential of persons in their eighties. At this point in the history of humankind, I think we do not yet know all that vigorous and engaged eighty-somethings might do with their lives or what their continued presence might offer to the rest of Western culture, which is unfortunately long accustomed to warehousing aging people and ignoring what they might want, say, or do.

Moreover, Callahan's claim emphasizes only the supposed collective consequences of extending the average life span. Even if he were correct (and at the very least I think he lacks evidence) that such an extension would not lead, collectively, to "greater economic productivity" or "a richer cultural and scientific life," such an argument unjustifiably ignores the potential advantages and benefits for individual elderly people, who just might want, as individuals, to live longer. If an eighty-year-old woman wants to continue to remain alive simply in order to spend time with her children and grandchildren, read books, watch television, and enjoy the sunshine on a warm spring day, I defy apologists such as Callahan to show that such a desire is unreasonable, unjustified, or immoral. Callahan's claim that "more life beyond a certain point seems to offer no proportionate gains" (Callahan 1998, 134) takes a merely quantitative view of longevity and ignores or denies the potential qualitative advantages of a longer life even to those in their eighties or nineties.

WHY THE SOCIAL COSTS OF
PROLONGING HUMAN LIFE ARE TOO HIGH

The final set of arguments against prolonging human life could just as easily have been mentioned first. In fact, in popular disputes about apologism, these arguments usually lead off the debate. The arguments in this category are consequentialist. Apologists believe that "senescence and death are necessary and even advantageous to the individual and to the human race" and, therefore, that it is unjustified to attempt to prolong human life (Gruman 1977, 10). How are they advantageous? The vigor and vitality of the human species are renewed, it is claimed, through the ongoing deaths of the old and the births of new human beings. As Callahan (1998, 131) expresses it, "The coming and going of the generations creates genetic and cultural vigor in human life." Even more fundamentally, it is argued that each generation must grow old and die simply in order to make room for a new generation, a claim attributed to Lucretius by Gruman (1977, 14), but one that may be easily reinforced by the previous two centuries' growing fears of increasing global overpopulation. In a context of finite or even diminishing resources, populations must be contained and the balance between the generations preserved. If elderly people live longer, it will become harder and harder for younger generations to support them.

Apologists claim that despite its sunny outlook, at the heart of prolongevitism is pure selfishness, which disregards the negative outcomes of the enactment of prolongevitism. The enthusiasm for prolongevitism is said to be a trait of the baby-boom generation in particular, whose members could not bear to leave their childhoods, let alone become adults, grow old, and die (Ross 1998). Journalist Jon Spayde (1998, 18) writes, "You know the cliché about the baby boomers: They never wanted to grow up in the first place, and they certainly don't want to grow old. Yet whether it's pure coincidence or some fluke of the zeitgeist, researchers are finally zeroing in on the bodily mechanisms that cause aging—and offering some hints about how it might be arrested or reversed—just as the mother of all generational cohorts squeezes into its 50s." Kai Nielsen (1994, 255) pours scorn on "the egoism of healthy individuals, living what would be otherwise normal lives, having obsessive hang-ups about the fact that they will eventually die. . . . The temptation is to tell them to get on with it and stop sniveling."

Prolongevitism is claimed by apologists to be the fad of the members of a demographic bulge who are determined to have it all and, in having it all, implicitly committed to denying opportunities for the generations who follow them.[15] Thus Nuland writes, "There is vanity in all this, and it demeans us. At the very least, it brings us no honor. Far from being irreplaceable, we *should* be replaced. Fantasies of staying the hand of mortality are incompatible with the best interests of our species and the continuity of humankind's progress. More directly, they are incompatible with the best interests of our very own children" (1994, 86, his emphasis). Nussbaum (1994, 223) suggests that a genuine concern for the resource depletion that may be occasioned by death resistance requires from us "a deeper and more consistent love of life and change, a love that is willing to confront one's own small place in the whole." According to this perspective, one's own loss of life is "someone else's good, [and] what you most wish to avoid is necessary and good for unborn others, [for] nature's structure contains an always tragic tension between the desires of the part and the requirements of the whole."

From this point of view, prolongevitism is something of a Western luxury, a goal founded on and necessitating not only major generational injustices but also class inequities. Neither the people inhabiting poor countries nor the occupants of the underclasses in our own have the luxury of worrying about obtaining extra years for their lives, for they are concerned primarily with surviving during the years they do have.[16]

The prolongation of human life requires, according to apologists, enormous physical and medical resources that could better be devoted to other human goals. The problem, they say, is that prolonging human life will extract high human costs, literal costs, because of the so-called burden of sustaining and caring for elderly people. Spayde (1998, 20) writes:

> Japan is worried about supporting its growing army of retirees, Russian pensioners have been reduced to hawking old clothes to get by, and the survival of the U.S. Social Security system is in doubt. . . . Add more and more years to the average life span and you will create armies of old people without pensions staying in the workforce decades longer, duking it out with rising generations for shrinking pieces of the economic pie. The delay of death may become as heavy a burden on planetary resources as high birthrates are now, and the quality of life for the elderly—and everyone else—may erode steadily.

Smith (1993, 3) notes that "it is widely recognized that we live in an 'aging society,' and the increasing numbers of elderly people present problems for everyone." Even such an author as Mothersill, a self-identified "old person" who does not explicitly adopt an apologist stance, follows the party line on the difficulties allegedly posed by elderly people:

> We, the oldies, are very expensive. We do not pull our weight. We are mostly unemployed and assumed by those whose opinions count to be unemployable. We are unproductive. Some of us live off pensions and annuities; others (not everybody) have social security which, as we are reminded daily, is running out of funds. We have a disproportionate number of medical problems, many chronic and severe. Some of us need part-time caregivers; some need round-the-clock institutional care. (Mothersill 1999, 13)

Meanwhile, even those who publish in self-declared feminist venues do not hesitate to describe the old, including old women, as a "burden." The difference, perhaps, between nonfeminist and feminist interpretations of this "burden" is that feminists tend to stress the ways in which the burden will affect young and middle-aged women as the caregivers of the old (Holstein 1999; Post 1990).

Callahan worries specifically about the costs of "new diagnostic and therapeutic options" directed at saving elderly lives. According to him, these options create an additional level of costs for the health-care system: "We will now have two costs on our hands: the cost of the treatment that saves a life now, and the cost of whatever subsequent conditions will eventually kill the patient—the costs, that is, of what I have elsewhere called the 'twice cured, once dead' phenomenon. The cost of death is deferred to a later illness, while in the meantime we must pay for the successful treatment that makes the deferral possible" (1998, 94).

Thus, in making projections for his ideal future, Callahan (1998, 255) writes, "It will be in the care of adults (roughly, people between twenty-one and sixty-five years old) that technological medicine will be most prominently and justifiably used, even in a steady-state medicine that seeks to limit it."[17] Hence, the quick and relatively easy (though surely not painless, at least for some) solution to the purported "problem" of the costs of a growing cohort of aging people is to refuse to develop or support measures that will keep them alive longer. "Once people have made it past the point of a premature death (a point I would set in the range of sixty-five to seventy years), then the highest priority for medicine should become not to avert death but to enable people to live as comfortable and secure a life as possible" (Callahan 1998, 256). For Callahan, a fatalistic acceptance, if one is old, of one's impending death "make[s] equity more possible." He believes that high-tech medicine should be rationed for those in their late seventies or early eighties, and, at that time of life, if you want expensive forms of health care, you should have to pay for them (Callahan 1998, 248, 256).

Although I accept that the costs of overpopulation within the contemporary human species may indeed be serious and that these problems may be exacerbated by the fact that human beings live longer, at least in the West, than they did in past times, I do not find it self-evident that we must let people die for the sake of alleviating overpopulation and certainly not that the burden of so doing should fall disproportionately and necessarily on older people. As Copper (1988, 84) points out, with deliberate irony, "Apparently only old people die. Death does not hover near the cradle, the motorcycle, the toxic workplace, high bridges or battlefields. . . . Death is a forbidden subject with all but the old, who are expected to bear the burden of this social suppression." She believes that old people are unfairly and inappropriately associated with death, and I suggest that this association helps to account for the unthinking assumption that the social and medical costs of overpopulation require the deaths of older people. The notion that it is "natural" to die in one's seventies or eighties is accepted with alacrity, in a way that the notion that it is "natural" to die at a younger age is not.

Indeed, if one were to take a ruthless view about the necessity for human sacrifices in response to the need for space, the need to preserve the means of survival for more and more people, and also the need to create and sustain people who are vigorous and strong, it seems just as practical to call on those with disabilities or severe illnesses to pass on, or perhaps those who carry genetic liabilities or those who cannot prosper because they are too poor to afford food and medical care. If those suggestions seem morally outrageous, as they should, I invite you to ask yourself whether it is not similarly outrageous to expect people of seventy-five or eighty years to accept death for the sake of alleviating population pressures, opening up jobs, or reducing medical costs. The very fact that old people are expected, without need for further argument, to accept their deaths and not struggle to prolong their lives—an expectation that is not foisted on individuals belonging to other social groups—is indicative of the deep, naive, and unquestioned ageism that lies at the heart of many of the claims on behalf of apologism.[18] In general, I see no reason to decide on the basis of age that certain individuals must be prepared to die for the alleged greater benefit of the human species. (In Chapter 3 I explore this issue further in the context of the idea of a "duty to die.")

I doubt, for example, that apologists would be willing to say that growing numbers of women or disabled people or people of some ethnic minority "present problems for everyone," as Smith claims old people do. And I doubt that any other group in society could be described, with acceptance and impunity, as a "burden." The widespread claim that elderly people are a burden is founded on a number of questionable, if not downright false, assumptions. It fails to question the biologistic premise that a Darwinian "balance" of generations requires a large demographic base of young people and only a small cohort of elderly people. Changing population demographics have already shown that there is nothing either inevitable or necessary about such a proportion between young and old, and, indeed, less developed countries, where such a profile persists, are seldom models of prosperity and abundance. The notion that elderly people are a burden also assumes that such people are all alike and, in particular, all alike in constituting a drain on social resources. It assumes that all old people are sick or incapacitated or both, an assumption that I have already argued is open to question. It also falsely assumes that old people do not and cannot contribute to their society through either paid or unpaid labor.[19] It assumes that certain crucial forms of health care are a legitimate benefit only for the young and middle-aged and can reasonably be denied, across the board, to elderly people, without consideration of elderly persons' individual conditions, needs, wants, or prospects. On the level of social policy, it also assumes that no changes in our social and financial arrangements are possible, that there is no potential for rearranging how we share resources and how we care for one another. In particular, it takes for granted that the overuse of finite resources and the uncontrolled pattern of consumption by members of all generations, which is the norm in the Western world, is a given that cannot be altered. All these assumptions are, at best, unproven and, at worst, false.

Moreover, because the large majority of elderly people are women, apologist claims that the prolongation of elderly people's lives creates a burden are really claims about the burden that elderly women (not persons in general) supposedly constitute. As anthropologist Margaret Lock notes, "It is the specter of *old women* in ill health and the burden that this burgeoning population of baby boomers is expected to place on the health care system in the near future that is of primary concern" (1998, 180, my emphasis). Copper (1988, 85) writes that we are "at the beginning of a world-wide demographic boom of old women. It is easy to predict that our society will soon be subject to all kinds of 'new looks' at death and dying. . . . The old are seen as half dead already." Bell points out that, in the United States, "older women are poorer, more apt to live alone, and less likely to have informal social and personal supports than their male counterparts. Furthermore, a disproportionate number of nursing home patients are women. Older *women*, therefore, are more likely to make the heaviest demand on health care resources." Bell worries that "it is easy to imagine someone arguing that a woman who is single, or who outlives her spouse, or whose children are independent has outlived her useful-ness and her obligations. Women could also be perceived as undeservedly requiring more in the way of others' responsibilities *to* them" (1992, 85, 87, her emphases).

In a culture that is accustomed to taking for granted the self-effacing caregiving behavior of women, the prospect of losing that caregiving and instead having to care for and support old women may help to generate an implicitly gender-biased argument against prolonging human life be-cause such prolongation in fact may primarily benefit women. As Bell (1992, 88) says, the perceived absence of value for very old people and the reluctance to provide the services to sustain their lives may be "due in large measure to the fact that there are few male competitors for these services." With no little irony, Emily Nett remarks that gerontologists are puzzled that elderly people seem to have a lower status as they ac-quire greater longevity. She suggests that this low status exists not be-cause elderly persons are near death and therefore remind younger people that they too will die nor because modern times require youth-ful strength and energy nor because there is any inevitable struggle for power between the young and the old. "Rather we [women] believe it is our comprising such a large proportion of the elderly in contemporary societies ('modern' or not) which accounts for the 'spoiled' identity . . .

of elders. Similar to what happens to the prestige of formerly male occupations 'opened up' to women, such as teachers, secretaries, tellers,
etc., 'opening up' old age to females inevitably alters the evaluation of
the position" (1982, 225).

An additional and even more worrying hypothesis about the role of
sexism in the attribution of "burden" status to elderly people can be derived from Gullette's work. In a discussion of how women are "aged by
culture" through what she calls the "menoboom"—the media creation of
menopause as an allegedly significant passage in women's lives—Gullette
suggests, "Menopause discourse flourishes at a moment when (some)
women are seen to be powerful, rich, and attractive. (Some) men start worrying that women are getting too much of the good things of life: they
assume men must be losing out. These worries center on midlife women,
because now . . . it's in their middle years, if ever, that women get power"
(Gullette 1997a, 99).

Gullette is suggesting a form of culturally devised reactive repression,
which has the effect, if not the intention, of responding to and damping
down the perceived recent growth in women's freedom, independence,
and power by inducing within women considerable anxiety and fear in
connection with the alleged physical, mental, and psychological declines
to be anticipated in midlife. "What woman, sniffing the stale sweat of
male alarm, can't anticipate the backlash? Gender backlash by definition
targets women, but as far as age is concerned, it's different strokes for
different folks. . . . Midlife women get hit with middle-ageism in the form
of widespread public menopause discourse, male science that assumes
we've all got a deficiency disease, and male commerce that sells us the
supposed remedies" (Gullette 1997a, 100–101).

Could it be that the labeling of elderly people as a burden—a description ostensibly attached to the undifferentiated group of persons of both
sexes—is an additional way of intimidating midlife women, who will become the vast majority of the aging population? Could it be a method of
warning women not to get too uppity because their pride will lead to a
fall, a fall in capacity, power, self-respect, and autonomy? Another pos-

sibility is that the language of burden is not part of a backlash against midlife women but an anticipatory preemptive strike against old women. Right now elderly women, as a cohort, may appear to be relatively powerless, but elderly women as a majority component of the supposedly assertive and self-aggrandizing baby-boom generation may appear to be a greater threat. Better to attempt now to put them in their place.

I make no judgment of the truth of this hypothesis, and to some it may seem preposterous. Nonetheless, I take from Gullette the idea that large changes in the cultural discourse about life stages, aging, midlife, and the requirements of those who are elderly are not inevitable and by no means natural but need to be explained. And the explanation for the dissemination of the language of burden may, in the end, have something to do with keeping women down. The implications for cultural attitudes toward increasing longevity are stark: longevity, "because it's female, [is treated] as if it were solely a disaster. (Perhaps men should congratulate themselves on dying younger!)" (Gullette 1997b, 186). And any system aimed at confining the average human life span will cause women to suffer disproportionately to men (Dixon 1994, 616).

When Smith says that increasing numbers of elderly people present problems "for everyone," I wonder whether he thinks that these increasing numbers also present problems for elderly people themselves. Are the growing numbers of their own cohort a problem for them? Is it in the interest of individual old women or old men not to have the lives of their age peers prolonged? Is it in their interest to see the group to which they belong stereotyped as a nonproductive, homogeneous, lower-value burden? Alternatively, given the standard cultural assumption that "problem" groups of people are not really persons, perhaps what Smith means is that the increasing numbers of elderly people present problems for everyone else; implicitly, elderly people, constituting the burden, are not a part of the "everyone" to whom they are a burden.

Although most apologists have unashamedly worried about the burden that old people constitute for others who are not old, a few have argued that prolonged age can be a burden for old people themselves. In effect, they suggest, the medical compulsion to prolong life becomes a new form of discipline of the flesh, a discipline that may weigh heavily and painfully on old people and perhaps especially on old women, who have already experienced a lifetime of social pressure to conform to sexist social norms for their physical selves. According to Copper, for example, old people may often be kept alive against their real interests: "old women, as they are dying, are the victims of medical technology—kept alive to fill hospital beds profitably." She believes that "government subsidies for medicine and institutional care have created a highly profitable industry of geriatric technology, with the elderly aid recipients captive to the modern Grail, longevity" (1988, 62, 74).[20] Macdonald concurs:

> We, as women, may look at this new aging population and think
> poor and think women. But that's not what the boys are thinking.
> They are already thinking of a whole new building industry, of new
> housing and nursing facilities. They will invent every kind of gadget
> ever dreamed of to help the elderly. They will design special chairs,
> dishes, clothes, beds. There is no end to what the male mind can
> come up with where there is a market and where public monies
> flow. (Macdonald 1991, 51)

To this list we could add the enormous potential for the pharmaceutical industry to generate large profits through the marketing of medications.

Another worry is that the lives of women could be sustained simply in order to enable them to continue with their customary caregiving and nurturing responsibilities. Indeed, plenty of evidence indicates that women are both more likely than men to need extended care late in life (because women live longer) and much more likely than men to be the ones who, because of gender norms, provide that care to persons of both sexes (Holstein 1999). The current emphasis on the burden that elderly women will allegedly constitute has, in fact, likely served to mask the many ways in which such women contribute service, care, and support to the society in which they live. Arlene McLaren writes:

> By providing services to their children, grandchildren, spouses, siblings, relatives, neighbours and friends, [elderly women] are not merely helping out the individuals concerned. They are also relieving the state and the economy of the need to offer such services. The provision of baby-sitting reduces the perceived need for organized day care; the nursing of spouses or friends reduces the pressure on medical services, and the exchange of services among themselves reduces the need for financial assistance. The hidden economy of elderly women has helped to sustain the current political and economic system. Why then have the defenders of the modern industrial society insisted on the "functionlessness" of such women? (McLaren 1982, 214)

Arguably, those who worry about the "burden" of old women may be benefiting, directly or indirectly, from their labor, while also stirring up hate against the very people who benefit them.

Applied to elderly people, especially elderly women, the language of "burden" is inappropriate and prejudicial. I grant that if old people, and old women in particular, were to be kept alive merely in order to provide material for scientific research, resources for capitalist expansion, jobs for needy baby boomers and their generational successors, or traditional feminine caring services, then the large numbers of old people could indeed become a burden—that is, a burden to themselves. The point behind prolongevitism is primarily to benefit those whose lives are prolonged. If it fails in this primary endeavor, then it is not justifiable.

INTERIM CONCLUSION

I conclude that the proponents of apologism have failed to make an adequate case for accepting the length of human life as it is and for repudiating deliberate efforts to increase it either individually or as a matter of social policy. Apologists like Callahan are mistaken when they claim, across the board and independent of personal or social conditions or individual capacities, that human lives should not be prolonged. They are guilty of making unjustified generalizations about aging and about the value of extended life. In the next chapter I turn to a discussion and assessment of the concept of a "duty to die" as an argument against prolonging one's life and that of others.

THREE

Age Rationing and "Generational Cleansing"

Evaluating the "Duty to Die"

In Chapter 2 I evaluated four main groups of arguments that are advanced in favor of apologism. I concluded that these arguments fail to provide any significant support for the belief that, other things being equal, human life should not be extended. But apologism is not merely inadequately justified. In its practical social applications it is morally untenable. The belief that human lives should not be prolonged implies that at a certain point in life it is better for people to die. Indeed, a number of ethicists have gone so far as to explicitly argue that old people, in particular, may have a real and compelling duty to die.[1] This chapter explores the question of whether there is such a duty. I examine arguments given by John Hardwig, John Beloff, Margaret Pabst Battin, and John Harris that purport to show that there may be a widespread duty to die.

In 1997 Hardwig published an article entitled "Is There a Duty to Die?" and in 2000 a book by the same title. Hardwig's answer to his question is an emphatic yes. He begins with the case of Captain Lawrence Oates, a member of Captain Robert Scott's expedition to the South Pole. After becoming too ill to continue, Oates walked out into the blizzard and perished. According to Hardwig, Oates was fulfilling his duty to die. Hardwig also cites cases of persons with deteriorating and incapacitating illnesses, which would seem to be far more common in the West than situations like that of Oates. Hardwig (1997a, 35) writes, "If further medical advances wipe out many of today's 'killer diseases'—cancers, heart attacks, strokes, ALS, AIDS, and the rest—then one day most of us will survive long enough to become demented or debilitated. These developments could generate a fairly widespread duty to die."

One might cavil that if Hardwig has so much confidence in science's capacity to obliterate disease, it is strange that he has so little hope that science could also prevent or significantly ameliorate dementia and debilitation. But, this reservation aside, let us give him the assumption that dementia and debilitation will increase in the future and that sudden deaths that avoid these fates will be reduced. Does it follow that more and more of us will have a duty to die?

Hardwig's ethics is firmly situated within a context of apologism, and he makes it clear that he supports the apologist views that many human beings unjustifiably fear death and that they irrationally fail to accept the "rhythm of life": "We fear death too much. Our fear of death has led to a massive assault on it. We still crave after [*sic*] virtually any life-prolonging technology that we might conceivably be able to produce. We still too often feel morally impelled to prolong life—virtually any form of life— as long as possible. As if the best death is the one that can be put off longest" (Hardwig 1997a, 40). However, as we shall see, Hardwig's case for the existence of a duty to die relies chiefly on the fourth theme discussed in Chapter 2: the burden on society that elderly and disabled people allegedly constitute.

If Hardwig were correct about the existence of a moral duty to die, then his thesis would pose a serious threat to the values and goals of pro-longevitism. Prolongevists could perhaps try to dodge Hardwig's claims by pointing out that prolongevitism advocates the extension of life only if it can be lived in a healthy, functional state. They advocate the extension of life only if it will not involve the severe illness, unrelieved pain, or disablement that undermine an individual's capacity to pursue his or her life projects. Hence, the prolongevist might argue that the problems Hardwig hypothesizes as arising from progressive mental and physical deterioration, and their alleged moral significance with respect to the prolongation of human life, do not have any force against prolongevitism. However, dodging the claim in this way simply avoids the serious problems about life extension that Hardwig raises, without in any way laying them to rest. His arguments for a duty to die demand an evaluation, for, as we shall see, he does not confine the purview of the duty to die only to those who are seriously ill.

SLIPPERY-SLOPE ARGUMENTS

An immediate and perhaps too easy criticism of Hardwig's thesis would invoke a typical slippery-slope argument about the threat it constitutes to people's psychological state and life choices. Indeed, I think that the idea of a duty to die would be easy to misinterpret. Just think of a person of any age who is already contemplating suicide: Could the idea of a duty to die become one of the proverbial last straws that could precipitate that act? Do we want to create a climate in which killing oneself is made to look, on a general basis, both more rational and more moral than it now appears? Although suicide may be rationally justified on occasion, including at the end of life (Prado and Taylor 1999), I deny that it is good, either for communities or for individuals, to create general normative pressures to end one's life that are prescriptively applied to all members of a large group and that may negatively influence those who are already vulnerable to suicidal ideation.

In response, Hardwig might argue that his concept of a duty to die will not ordinarily influence or affect the young and the healthy because it is directed mostly at the aged and the seriously ill. And if it does influence older people, Hardwig could say, that is precisely the effect he is looking for: to persuade people near the end of their lives that they should not be seeking or even wanting to prolong their existence. It's worth pointing out that not all seriously ill people are elderly. But Hardwig might well be undisturbed by this observation because his goal is not merely to encourage elderly persons to die but to persuade those of any age who face the prospect of constituting an unrelieved "burden" to their families and other loved ones that they have a duty to do so.

However, just as important as the effect the promulgation of a duty to die would have on potential suicides is its effect on the general population. I am troubled by the possible consequences that this sort of perspective, if it becomes part of the cultural fabric, could have on common social attitudes toward and evaluations of people who are very old or very sick or seriously disabled. If there is cultural acceptance of the moral concept of a duty to die, we can anticipate that more and more sick or elderly people (or those who are both) will feel pushed or even compelled to take their own lives or to find ways to get others—family members or health-care providers—to assist them to end their lives (Beloff 1988, 3–4).[2] Alexander Morgan Capron (1987, 51) thinks this tendency could become more pronounced with the aging of the population in developed countries and the consequent increases in health-care costs.

So, in an ageist and ableist culture we cannot be sanguine about the potential effects of emphasizing the supposed selfishness of elderly and sick people who persist in wanting to live. Although Hardwig (1997a, 42, n. 1) states that he is not claiming any right of others corresponding to the duty to die, it is not farfetched to suppose that the widespread acceptance of a duty to die could lead many people to believe that relatives of and caregivers for those who are elderly and very ill are entitled to the death of anyone who is a burden.

Nonetheless, Hardwig might respond that, even if true (and it would likely be difficult to establish its truth without a real-life test), the empirical claim about the slippery-slope dangers of widely advocating a duty to die does not show anything about the legitimacy of the purported duty to die itself. In particular, it does not show that a duty to die is not widespread, as Hardwig claims. At most, it would show something about the promulgation of the idea of the duty to die: specifically, that it would be necessary to be careful about how the idea is disseminated. In this case, then, a slippery-slope argument does not suffice to defeat the claim at issue.

THE "INDIVIDUALISTIC FANTASY" AND THE "BURDEN" OF AGING PEOPLE

Hardwig (1997a, 35) claims that the failure of contemporary bioethics to take seriously the idea of a duty to die may be a product of "the individualistic fantasy": "This fantasy leads us to imagine that lives are separate and unconnected, or that they could be so if we chose. If lives were unconnected, things that happened in my life would not or need not affect others." But I am not persuaded that such a fantasy lies behind bioethicists' failure to embrace a duty to die. First, various versions of consequentialism are widespread within contemporary ethics, including bioethics, and consequentialism requires its adherents to consider the ways in which lives are connected and actions influence others. We need think only of the deployment of consequentialist principles of beneficence and nonmaleficence, which are customarily emphasized even in basic bioethics textbooks. Second, I believe that feminist critiques of atomistic views of the human individual have been largely successful in alerting ethicists, since the 1990s at least, to take into account the varied social and technological contexts in which moral questions arise, not to consider human persons in isolation from other human persons, and to widen the scope of consequences that are evaluated when making moral decisions to include matters of social power, oppression, and inequity (Sherwin 1992). Hence other, much better, reasons may exist for the refusal of most contemporary ethicists to rally around the idea of a duty to die than a failure to notice that human decisions have effects on other people. Ironically, however, as I later show, Hardwig himself is guilty, in his discussion of the social context of the duty to die, of the very "individualistic fantasy" of which he accuses other bioethicists.

Hardwig says that the source of the duty to die is the impact of one's decisions on family and loved ones (1997a, 36), and the centerpiece of his argument is the concept of burden. Hardwig notes, correctly, I think, that many people, especially older ones but also young ones, fear the prospect of becoming a burden to those they care about. All of us, he says, have "a responsibility to try to protect the lives of loved ones from serious threats or greatly impoverished quality, certainly an obligation not to make choices that will jeopardize or seriously compromise their futures" (36). One has a duty to die—even if one does not want to die— "when continuing to live will impose significant burdens—emotional burdens, extensive caregiving, destruction of life plans, and . . . financial hardship—on [one's] family and loved ones" (38). As an example of an extreme and unpardonable burden, he describes an eighty-seven-year-old terminally ill woman whose determination to cling to life eventually costs her fifty-five-year-old daughter all the younger woman's savings, her home, and her career (37). An elderly and sick individual such as this is a prime example of a person who has a duty to die.

I am convinced that personal and financial costs such as those incurred by the daughter are indeed excessive and unjustified, and I concede that caregivers sometimes (have had to) make sacrifices that no human being should be expected to endure. But we should not overestimate the extent of caregiving. Anne Martin-Matthews (2000) argues that the concept of caregiving has been unjustifiably extended in such a way that "care" for elderly people is seen as analogous to care for children. However, for the most part elderly people are not dependent in the ways that children are. Behaviors such as visiting, providing transportation, and filling out forms for elderly persons get described as "caregiving," yet they may be intermittent, and old people do not require the twenty-four-hour presence and vigilance that children demand. As a result, old people come to be perceived as much more burdensome than most of them actually are. It is ironic, says Martin-Matthews (2000, 69), "that the widespread use of a concept that perpetuates images of older people in dependent roles and non-reciprocal relationships should come at a time when, despite cutbacks to many services and programs, the ability of older people to live independently into advanced old age is greater than it has ever been."

The justificatory role in Hardwig's arguments played by the concept of being a "burden" is inappropriate. When individuals say that they do not want to be a burden to their loved ones, I believe what they primarily mean is that they dread a time when their personal autonomy is severely diminished and their capacity to care for themselves is deeply impaired. The loss of independence and self-determination is the principal problem; becoming a "burden" who must be cared for by others is the inevitable result of a high absence of autonomy, but the autonomy itself is the primary value, and its loss is the primary fear (Cowley 1980, 57). So Hardwig may be overestimating the moral significance of people's supposed desire not to be a burden. Those who say they fear being or becoming a burden do not necessarily feel any duty to die; rather they are expressing the desire to continue living in an independent and autonomous state of health.

The claim of burdensomeness generates epistemological problems concerning who determines what constitutes a burden, how the scope of that burden is assessed, and when the burden becomes so intolerable as to trigger the duty to die. What, for example, should happen if the elderly person's family is divided, with some finding the individual an overwhelming burden and others not (Callahan 2000, 142)? Because caregivers vary in their capacity to tolerate constraints and demands, the duty to die would seem to depend on "the emotional vagaries and differential values" of those who care for them (Callahan 2000, 142). Imagine two elderly persons with comparable health problems. One is cared for by a strong, resilient, and resourceful person. The other is cared for by a vulnerable and easily depressed person. Imposing a duty to die based on burdensomeness implies that the second elderly person, but not the first, would have a responsibility not to go on living. So problematic moral outcomes are created when the duty to die is determined by the extent of burdensomeness as it is experienced and assessed by family members.[3]

And as Callahan argues, if the person burdened should decide—and it is, after all, for the sake of rescuing him or her that Hardwig chiefly makes his case for a duty of ill persons to die—then that person could demand that the burdensome individual commit suicide, whether or not the burdensome one wants it. This "logic" leads, says Callahan (2000, 141), to "family tyranny."[4]

But the situation is not improved if the responsibility for determining when one is an insupportable burden falls to oneself (Callahan 2000, 140). Bill Hardwig, John Hardwig's own son, expresses trepidation about the prospect of "burdensome" individuals' attempting to interpret the behavior of their families in order to try to determine when they have become too much of a burden to deserve further life. Bill Hardwig is worried about the likelihood that the "burdensome" individuals might err on the side of overestimating the trouble they cause their families (Hardwig 2000, 191) and hence might attempt to kill themselves prematurely and unnecessarily.

John Hardwig's ready answer is that all these questions about burdensomeness should be discussed by the elderly person with the members of her family. He does not explain how such a discussion would be possible when the elderly person is sick and vulnerable and hardly in a position of equality and independence with respect to her caregivers. Moreover, that recommendation provides no method for resolving the epistemological problems of determining the extent and scope of burdensomeness. Nor does it in any way mitigate the morally problematic role played by the concept of burden.

In Chapter 2 we saw that ageist claims about the burdensomeness of old people have been invoked in order to provoke fears about an upcoming population that is top-heavy with elderly and declining people. The mistake imbedded in these ageist claims is supposing that all persons are, by virtue of great age, inevitably and unavoidably an unacceptable burden to the younger cohorts of the population. Hardwig does not make that mistake. Instead, his mistake is to assume that the imposition and assumption of burdens are not a normal part of human life, of what he poignantly calls the "ties of care and affection, . . . legal relations and obligations, . . . interlocking finances and economic prospects, . . . common projects and also commitments to support the different life projects of other family members, . . . shared histories, . . . ties of loyalty" (1997a, 36). I contend that living and working with other human beings inevitably generates burdens that are imposed by some, adopted by others, and that both being the burden and caring for the burden are roles that we may enter into or adopt at various times during our lives.

Let us examine what being a burden usually means within familial contexts. In contemporary Western culture, children, to take one example, inevitably start out as burdens in that parents incur financial, temporal, opportunity, and caregiving costs. Raising children has been shown to be enormously expensive, costing thousands and thousands of dollars over the course of an individual's first eighteen years.[5] But the personal and financial costs of children's dependence are not necessarily construed in a negative fashion. First, provided that they are reasonably healthy, children are ordinarily not burdens in the financial, temporal, opportunity-cost, and caregiving senses forever. Second, virtually no child is only or nothing but a burden. Although costs, difficulties, and challenges are inevitably incurred during child rearing, most parents do not think of their children as burdens but as blessings. And one reason is that children are not just the passive recipients of care. They can and do give back to their parents and caregivers, almost from the time of birth, everything from smiles and personal responses to interesting conversations and great opportunities for revisiting childhood play and sport. Third, to the extent that children are burdens they are nonetheless willingly assumed burdens. The demands of child rearing are part of what one takes on when one makes a commitment to raising a child; those demands are part of what being a parent entails.

In general, then, as the example of child rearing shows, close social ties generate and in part are constituted by the sharing of burdens and by taking turns being the burden and taking care of burdens. Both being and assuming a burden are an ordinary, expected, even essential part of family life. Being dependent on other people is not necessarily bad. We all start out life by being a burden, and most of us eventually also take responsibilities for the burden that one or more other family members temporarily impose. Caring for a "burdensome" person is part of the commitment we take on as a component of living in families, however those families may be constituted. Even Hardwig (1997a, 36–37) is willing to concede that "our families and loved ones also have obligations, of course—they have the responsibility to stand by us and to support us through debilitating illness and death. They must be prepared to make significant sacrifices to respond to an illness in the family."

Hardwig (2000, 170) is highly critical of situations in which an ill person is the center of his family, to whose goals all else is subordinated. But in fact no sick person is a burden forever, and few sick people are nothing but a burden. As many caregivers have told me, a sick or disabled person may still give love, conversation, support, and even joy to those who care for him. Martin-Matthews (2000, 68) remarks that in her research " 'caregivers' constantly reminded us of what they received from their elderly relatives in return, either tangibly in the present or in terms of reciprocal 'credentials' from the past." Caregivers may not even be willing to describe the person dependent on them as a "burden" at all.[6] Hardwig's concept of the moral responsibilities of patients countenances only the possibility of their dying to save others from trouble and financial costs, not the possibility of their living and enhancing others' lives.

Also, no evidence indicates that caregivers usually want the "burdensome" person for whom they are responsible to die. People to whom I talk about the demands of long-term caregiving often express a wish that their work could be reduced and that they could receive more social support but not that the individual for whom they care would die. Perhaps they are not being honest about their real feelings, but I doubt it. If you love someone enough to make sacrifices in order to care for them, you are unlikely to want them dead—unless, perhaps, their suffering is so great that they would be better off dead, but that is a far different reason for dying than an alleged duty to die. Says Callahan (2000, 145), "If it can be a legitimate expression of moral agency to care for a sick person at high personal cost, something good to do, then it is hard to see why it would be wrong for the sick person to accept that care; and it is imaginable that, in some cases, it would be wrong to deprive a family of that moral possibility if they chose to accept it."

So in choosing to fulfill a so-called duty to die one could potentially be both diminishing the moral agency of one's caregiver as well as greatly increasing the suffering, the sense of inadequacy, and the probably overwhelming guilt that the caregiver might feel if one became convinced that one was too burdensome to live. Although the loss that one's loved ones will feel at one's death cannot be avoided, only postponed (Hardwig 1997a, 39), their sense of loss is likely to be exacerbated and complicated if one has committed suicide, and even more so if the suicidal person has acted out of a conviction that he has a duty to die. I would be horrified to find that someone I love has ended his life in an effort to save me from making sacrifices for him—sacrifices that I would likely want to make. And imagine the horror of a situation in which the "burdensome" individual tries to kill himself and fails (Linehan 1997, 5).

The very nature of collective human life lived in groups means that people have—fortunately—the opportunity to depend on others and to be depended on. I therefore contend that the status of being a burden, even a serious burden, is not a sufficient reason to believe that one has a duty to die.

HUMAN DIGNITY, CONTRIBUTIONS, AND INDIVIDUAL AGENCY

In considering counterarguments to the duty to die, Hardwig (1997a, 37) notes that some might object to an ostensible duty to die on the Kantian grounds that it would be "incompatible with human dignity or would embody a failure to recognize the intrinsic value of a person." He responds in the following way:

> I do not see that in thinking I had a duty to die I would necessarily be failing to respect myself or to appreciate my dignity or worth. Nor would I necessarily be failing to respect you in thinking that you had a similar duty. There is surely also a sense in which we fail to respect ourselves if in the face of illness or death, we stoop to choosing just what is best for ourselves. Indeed, Kant held that the very core of human dignity is the ability to act on a self-imposed moral law, regardless of whether it is in our interest to do so. (Hardwig 1997a, 37)

The flaw in this response is that it fails to constitute any genuine refutation of the Kantian objection. Hardwig simply claims that in assuming a duty to die he would not be failing to respect himself or others, but he does not show where the objection fails or why assuming a duty to die is compatible with an appreciation of one's own dignity and worth. Indeed, the objection can even be reinforced by pointing out that belief in the duty to die requires that one regard oneself, in Kantian terms, mainly or only as a means rather than as an end. In believing that I have a duty to die because of the burdens that I impose on my family, I would be regarding myself as a means to evil (the task of caring for me) while I am alive and as a means to good (removal of the burden) by ending my life or allowing it to end. Far from asserting my own value as a person by acting on a supposed duty to die, I would in fact be seeing myself solely in terms of the costs and benefits that I generate for other people. The argument applies even more clearly if a duty to die is imputed to another person. To say that an individual has a duty to die is to say that his existence is a liability and his death a benefit. In both instances, the individual is treated solely as a means rather than as an end valuable in himself.

Hardwig (1997a, 40) claims that recognizing a duty to die affirms one's moral agency and demonstrates that one can make a difference in the lives of one's loved ones. But if one is still sufficiently functional to recognize and even act on a duty to die, it is hard to believe that there are not other, less destructive, ways to affirm one's moral agency and positively affect the lives of one's loved ones. Hardwig (1997a, 40–41) writes as if the only alternative to recognizing a duty to die is to treat ill persons (and for them to treat themselves) as if they had no moral responsibilities and should merely be given what they want. But he has created a false dichotomy. A seriously ill yet competent person may very well still be capable of listening carefully and empathically to her loved ones, offering them emotional support, assuring them of her love and trust, and providing advice and counsel. Perhaps Hardwig's failure to recognize these possibilities arises from his implicitly ageist assumptions about elderly and chronically ill people. He states, "As we age or when we become chronically ill, connections with other people usually become much more restricted. Often, only ties with family and close friends remain and remain important to us" (41–42). But as I stressed in Chapter 2, there is no good reason to suppose that old or ill people (or those who are both) are necessarily less capable of having or less likely to have the kinds of relationships that younger and healthy people have. It is ageist and ableist preconceptions and structures that chiefly make it harder for such people to continue to be fully functioning members of the human community.

Hardwig (1997a, 39) suggests that one's duty to die is stronger when one's loved ones have already made great contributions, or even sacrifices, to enable one to live a good life, "especially if you have not made similar sacrifices for their well-being or the well-being of other members of your family." But he appears to underestimate what the "burdensome" person may have done for her loved ones and the sacrifices she may already have made in her personal life, education, job advancement, finances, in order to enable loved ones to have a better life. As Letty Cottin Pogrebin remarks, "After our older citizens have given their all to their country—their labor and loyalty, their ideas, their offspring, their creativity and spirit—health care is not something to begrudge them, but something we as a people should *want* to provide as a gesture of recognition and thanks" (Pogrebin 1996, 308, her emphasis). I will not at this point discuss the general matter of intergenerational justice, which I explore in Chapter 7. I am simply pointing out that Hardwig's defense of the duty to die appears to assume, without argument, either that morally significant sacrifices in a relationship are inevitably one-way and one-sided or that earlier sacrifices made by the one who is cared for need make little or no difference to the later moral reckoning of a duty to die.

Hardwig (1997a, 38) wants to emphasize that each of us has a responsibility to endeavor to protect the quality of our loved ones' lives. He is correct in thinking that this is an important responsibility. But rather than claim that an implication of this responsibility is that individuals always have a duty to die at the time or even in anticipation of the time when they become heavy burdens to their family members, it would make more sense to say that individuals have a responsibility to take steps to reduce the likelihood that they will become burdens. Individuals have a responsibility to avoid, wherever possible, letting themselves arrive at a condition where they cause harm to others.[7] This responsibility would include planning, wherever one's income allowed it, for one's material support and health-care needs after retirement or at any time when paid employment is either inadequate or no longer possible. For middle-class people it might mean postponing some material acquisitions during young- and middle-adulthood in order to save money for later life. It would certainly mean acquiring appropriate health-care and long-term disability insurance. We do have responsibilities to plan for our futures—although some people, especially some people of color, poor people, and women of any race, may have so few material resources and such low incomes during their working lives that the extent of such responsibilities is limited. However, even if we have culpably failed to engage in such long-term planning, it does not follow that we then have a duty to die, any more than a parent's failure to obtain long-term life insurance to support his dependents requires that he die before his short-term life insurance expires.[8]

WHAT TYPES OF PERSONS
HAVE A DUTY TO DIE? AND WHEN?

Hardwig (1997a, 39) concedes that a person who has never been able to understand moral obligation at all cannot have a duty to die and that "moral dangers" probably behoove us not to say that any incompetent person, even one who was formerly competent, can have a duty to die. The empirical implication, I think, is that a large number of people among the ranks of the highly "burdensome" likely cannot have a duty to die. Indeed, such people would seem to have been the original target of Hardwig's concern, for he was worried about the burdens that individuals with dementia would impose. So, ironically, the very people about whose impositions Hardwig is most concerned are also the very people who cannot possibly possess a duty to die. As a result of the latter concession, however, Hardwig claims that a person such as himself may have a duty to die while he is still competent—that is, before he becomes unable to rationally formulate and execute such a decision (1997a, 39). He therefore foresees, and approves of, a future in which competent and healthy people are morally obligated to choose to end their lives on the basis of, so to speak, a preemptive duty to die.

But at the very least such a moral requirement suffers from epistemic instability. Deciding when to end one's life could be so difficult to determine as to be almost impossible. Surely one would need strong evidence to justify the taking of such a drastic and irreversible step. How likely is it that most of those who are now competent (other than, perhaps, those with the gene for afflictions such as Huntington's disease) know, with the degree of certainty necessary to buttress the taking of one's own life, that they will become cognitively and morally incompetent at a certain future point in time?

More specifically, how can now-independent persons know with sufficient assurance that they will in future constitute an unbearable burden? Or, perhaps more relevantly, how can their family members know it? For the important factor, on Hardwig's moral assessment, is not whether I think I am a burden but whether those who care for me will find me a serious burden. So if I am trying to decide whether to go on living, I have the responsibility, according to Hardwig, of trying to estimate the point at which I will become so incompetent as to be considered an intolerable burden by significant other persons in my life.

Moreover, to kill oneself while still competent is surely a sacrifice that is not a matter of moral obligation but at best of supererogation. If I were sufficiently competent to understand the nature of moral obligation, then I would be sufficiently competent to recognize the loss of the remainder of my life as a deprivation, perhaps an enormous deprivation, for I would be fully aware of what I would be giving up, and I would inevitably be sacrificing a period of time during which I am competent and autonomous. Therefore, serious epistemological and moral problems are associated with the questions of what kind of persons have a duty to die and when they possess that duty.

GENDER AND CLASS DIMENSIONS

Hardwig (1997a, 39) states, "A duty to die becomes greater as you grow older. As we age, we will be giving up less by giving up our lives, if only because we will sacrifice fewer remaining years of life and a smaller portion of our life plans." Hardwig is correct in saying that the older one is, the fewer years of life one has. However, he is not correct in assuming that in the case of every individual, the older one is, the smaller portion of one's life plans one is sacrificing. As I pointed out in the discussion in Chapter 2 of the apologist argument that human life is already long enough, the existence of gendered expectations about women's biological and cultural roles, for example, makes it less likely that women will have had as full a human life as many men will have had and more likely that the quality of their lives will be lower than that of men (Bell 1992, 86). Unfortunately, almost nowhere in his discussion of the supposed duty to die does Hardwig consider the ways in which differences of gender, race, or class might affect people's material circumstances or moral obligations. He describes himself as espousing a "family-centered" bio-ethics (Hardwig 2000, 166), but it is one that apparently recognizes no significant gender differences among family members.[9]

But it may be both sexist and classist to assume that people inevitably have opportunities, in young adulthood and middle age, to implement their life plans. Hardwig (1997a, 40) admits that he himself, at the age of fifty-six, has "lived a very good life." He is fortunate to have done so. But material scarcity, lack of income, lack of opportunities, and the requirement of tending to the needs of others may compromise a person's ability to carry out his own life plans. For those reasons, it cannot be assumed that an elderly person has little left to do or experience; the sacrifice of even six months of life may mean the loss of a priceless opportunity to partially make up for what he did not have earlier in life.

However, Beloff, also an advocate of the duty to die, argues that there is a gender dimension to the cultural context of aging that serves to generate what he takes to be the duty to die: the fact that women are more likely than men to bear the responsibility for caring for the very old and ill (1988, 6). Similarly, Stephen Post worries about the potential changes in women's moral obligations wrought by increasing human longevity. He writes, "I am especially concerned with moral questions the aging society creates for young women who will be confronted with potential 'obligations' to elderly parents far more burdensome than they may have anticipated. Are there clear 'obligations' in this sphere . . . ? Does the extension of the life span and the reality of the rising numbers of elderly enlarge these possible 'obligations' beyond what can fairly be asked of adult children?" (1990, 84).

My rejection of the duty to die is in no way an endorsement of the traditional stereotypical ethic of feminine self-sacrifice. Although the possibility of increasing the responsibilities women already carry is a real one, and women are routinely expected to sacrifice their own lives in order to care for others, such a concern is out of place in the discussion of the duty to die. As a feminist, I would reject any attempt to justify a duty to die on the basis of the costs to women of caregiving.[10] Indeed, such a justification sometimes sounds suspiciously like woman blaming. Consider, for example, Ruud ter Meulen's comment that "the willingness to provide informal care is also lessened by a decline in the number of children and *the emancipation of women*. . . . Because employment opportunities will not likely increase in the future (*partly because of the increasing participation of women*), the pensioning age will probably not be changed in the coming decades" (1995, 75, my emphasis). Such statements attribute declines in the availability of caregiving behavior and social security to women's greater freedom rather than to insufficient community support for families.[11] They imply that women are responsible for the plight of elderly people. Instead, I suggest that efforts to create more humane policies with respect to health care and long-term care need to be based on an awareness of the asymmetrical caregiving roles of women and men, roles that are generated partly through gendered expectations of women's nurturing work.

One reason I am deeply suspicious of gendered arguments for the duty to die that appeal to the supposed benefits to women of entrenching such a duty is that there is another side to the gendered nature of the social context of caregiving and the supposed "burden" of elderly people. Both Beloff and Hardwig ignore the crucial empirical fact that women live longer than men. They therefore overlook a significant implication of the claim that there is a duty to die: the fact that it would apply disproportionately to women because women constitute the great majority of elderly people.

It might be argued that there is no imbalance here, on the grounds that men simply develop serious dementia or debilitation (or both) earlier than women and hence would incur the duty to die as frequently as women but sooner in their lives. For two reasons, I don't think this claim removes the prospect of gender discrimination. First, by virtue of living longer, women have more opportunities over a lifetime to incur the duty to die, whereas men die sooner and have less time in which to run the risk of having a duty to die. Second, because their wives outlive them, men are more likely to have women to care for them, and if those women do so willingly and without a sense of burden, then the men are not as likely to meet the condition of burdensomeness as women are because women are less likely to have a partner to care for them.

Now, Hardwig and Beloff could just bite the bullet and say, so be it; the duty to die is an obligation that women will incur more frequently than men because women live longer. But surely there are good reasons to be worried about a moral injunction that would weigh disproportionately on persons of one sex rather than the other, persons who are, in any case, systematically disadvantaged throughout their lifetimes for being female and who are then to be asked to pay a further penalty because of what is arguably an advantage accruing to being female, that of having the capacity to live, on average, longer than men do.[12]

In his book, Hardwig appears to briefly recognize the possibility that near the ends of their lives not all elderly people will have had the same opportunities. Yet that recognition in no way mitigates his affirmation of a duty to die:

> Even if you have not lived a full and rich life, there is more duty to die as you grow older. As we become older, there is a diminishing chance that we will be able to make the changes that would now be required to turn our lives around. As we age, we will also be giving up less by giving up our lives, if only because we will sacrifice fewer years of life. (Hardwig 2000, 90)[13]

Such a response is both insensitive to the real impacts of inequity on the lives of elderly people and ageist in its assumption that old people cannot make significant changes in their lives. In advocating a duty to die even for those who have not benefited from life's opportunities, Hardwig manifests both his unwillingness to challenge the injustice of the status quo and his willingness to see it reinforced. Those who are most likely to have a duty to die will be those who have already been deprived throughout their lifetimes: the poor, the unemployed, those with mental and physical disabilities, and those who may have suffered other disadvantages because of their gender, race, or sexual orientation.

Although wealthy people do get old and become chronically ill or disabled, they are less likely to incur a duty to die on Hardwig's terms because they are less likely to have to be dependent solely on their families for long-term care. To advocate a duty to die is, then, to contribute to social inequalities and to require already-marginalized persons in our society to end their lives prematurely. Indeed, Hardwig goes so far as to point out that if the idea of a duty to die is widely accepted, wealthy people in the United States will be able, through the purchase of excellent health insurance and extended-care insurance, to buy a "personal exemption from a duty to die" (Hardwig 2000, 184, n. 9). So wealthy persons, who may already have had a full and rewarding life, will be enabled to prolong their lives further, while poor people, who may have been deprived of many of life's rewards, will be unable to stave off death despite their lack of access to material and social opportunities. For example, in the United States, women in their forties and older are much less likely than men of similar ages to have health insurance "either because they are more often part-time employees or because their coverage depended upon their relationship with a man, and the coverage ceased when the man died or otherwise left the relationship" (Nelson and Nelson 1996, 355). Such persons are less likely to have been able to accumulate the funds to pay for long-term professional care and may be more likely to face debilitating illnesses, especially if their health was poor early in their lives. Hence, the duty to die is both a flagrant consequence of and a contributor to social injustice.

PRACTICAL PROBLEMS
AND SOCIAL-POLICY IMPLICATIONS

Advocacy of a supposed duty to die raises some difficult practical questions about how individuals should and could act on that duty and about how the society in which they live would go about creating conditions to make it possible for them to carry it out. Creating social policies would require answering questions about whether and under what circumstances those with an ostensible duty to die must simply refuse life-prolonging treatments (and complete, in advance, directives that would reject such treatments) (Hardwig 1997a, 35) or must deliberately reject food and water and suffer a slow and drawn-out death (Hardwig 1997b, 7) or must in some cases fulfill a direct obligation to commit suicide or to demand physician-assisted suicide.

To commit suicide is difficult, perhaps even impossible, for those who are already ill and weak. If one is not capable of solo self-destruction then the duty to die implicates others—sometimes physicians, sometimes family members—who must become the instruments of one's death, whether or not they would ever seek out that role. The demand for physician-assisted suicide, moreover, is an enormous issue in its own right, made more complicated while it remains illegal (Linehan 1997, 4–5).[14] Hardwig (1997b, 7) asserts that we could have the duty to die "whether or not the assistance of a physician is (legally) available." He helpfully provides a detailed discussion of the pros and cons of "taking responsibility" for our death in three different ways: by killing ourselves directly, by means of the ominously named "family-assisted suicide," and by physician-assisted suicide (2000, 90–96). He argues that each could be the best approach in different cases, although "family-assisted suicide" is the most fraught with moral and legal obstacles.

Yet Hardwig remains curiously detached from the legal and political implications of his duty-to-die recommendations. He claims that he "intend[s] no implication that there is a corresponding law that grounds [the] duty [to die]" (1997a, 42, n. 1). In other words, he denies that his advocacy of a supposed duty to die has implications for social policy. But having defended the idea of a duty to die as a general moral obligation potentially incumbent on many thousands of people, he has some responsibility to address its implementation through laws, policies, and social practices. Because Hardwig himself fails to do so, I now turn to a discussion of the work of ethicists who do explicitly discuss the practical and cultural ramifications of accepting a duty to die.

As we saw in Chapter 2, some ethicists have argued that the prolongation of human life will eventually be unacceptably costly to the lives of others if resources are redirected from the care of the young and middle-aged to sustaining the lives of the very old and vulnerable. Thus, a duty to die would be generated not, as Hardwig argues, through the burdens imposed by elderly or disabled individuals on individual friends and family members but rather through the collective social costs of supporting large groups of such persons. Hence, Beloff (1988, 6) argues, "since at the present time death control seems to be much more effective than birth control, we may anticipate a sharp increase in population. Eventually, society may, in self-defense, try to promote voluntary euthanasia, as a sort of demographic duty if we are to avoid letting our present aging population create a demographic disaster!" Similarly, Harris presents a chilling depiction of one possible way in which the requirement to die might be imposed as a matter of social policy. He calls it "generational cleansing": "This would involve deciding collectively how long it is reasonable for people to live in each generation, and trying to ensure that as many as possible live healthy lives of that length. We would then have to ensure that, having lived a fair inning, they died—either by suicide or euthanasia, or by programming cells to switch the aging process on again after a certain time—to make way for future generations" (2000, 59).

It is difficult to be sure of Harris's attitude toward "generational cleansing." He describes it as "seem[ing] desirable" but also acknowledges that it is hard to square with any commitment to the sanctity of life (2000, 59). But surely he has chosen the term deliberately. The idea of "generational cleansing" harks back to extremist ideas in early twentieth-century eugenics, which sought to purify the population by prohibiting the reproduction of those deemed inferior.[15] "Generational cleansing" would share with ethnic cleansing the deliberate murder of hundreds, perhaps thousands, of people, whose only "fault" was that they were considered a burden and were not wanted in society.[16]

Battin also advocates a version of the duty to die as a matter of social policy. She argues that if health-care funding were severely limited and the rationing of resources were necessary, society would be justified in deciding to remove resources from older people and to redirect them to the promotion of health care for younger people, by which she means, roughly, those who are under the age of sixty-five. The reason is that "medical care is less efficient in old age, more efficient at younger ages, and . . . a unit of medical care consumed late in life will have much less effect in preserving life and maintaining normal species-typical function than a unit of medical care consumed at a younger age" (1987, 333). So this form of rationing would liberate resources to be used against diseases that cause death or "opportunity-restricting disability" early in life, thereby "maximiz[ing] one's chances of getting a reasonable amount of life within the normal species-typical age-relative opportunity range" (322). What would happen to elderly people? Policymakers who are rational self-interest maximizers would, she says, prefer to introduce forms of "voluntary but socially encouraged killing or self-killing of the elderly as their infirmities overcome them" (340) in preference to merely letting old people die without treatment, which would occasion great suffering. The elderly person who is expected to end his own life and thus perhaps to give up some benefits attached to living longer would have to recognize "the benefit he has already gained from policies which have enhanced his chances of reaching his current age" (333).

To be entirely accurate, Battin denies that under her hypothesis any individual would actually have a duty to die; such an individual would merely have, she says, "a duty to refrain from further use of medical resources" (1987, 337). The existence of such a duty would then act as motivation for such an individual to resort to the "direct, painless termination of his life." An inducement for recognizing the appearance of such a duty would be the fact that if such persons chose not to die, they would be deliberately "disenfranchised" from full medical treatment (337) and would have to endure the sequelae of illness and increasing disability without the full panoply of available medical treatments.[17] Individuals would be further assisted by the collectively engineered "development of social expectations around the notion that there is a time to die, or . . . that it is a matter of virtue or obligation to choose to die" (335). These expectations would be supported by social practices such as "predeath coun-seling, physician assistance in providing the actual means of inducing death, or ceremonial recognition from such institutions as churches" (336). According to Battin, then, even if individuals did not have an ac-tual duty to die—and they would still be free, or at least experience them-selves as free, to choose not to die (337)—they would encounter the ap-pearance of such a duty, probably during "the last month, half-year, or year of life" (338).

This set of proposals presents many problems. One must wonder how free individuals would be to choose not to die, given that the alternative path might be a slow, painful, and almost-unaided deterioration in health until merciful death arrived of its own accord. The policy would punish the decision not to die. "Instead of an ongoing presumption in favor of life, any member of society could be required to make a case for his/her continued existence (at least to himself/herself and probably to his/her family)" (Cohn and Lynn 2000, 147). As Nat Hentoff (2000, 138) dryly inquires, "Will octogenarians who are not ready to die be publicly shamed as the moral community shuns them?"

But even if it makes sense to say that such individuals are free—for they will not, according to Battin, be murdered if they fail to choose death—the distinction she is making between there being a duty to die and there being merely a socially engineered "expectation" that "there is a time to die"—hence, that there would *appear* to be a duty to die—is obscure. From their subjective point of view as citizens who are social-ized to conform, individuals will simply perceive a moral pressure to die; they will not likely be able to distinguish between the existence of a duty and the existence of the appearance of a duty. Moreover, from an objec-tive point of view, just as a class of actions does not become a moral duty by virtue of being compulsory—by virtue, that is, of individuals' having no choice but to carry out the actions—so also the presence of freedom to act otherwise does not obviate the existence of a duty. On the con-trary, it seems more plausible to say that the existence of a moral duty presupposes the freedom to choose whether to carry it out. So Battin's appeal to freedom not to conform does not mitigate either the subjective force or the objective existence of a duty to die within her proposed social arrangements. Battin's appearance of a duty to die is, then, indistinguishable, within the context of her moral framework, from a genuine duty to die.

In Battin's scheme, the justification of the imposition of (at least) the appearance of a duty to die depends on a condition of "scarcity" with respect to health-care resources (1987, 319). But a policy of age rationing may not even be successful in its stated goal of reducing the collective costs of supporting large groups of elderly people. If, as seems likely, such a policy contributes to reinforcing negative views of old age and of elderly people, it could very well generate in the individuals who are targeted a decreased sense of self-worth, increasing depression, and suicidal thoughts and attempts. Hence, we could see a growth in the number of visits by elderly people to physicians, health-care centers, and emergency wards (ter Meulen 1995, 80). The supposed solution would exacerbate the alleged scarcity that it was intended to remedy. It would also likely generate more, not less, work for family members, who would have to care for elderly relatives who no longer had access to medical care.

But in Western nations the existence itself of a condition of scarcity is open to question. As Battin (1987, 339) acknowledges, "Age rationing is a rationally defensible policy only if the alleged scarcity is real and cannot be relieved without introducing still greater injustices." To claim a severe shortage of health-care resources is to assume that "health care" is a sealed envelope to which no new funds can be added from envelopes now devoted to, for example, military spending, or from savings generated by reducing financial incentives and tax breaks to large corporations. Even if there are genuine problems of resource scarcity, it ought not be assumed that age rationing is the only method of responding to them, especially when age rationing entails coercive pressures on older people to die.

In general, so far no clear evidence indicates that Western cultures have succeeded, under present conditions, in maximizing the fair distribution and use of health-care resources even within age groups: for example, it is not the case that all individuals in the twenty-to-forty age group or the forty-to-sixty-five age group have fair and equal access to health-care services. Quite the contrary. Studies suggest, for example, that even in Canada, with its publicly supported health-care system, wealthier citizens (who are rather modestly defined as individuals in three-person households with an annual income of $40,000 or more) are almost 30 percent more likely than lower income Canadians (those with an annual income lower than $40,000) to see health-care specialists. Those Canadians who do not have a regular family doctor are less likely to receive both primary and specialist care (Priest 2000, A1, A4). Findings such as these show that under the present circumstances some economic classes of individuals benefit more than others from the current distribution of health-care resources. Until existing health-care assets are fairly distributed, it is at least premature to make absolute claims about a scarcity of resources. This is not to say that health services are an unlimited resource or that every possible health-related demand or desire can be met. In Chapter 7 I discuss some general ways of making a more just distribution of health-care resources, a distribution that takes into account and attempts to rectify the social disadvantages inflicted on some specific economic and racial groups, disadvantages that have affected the longevity and quality of their members' lives.

But perhaps the greatest problem with respect to Battin's proposed policy of creating (the appearance of) a duty to die is that its implementation would require an enormous and unconscionable sacrifice on the part of the first generation of elderly people who would be expected to give up their lives. The members of this cohort would not have benefited from the redistribution of savings to younger people and so would not have received improved care in their youth and middle age. In addition, they would be expected to give up their lives prematurely for the sake of those who would then receive both better health care earlier in life and improved life expectancy as a result. Moreover, their friends and relatives could likewise not be expected to see the imposition of this requirement as a good thing because they would prematurely lose loved ones in this first cohort. There is no reason that the members of this first cohort would agree to such a sacrifice (short of a belief in altruistic self-sacrifice), and no reason that they should be expected to. At most, agreeing to be among the first generation of suicides in response to Battin's "time to die" would be supererogatory, not morally obligatory.

Now, despite all my foregoing arguments, I want to concede that caring for a seriously and chronically or mortally ill person can be extremely hard on the caregiver. The demands of such work show the enormous need for suitable health-care arrangements that provide not just respite for the caregiver but also alternative forms of care that would reduce the demands on individual family members while providing enhanced well-being for those who are very elderly or seriously disabled or both. A sign of Hardwig's own implicit commitment (despite his disavowals) to the "individualistic fantasy" that all our lives are "separate and unconnected" is that he nowhere takes seriously the need for advocacy of major policy changes that would reduce and redistribute the caregiving challenge and instead makes caregiving a social rather than an individual responsibility. Although he acknowledges that his arguments might be interpreted as requiring "the sick and debilitated to step in and accept responsibility because society is derelict in its responsibility to provide for the incapacitated" (Hardwig 1997a, 40), he insists nonetheless that it is irresponsible to assume that existing social institutions will protect one's family from one's own illness and debility. Indeed, he adds as a warning that in the United States, at least, the tendency is to shift the responsibility for caring for seriously and chronically ill persons onto family members in order to reduce costs to the health-care system (40).[18]

The consequence of the lack of social provisions for aging persons is that more and more people will have, according to Hardwig's reckoning, a duty to die. But, by advocating and arguing for a duty to die, Hardwig himself is possibly contributing to the creation of conditions that will make it that much easier for a nation like the United States to divest its health-care system of any vestigial responsibility for elderly and ill persons. As he says,

> Our political system and health care reform (in the USA) are also moving in a direction that will put many more of us in the position of having a duty to die. Measures designed to control costs (for the government, and for employers who pay for retirement benefits and health insurance) often switch the burdens of care onto families. We are dismantling our welfare system and attempting to shift the costs of long-term health care onto families. One important consequence of these measures is that more of us will one day find ourselves a burden to our families and loved ones. (Hardwig 2000, 97)

This statement makes absolutely clear that the supposed duty to die is a direct result of policy choices. The goals of "cost containment," lower taxes, and the maximization of profits for private corporations in the health-care business (Hardwig 2000, 175) trump individual and collective well-being. In fact, the promulgation of a duty to die might be regarded as the reductio ad absurdum of a social policy that says that individual responsibility must always replace collective responsibility. Hardwig himself states,

> The renewed emphasis on individual responsibility brings with it the consequence that many more Americans will face a duty to die. Each of us must live and die in the social context we create together: Either we will bear responsibilities collectively or we will have to face them individually—often in terms of personal caregiving, sometimes in the sacrifice of health, and even—if I am correct—in decisions to lay down our own life. (Hardwig 2000, 178)[19]

The questions with which the arguments of Hardwig and other advocates of the duty to die leave us are these: Should we commit ourselves to the passive acceptance of existing social conditions, merely preparing, individually, for future debility and resolving to accept an early death as the personal cost of tolerance for the absence of collective responsibility? Should we collectively confront the impending demands of an aging population by creating a requirement that they sacrifice their health and their lives? Or, instead, should we take seriously the possibility of social change? Should we choose to advocate on behalf of antiageist, antiableist policies that offer opportunities for the flourishing of all citizens, of all ages, health conditions, and abilities? Should we support political and moral principles that do not require people to prematurely shorten their lives? In Chapter 7 I return to a discussion of the policy implications of rejecting the duty to die.

CONCLUSION

I have argued that none of Hardwig's arguments for the existence of a broadly distributed duty to die are successful. Given the potentially noxious consequences of any widespread adoption of support for and social expectations about a duty to die, in this case, even more than in many other instances of existential claims, the burden of establishing the existence of a duty to die clearly rests firmly on those who believe that there is one. I conclude that dying is not, under most circumstances, a duty that any of us have, even if at times we may constitute a burden to our loved ones.

In some circumstances an individual might deliberately choose not to prolong her life out of a sense that to do so would require large sacrifices from her loved ones. She might, for example, choose to forego expensive and complex technological interventions that would prolong her life for only a few more months. Choosing to die could, in a few of the kinds of cases Hardwig is worried about, be an honorable and highly moral decision if doing so would save certain people a great deal of psychological anguish and material loss. The individual might thereby be making a virtuous and morally justified choice (Beloff 1988, 5), providing she were to fully take into account the effects of her decision and of the manner of her dying on those who are close to her. But she would not thereby be fulfilling a duty to die. Choosing to die would almost always be, at best, an act of supererogation.

In arguing against Hardwig and other supporters of the duty to die, I have not tried to show that there is never any duty to die. I agree that on occasion some persons may have a duty to die, but I believe that those situations are far more rare, in the prosperous West, than Hardwig's arguments would indicate. A duty to die could be triggered if the harm caused by a person's existence included serious and widespread mortal injury and death and if that harm were unavoidable.[20] I might, for example, have a duty to die if I were ravaged by a perilous disease that was both unavoidably highly contagious and certain to cause death to others and myself. I would have a duty to die in order to protect people from contagion. In such a case, because, *ex hypothesi*, I am going to die anyway, my duty would consist in the obligation to hasten my own death in order to reduce the danger I pose to others. In other words, I am willing to acknowledge rare cases in which a duty to die may be incumbent on me—those cases, that is, when the continuation of my life is an immediate mortal threat to other persons. This was probably the danger posed by Captain Oates in his sick and debilitated state. However, no good grounds exist for belief in and adherence to any more broadly based duty to die. The threshold of harm necessary to trigger any duty to die is very high indeed.

I conclude that the case against apologism and in favor of prolongevitism is not weakened by the existence of a putative duty to die. In general, as I argue in Chapter 4, people do not have a duty to die chiefly because the loss of one's life means the loss of all other possibilities. Life is the precondition for all other goods. Any moral and political principles that treat elderly or disabled people as if they are social liabilities who must give up the entitlement to go on living and to enjoy life's possibilities are unjust and prejudicial in ways we would never countenance, at the policy level, with respect to other groups. Policies intended to ration health care on the basis of age and to thus engage in "generational cleansing" by means of social expectations about a supposed "time to die" are pernicious expressions of ageism and ableism.

FOUR

"One Swallow Does Not Make a Summer"

Arguments in Favor of Prolonging Human Life

One swallow does not make a summer, nor does one day;
and so too one day, or a short time, does not make a man
blessed and happy.
                Aristotle, Nicomachean Ethics *(1941, 1098a 15)[1]*

In Chapter 2 I examined the four main groups of arguments in favor of apologism, showing that they are unsuccessful, and in Chapter 3 I argued that there is no duty to die. If apologism is not adequately justified, can prolongevists justify extending human life? In this chapter I present and assess prolongevist arguments. Although I think a good case can be made for extending human lives, I shall show that not all the arguments in support of prolongevitism are sound.

Whether a longer life is worth having is at least partly distinct from the question of whether the resources currently exist to provide it. I have already argued that the widely prevailing notion of elderly people as a "burden" is exaggerated and stereotyped. True, social conditions—access to good health care, the availability of long-term care, the presence of appropriate housing, the provision of social networks and cultural services, and so on—can be so poor that a longer life is not worth living. And a prolonged life will not even be possible in extreme conditions such as war, pandemic illness, and catastrophic climate change. But the issue for consideration here is whether a longer life is worth having, given the existence of suitable and relevant supporting conditions, and if the answer tends to be positive, then appropriate policy changes sufficient to bring it about would be warranted. So, in general, it is not possible to circumvent the discussion of the ostensible justification of prolongevitism merely by claiming that the conditions for a longer life are not present; as we saw in the discussions in Chapters 2 and 3 of the stereotyping of elderly people as a "burden," such conditions could be at least partly a product of ageism and an unreflective acceptance of apologism.

My thesis is that, *ceteris paribus*, not wanting to die can remain a rational wish, even in very old age, and there are good reasons to (attempt to) extend the length of human life. The other-things-being-equal provision is essential. I want to argue in favor of a longer life with the following proviso: the longer life would not be lived with severe illness or unrelieved pain or a disablement that undermined the individual's capacity to pursue his or her life projects. Instead, long-living persons would have the opportunity to live comfortably, to enjoy interests of their choosing, and to decide whether and to what extent to be a part of a community of similar long-lived persons or other communities. They would also be able to know or to have strong reason to believe that they would live long. At the same time, they would not be forced to go on living and would, if necessary, be able to opt out through the refusal of life-extending treatments.

Let us now examine the arguments in favor of an extended life.

THE INTRINSIC VALUE OF LONGEVITY

Mothersill (1999, 9) asks, "How is temporality related to value? Is longevity, other things being equal, a positive good? . . . Is sheer longlastingness ever a feature to be admired?" Prolongevitism requires us to consider these general questions. Perhaps prolongevitism can be justified by virtue of an appeal to the intrinsic value of longevity. According to this approach, life should be prolonged because great longevity is inherently good.

Great age would seem to make some objects more valuable; furniture, buildings, and art works are examples. But their extended age is not valuable for its own sake; rather, in some cases the relative rarity resulting from their age increases their monetary value, and in other cases their connection with earlier eras increases their historical, scholarly, and artistic value. In addition, a biologist might value an old tree or a long-lived turtle, to use two of Mothersill's examples, but the scientist likely values them not for their age per se but rather because they are living beings and because they can teach us about the species to which they belong and the conditions that make enduring survival possible. Some cultures—although mainstream Western culture is not among them—value great age in human beings, but their high esteem for elderly persons appears to be directed primarily at what such people are thought to possess—that is, wisdom, experience, and a knowledge of history—rather than at the sheer accrual of years.

Yet old age itself—the accumulation of years of life—can be viewed as an accomplishment of sorts. Mothersill (1999, 19) claims, "Having lived longer than anyone else makes you an object of interest but is unlike showing that you can, for example, run faster than Roger Bannister. It is not counted as a significant achievement." As an empirical generalization this statement appears to be false. Media accounts of very old people often, rightly, treat extreme old age, especially if the individual is still fairly healthy, as an accomplishment, on the grounds that it may take a certain kind of character or perhaps particular choices, efforts, and ways of life to live for a long time. But, once again, what is valued is not sheer temporal endurance itself but rather something that is connected to that endurance, in this case, the living of life in an exemplary way. (We would likely be disturbed to contemplate a very long life lived by a ruthless dictator or a mass murderer, although we might be reluctantly impressed by such a person's capacity to endure.) Hence, Mothersill seems correct when she concludes, "True goods and ills are related only contingently to age" (19).

THE INTRINSIC VALUE OF LIFE

But a prolongevist argument based on intrinsic value might be formulated in another way. Proponents of prolongevitism might argue that all life, human or nonhuman, is intrinsically valuable, perhaps even "sacred," regardless of its specific qualities; that is, life is good independent of the value of other things with which it may be connected, the condition in which it is lived, or its effects on individuals. Some physicians who offer costly high-technology medical treatments to sustain patients who are very close to death act as if they believe that life is intrinsically valuable, and sometimes relatives of very sick people, and the patients themselves, act as if they also think so and hence believe that life must be preserved at all costs, even if it is lived in a condition of great pain or unconsciousness. Hence they take steps to extend human life as long as possible.

Momeyer (1988, 23) suggests that this view has an untenable implication: "If life were absolutely good, we would *prima facie* be justified in any effort, at whatever sacrifice and expense, without regard to all other (nonabsolute) values, to preserve an individual life. . . . We might be obligated to such ceaselessly heroic endeavors for the sake of sustaining any life, even at the cost of overwhelming suffering to the one whose life is sustained." Preserving life in any form and any condition would be an overriding value defeasible only, if at all, by another intrinsic value. As Jay Rosenberg (1983, 134) points out, if life had intrinsic value, then what we now regard as humane practices, both when we deliberately end the lives of suffering animals and when we choose to allow suffering terminally ill human beings to die, would be morally indefensible or at least problematic. Although one must be cautious about judging when life is no longer worth living, it is implausible to suppose that such a point is never reached—for example, by beings in an irreversible persistent vegetative state, by beings in irremediably severe pain, and by beings in an irrevocable condition of physical and mental deterioration. So these plausible sorts of instances where human or nonhuman life is allowed to end or is even hastened toward its ending are evidence against the idea that life itself has intrinsic value and suggest that the preservation and prolongation of life cannot be warranted on that basis.

Moreover, to claim that life has intrinsic value would commit the prolongevist to too much, for, according to the view that life has intrinsic value, a world with more life and longer life is a better world. If life were intrinsically valuable, then its loss, in whatever form the life takes, would always be a prima facie evil. Although prolongevitism advocates the extension of human lives, the typical prolongevist would probably not wish to advocate the prolongation of all forms and instances of life, including, for example, that of mosquitoes, worms, bacteria, and viruses. The timely or even the premature death of, let's say, an ant or a slug, is most likely not a prima facie evil.

Feldman points out another problematic implication of the view that life is intrinsically valuable. If the existence of more life and longer lives automatically makes the world a better place, then human beings would have an obligation to have as many children as we possibly can, regardless of how unhappy they might be. "Our obligation to produce more children continues up to the point where there are so many children that they begin to crowd each other out and thereby shorten their lives" (1992, 176). More ridiculously still, the reductio ad absurdum of the life-is-sacred view would seem to be the moral obligation to encourage and facilitate the reproduction not only of our own species but also of members of all other species.

However, in making the claim that life is intrinsically valuable, the prolongevist might be saying that it is not life itself, undifferentiated and unspecified, that is valuable, but rather it is individual human lives that are valuable for their own sake. Because I am proceeding on the basis of an explicitly secular world-view, without any religious presuppositions, I will not explore theistic and mystical views about the intrinsic value of human lives. However, I have a pragmatic sympathy for this idea as a potential functional antidote to violence and killing and as an argument for peace and nonaggression. The idea promotes, or seeks to promote, increased respect for persons, and I think it could be worth supporting for practical moral reasons, even without the religious baggage often attached to it.[2] Felicia Cohn and Joanne Lynn (2000, 147) suggest, "Society is more humane, kind, and protective when its members hold that every life is precious, even when nearing the end. As we die, we continue living. This period of life should not be stripped of its value and meaning." However, I doubt that the only way of promoting respect for human life even near its end is to believe that human life is intrinsically valuable. This book is intended to demonstrate that there are other good reasons for changing prevailing social attitudes toward aging and toward elderly people and for valuing the lives of old individuals sufficiently to think them worth preserving.

Yet even if the claim about the intrinsic value of human life has pragmatic value in promoting respect for people up until their death, that pragmatic value demonstrates not the truth of the claim but merely its effectiveness in swaying human behavior. Once again, this claim is not immune to Feldman's argument: if individual human lives are intrinsically valuable, then the implausible implication is that we have a moral duty to create as many children as we possibly can. In addition, the claim also has the implausible implication that human fetuses and even the tiniest embryos are equal in moral worth to children and adults.

More significantly, the claim about the intrinsic value of human life probably cannot be made to serve the particular purpose of justifying the deliberate extension of the lives of those who are elderly. Although we could agree that all human beings are deserving of respect qua persons, it is less clear that people who are old are deserving of this generalized respect or of its material embodiment by means of enhanced access to resources to any greater degree than are those who are ten, thirty, or fifty.

The general concept of respect for human life does not appear to justify particular measures aimed at extending the last part of life. It might be suggested that elderly people are more vulnerable than those in other age groups (Battin 1987, 321) and therefore more needy and deserving. However, although elderly people may, on average, be more vulnerable than youth or the middle-aged, they are probably not more vulnerable than infants and children. In any case, elderly people are not all the same, and any moral perspective that treats them as if as individuals they do not possess just the same variety of differences as members of any other group is guilty of overgeneralization. Greater vulnerability may create a responsibility, on the part of individuals or more generally the culture, to care for those who are vulnerable, but it does not constitute an argument in favor of differential respect for all old people, nor is it adequate to justify special measures to extend the length of the last part of human life.

Now it is true, as Nagel insists, that only very negative experiences are sufficient to make the loss of one's life not an evil. Nagel takes this fact to imply that life itself has a positive value. He endorses the anti-utilitarian idea that it is "good simply to be alive, even if one is undergoing terrible experiences": "There are elements which, if added to one's experience, make life better, there are other elements which, if added to one's experience, make life worse. But what remains when these are set aside is not merely *neutral:* it is emphatically positive. Therefore life is worth living even when the bad elements of experience are plentiful, and the good ones too meager to outweigh the bad ones on their own" (1975, 402, his emphasis). Similarly Momeyer (1988, 22) points out, "We nearly always suppose that continued life, even with greater than ordinary suffering, deprivation, and hardship, is to be preferred to death." We regard the saving of lives, even those filled with misery, as ordinarily a benefit to those saved, and we do not accept facile calculations of good and bad as simplistic justifications for their deaths.

But these observations about human preferences do not show that some residue, mere life itself, something left when good and bad "elements" are set aside, is good in itself. Momeyer (1988, 25) goes on to argue that because some losses of goods—such as the loss of consciousness or the capacity to set goals—destroy our very humanity, the connection between such basic goods and human life is not merely accidental or contingent but necessary. He concludes that any fully human life—that is, any human life that possesses the features of "consciousness and its capacities and propensities to create projects, set goals, have an acute awareness of possibility and future" (25)—is intrinsically good. "The connection of basic goods to human life is not simply accidental, but necessary. It is what makes life intrinsically good, and when life is thus intrinsically good, it is in the fullest sense *human* life. There is no fully human life, no life of a person, that is not intrinsically good" (25, his emphasis).

This argument suggests that if there is any room for the concept of goodness in the case for prolongevitism, it does not belong in the claim that mere human existence, mere life that happens to be lived by beings belonging to the human species, is intrinsically valuable. Instead Momeyer's argument shows that it is the perceiving, planning, enjoying, and acting features of human lives that have a high degree of moral significance. Capacities such as sensing, remembering, anticipating, feeling, thinking, valuing, and choosing enable human beings to live lives that are fully realized. Although we may not be able to go so far as to say that these features, or human lives possessing them, are intrinsically good, the prospect of ongoing opportunities for experiencing and doing, competence and creation, makes the possession and extension of human life valuable. As Momeyer (1988, 22–23) says, "So long as there is the slightest prospect of satisfying experience—not even a majority of such experience, but the possibility of it—human beings endure abysmal suffering and hope for more and better life." Death means the end of the possibility of any more experience whatsoever, and this loss, not the end of sheer biological existence, constitutes the threat to human life. Death is an evil to the extent that it deprives us of values we would have enjoyed if we had not died (Feldman 1992, 140).

No friend, himself, to prolongevitism, Callahan (1998, 142) nonetheless writes, "The greatest threat to the self is that of death, the utter de-struction and disappearance of the self. This is not to say that death is necessarily the worst fate that can befall the self; sometimes it is a wel-come release. But that is the exception. Death in general remains an ob-vious threat because the possibility of life is the foundation for all other human possibilities." The reason we assume that a hard or pain-filled life can still be worth living is not that living is intrinsically valuable in itself nor even that human capacities for experience are intrinsically good but rather that as long as a life of human competence continues, a prospect, or at least a possibility, remains that the individual sufferer's experiences will change and that he or she can create a better existence. For this rea-son, we could say that as long as there is life there is hope. In some cases we might be inclined to judge, after a life is over, that a life of great and unrelenting "suffering, deprivation, and hardship" was not after all worth living. But we would be unlikely to make such a judgment as long as there was some reasonable prospect for improvement. So, life is not valuable in itself but, rather, for the potential it offers for experiencing and doing. Being alive is the precondition for having, obtaining, experiencing, cre-ating, and doing everything else that human beings hold valuable, what-ever those values might be.

In Chapter 2 I discussed at length the Lucretian claim that "we are continually engaged and fixed in the same occupations; nor, by the pro-longation of life, is any new pleasure discovered" (Lucretius 1997, 143). According to Lucretius, life's enjoyments and gratifications are fixed and limited; if we live too long we will have no choice but to simply repeat what we have already done, and such repetition would be boring and fu-tile. I argued that for most human beings this claim is simply false and that the wealth of opportunities to explore, experience, and engage means that ordinary human life, lived within its current bounds, is seldom if ever adequate for all that the world offers. For that reason, it makes sense to want to extend life for as long as life holds out the prospect of further opportunities.

Rosenberg (1983, 202) claims that because one could, in principle, have a long and miserable life or a short and happy one, it follows that "the quality of a person's life . . . is independent of its magnitude, that is, of its length." But although the quality of a person's life may in some cases be independent of its length, it is not necessarily and always independent: quantity of life can have an effect on quality of life. From a past-regarding point of view, one's life might turn out to be sad just because it is (too) short—if, that is, one were unable to see one's children grow up or unable to complete a long-desired artistic project or unable to have the life experiences to which one had looked forward. One is justified in being more than merely neutral toward the prospect of extending one's life. Death is not, as Rosenberg claims, "value-neutral" (1983, 209). To the extent that most people get some value or enjoyment out of their lives, death is in fact an evil for most persons, an instrumental evil. Most people want to go on living. It is not irrational to want to stave off death.

Death brings to an unequivocal end the chance to enjoy the goods of experience and action, and that fact is probably the strongest argument for prolongevitism. As Harris argues:

> All of us who wish to go on living have something that each of us values equally although for each it is different in character, for some a much richer prize than for others, and we none of us know its true extent. This thing is of course "the rest of our lives." So long as we do not know the date of our deaths then for each of us the "rest of our lives" is of indefinite duration. Whether we are 17 or 70, in perfect health or suffering from a terminal disease we each have the rest of our lives to lead. So long as we each fervently wish to live out the rest of our lives, however long that turns out to be, then if we do not deserve to die, we each suffer the same injustice if our wishes are deliberately frustrated and we are cut off prematurely. (Harris 1996, 436)

Members of many species of nonhuman animals also possess some or all of the same or similar capacities as human beings—for example, the capacities for perception, planning, remembering, choosing, and acting.

As long as they possess these capacities, and prospects for further experiencing and doing, their lives are worth preserving. Although I have rejected the idea that a prolongevist could be legitimately committed to extending the span of all forms of life on the grounds of their supposed intrinsic value, I do not assume that human beings have no obligations to avoid harming or killing nonhuman entities, whether by direct attack, indirectly through habitat destruction, or, in the case of animals directly dependent on us, through the failure to provide the necessities of life. Indeed, I believe that the burden of proof in the deliberate destruction of any form of life rests on the one who would do the destroying—the reason being that life itself is the condition necessary for the acquiring of the goods peculiar to each form of life. My point is not that such proofs cannot be given—if the use of antibiotics against harmful bacteria is morally controversial it is not because bacteria lose their lives—but just that the ethical onus is on the would-be destroyer, not on those who oppose destruction.

To say that the burden of proof rests on those who would end life is not to say that we always have a de facto obligation to prolong the lives of nonhuman animals. Nonhuman animals are obviously different from human beings in that people are capable of formulating a conscious and overt desire for a longer life and of deliberately seeking to extend that life. Although in many cases a longer rather than a shorter life is a good for an animal, no elephant, cat, or hamster regrets the short duration of its existence and wishes to exist for longer. While human beings can be prolongevists, no nonhuman animal that we know of possesses the conceptual sophistication to enable it to entertain the prolongevist point of view. No elephant, cat, or hamster experiences cognitive frustration or personal regret at the prospect of being unable to experience all that it wishes or to complete projects that it has only just begun. They do not form plans for the future whose value to them would give them reason to want to prolong their lives or whose value would otherwise compensate them for suffering or for the absence of hedonic goods.

Thus, if prolongevitism is extended to nonhuman beings, its extension is necessarily both desired and accomplished not by the beneficiaries themselves but by their human owners and caretakers. For example, an animal-loving prolongevist might seek a longer life for his pet cat or companion dog. But arguments would have to be made to show that such lives ought to be or become considerably longer than they now are by virtue of statistical normality. The justification of a prolongevist approach to the lives of nonhuman animals will depend on such things as the environmental and social costs of prolonging their lives, the quality of their lives, their proportion of positive to negative experiences, and the minimization of pain and suffering. The justification for such an extension will also lie, in part but certainly not exclusively, in the values possessed by nonhuman animals for human beings themselves. It would be fairly easy to justify measures to prolong the lives of animals whose existence is otherwise compromised by human neglect, predation, or environmental degradation. Moreover, some animals, especially so-called domesticated animals like cows and chickens,[3] may lead relatively impoverished and deprived lives and would benefit from being given new opportunities to enjoy such goods as comfort, adequate nourishment, and species-specific activities. Although there may be reasons, even strong reasons, for taking a prolongevist stance toward some nonhuman animals, the justification for that stance does not lie in any claim about the alleged intrinsic value of life itself or of individual lives. Instead it lies in the prospects for experiencing and acting, both for the animals themselves and for human beings.

THE RIGHT TO LIFE

Some prolongevists attempt to defend prolongevitism on the basis not of the supposed value of life itself but rather of a supposed right to life. Within the context of the possible prolongation of life, the idea of a right to life seems to be useful at the very least for purposes of defending people against deliberate, unjustified, unsought attempts to end their lives. If I have a right to life, then I have a right not to be killed—that is, I have a negative or what is sometimes called a "weak" or "liberty" right against other human beings that they shall not act in such a way as to terminate my life.

John Woods (1978) offers an interesting amplification of this idea, which makes a case for prolongevitism by linking the right to life in the negative or liberty sense to the idea of a right to go on living. Some people, he suggests, might compare the right to life to the right to make money. If, as some believe, one's right to make money "varies inversely with how much money one already has," perhaps it might also be argued that one's right to go on living varies inversely with how long one has already lived (122). Nonetheless, he states, one's age or temporal distance from death probably is not a relevant measure of one's right to live.

> It *may* be that one's right to make money does not always imply the right (or as strong a right) to make *more* money. But it surely cannot be true that the right to live does not imply the right (or as strong a right) to live *longer*. If I have no (or only a diminished) right to live longer than now, then in reducing (to zero or not, it doesn't matter) the protections of my longer life, you also reduce to that very degree the protections of my life, period. How else can you deprive me of my right to live longer than now without depriving me of my right to live now? It is not this way with the monetary case; the cancellation of my right to make more money than the amount I have now does not involve the cancellation of my right to make any money whatever; it does not deprive me of the riches accumulated to date. (Woods 1978, 122, his emphasis)

If a person reached the point at which he no longer had a right to make more money, then he might eventually get back to the point where he has the right to make money again, perhaps through the gradual spending or loss of money. "But if I have no right to live longer, then, since there is no prospect of my getting younger to the point where I recover my right to live on, the loss of the protections of a longer life are [*sic*] equivalent to the loss of the protections of my very life itself" (Woods

1978, 122). So, according to Woods, that a right to life in the liberty sense implies a right to go on living is shown by the fact that the negation of the right to go on living automatically negates the right to life.

I see one immediate problem with this argument. Woods's contrast between a right to life and the right to make money is not helpful. Contrary to Woods, the absence of a right to go on living could not deprive one of the years one has already lived. Apologists could say that just as no longer having a right to go on making money does not deprive you of the money you have now, so also no longer having a right to go on living does not deprive you of the life you have already lived. If my right to go on living ends at age seventy, I am not thereby deprived of the seventy years I have already lived; they are, so to speak, mine to keep, and, indeed, they cannot be cancelled. The cancellation of my right to live longer does not cancel my life as it has already been lived. I may (or may not) go on living; I just do not go on living by virtue of a right to do so.

However, I agree with Woods that the liberty right to life is not a function of one's age or distance from death. Killing a man who might have died a month later anyway is in moral terms just as bad as killing a man who would not have died for another thirty years. The likely number of years left in the victim's life neither increases nor attenuates the immorality of killing him, and there is and should be no moral or legal recognition of a mitigation of punishment for the deliberate and unsought killing of competent elderly people or those otherwise close to death. Whatever another person's prospects for longer life, his life is not mine to take, and in that sense he has a right to his own life. As the discussion in Chapter 3 showed, there is no duty to die, and there are no good reasons to suppose that people lose their entitlement to protection from deliberate, preemptive, unsought attempts to end their lives simply by virtue of reaching a certain age or by virtue of a particular condition of ill health or disablement.

But even if the existence of a right to life in the liberty sense is conceded, as I think it readily can be, it does not do a lot to enhance the case for prolongevitism. Although having a liberty right to life would seem, minimally, to mean that at any given time it is wrong to take my life away from me, having this right to life is not the same as having a right to extend my life if doing so requires not just protection from accidentally or deliberately inflicted mortal violence or even from normative social pressures to stop living but, in addition, access to supplementary health-care services and resources that will extend my life. To serve the case of prolongevitism we seemingly also need to establish the existence of further entitlements. Some prolongevists might therefore want to advocate the existence and acknowledgement of a right to life in a strong sense. Understood in the entitlement sense, as a welfare right, the right to life as a positive right would be the entitlement to all possible assistance to preserve, enhance, and extend life.[4]

Often a welfare right to life is ascribed to some groups of people rather than to others. Thus, young people are said to be strongly entitled to the continuation of life and to the goods that it offers simply because they have lived for so short a time that they have not yet had the chance to experience many of life's benefits. Their opportunities and capacities for experience have not been fully realized and developed. The shorter one's life is, the greater is the likelihood that one has missed out on life's bounties. As Feldman (1992, 183–184) puts it, "We may agree that something very bad happens when an old person dies—even if his death is quite painless. Yet many would hold that something even worse happens when a young person dies. Perhaps this intuition is based in part on the notion that the old person has already enjoyed his fair share of life, whereas the young person has been shortchanged."

Feldman is correct in saying that the death of a young person certainly shortchanges him or her. If the point of Feldman's claim that young people are entitled to more life is just that they are deserving because they have enjoyed less of life itself, then the claim concedes that quantity of life itself is prima facie desirable. This is at least part of the case that the prolongevist is making on behalf of elderly people. Recall Harris's argument that whatever age a person may be, she may want to go on living just as much as a person who is much younger because she has her own unique remaining life to live. It is unjust to discount the rest of her life simply because she happens to be old. According to Harris, from a future-regarding point of view, two persons of different ages may have the same entitlement to continued life, for respecting the wish to go on living is "the most important part of what is involved in valuing the lives of others" (Harris 1996, 440). Each of them has the prospect of further experience and action that is ended when they die.

The evil of a death is not a simple function of the length of the life that is lived, and the strength of the entitlement to life is not inversely related to years lived. We cannot assume that an old person, despite his age, has already enjoyed his fair share of life. It is true, as Feldman says, that "something very bad" happens when a person of any age dies, even if the death is painless. While Feldman (1992, 184) assumes, simplistically, that "the amount of life that a person deserves depends at least in part on how much life he or she has already experienced," the issue for prolongevitism is not only the quantity of life lived but also the content of that life and its prospects for the future. It is a mistake to think that only young people have not yet had the opportunity to enjoy the goods of human life. Although the shorter one's life, the less one is likely to have experienced, it does not follow that a long life inevitably means a fuller life. As Anita Silvers points out, such a belief assumes the existence of "a fair social system with a level playing field" (Silvers 1999, 217). Not all older people have received or experienced the things for which we automatically believe young people should have the opportunity. As I argued in Chapter 3, many elderly people have been deprived of material comforts, good health care, education, travel, fulfilling work, access to the arts and sciences, and so on. So if the absence of opportunity to experience these things makes life particularly of potential value to the young, it should equally make life of value to many who are old—perhaps even the majority of elderly people worldwide.

Silvers remarks, with deliberate irony:

On the "fair life's share" argument, older persons who have been wronged as a result of their membership in groups misperceived as weak and incompetent now should be offered *more* opportunity than members of present and past dominant classes. For example, as women belong to a class disadvantaged by being considered, until very recently, to be incapable and dependent, and thereby to be un-suitable recipients of the full range of competitive opportunities, the "fair life's share" argument suggests that aged women be compen-sated by receiving *greater* support for actualizing their opportunities to flourish than is afforded to both young and old men. (Silvers 1999, 217, emphasis added)[5]

In Chapter 7 I return to a version of the idea that disadvantaged persons may be entitled to proportionately more resources in later life. Here I want to emphasize Silvers's point that older women, older people of color, and older persons with disabilities, despite their age, may very well not have benefited from their sheer quantity of life and therefore are in no way necessarily advantaged as compared with young people (cf. Dixon 1994, 625). Hence, it is false to assume, across the board, that any young person is automatically more entitled to lengthened life than any old per-son. It is both unjustified and perniciously ageist to suppose that old people are a homogeneous group about whom overarching generaliza-tions about needs, desires, abilities, histories, health, and achievements can be made.

In a fascinating article entitled "Death's Gender" (1999), James Lin-demann Nelson contests the work of philosophers such as Frances Kamm, Daniel Callahan, and Norman Daniels, who, he says, assume that "death's significance is, in the general case, a function of age alone" (116). This purported "superfact"—"a fact that characterizes a set of people in a manner so relevant to distribution of goods or assignment of duties that none of their other traits, nor any of the traits of potential claimants not in that group can, singly or in combination, defeat its dispositive rele-vance" (116)—erases the significance for death of ethnicity, class, and gender. Rejecting this supposed superfact, Nelson claims that "different facts about death affect different people at different times in different ways" (119). He concludes, "Handing out resources in ways that favor the young cannot be justified as straightforwardly as proponents would intend. . . . In figuring out how to direct health care budgets or hand out transplantable livers, comparing the stringency of the claims of the young qua young to those of the old qua old is a form of 'false totalization,' and thus is disrespectful, particularly (though not solely) to people who happen to be old" (125). This argument supports the idea that if prolongevitism can be grounded in a suitably modified form of a welfare right to life, then that right should not be attributed to young people exclusively.

In defending his version of apologism, Callahan acknowledges that his proposed policy of reducing access for elderly people to high-technology medicine will disproportionately affect women because women live longer and also suffer more chronic diseases and disabilities. He has an ingenious (and possibly disingenuous) response:

> Women would fail to get what dead males already fail to get as well; it is thus not as if women are being denied a benefit that men get. Men would fail to gain the benefit by virtue of dying before needing it, women by virtue of rationing. Those men who managed to live as long as women would be denied the same high-technology benefit as the surviving women. It is, then, under this interpretation, hard to see where women would be victims of discrimination. (Callahan 1999, 194)

There are good reasons to be suspicious of Callahan's argument. First, although it is true that men who happen to live as long as women would equally suffer under this policy, the fact remains that the large majority of long-living human beings are women, and therefore a practice that denies long-living people life-sustaining medical care does as a matter of fact discriminate against women, even if the intention of the policy is to discriminate "only" against elderly people whatever their sex. Second, we could question why men's life expectancy should be taken to be the norm toward which women's life expectancy can legitimately be lowered. Why should men's relatively poorer health constitute the standard? It is easy to suspect that the answer, however covert or even unconscious, is just that men have always set the standard for human striving and that their biological needs and capacities are considered to constitute the human norm. But there is no good reason to think that men should be regarded as representative of the human race as a whole. Indeed, there are more reasons to take the contrary perspective: that women's higher life expectancy sets a standard that would be an appropriate goal for men because it would provide them with an advantage that they are otherwise missing, and it would even the playing field in a way that would not disadvantage members of either sex.

Third, although men's life expectancy is currently lower than that of women, this disadvantage is not (in contrast to Callahan's proposal) deliberately socially engineered, at least not through any direct policies or resource-allocation decisions. Callahan is proposing to take calculated steps to even the playing field through inequitable social engineering by disproportionately disadvantaging women, a proposal that reflects intentional gender discrimination. Callahan's defense against the charge of gender discrimination in denying a welfare right to life to elderly people is a failure. In Chapter 7 I discuss further the nature of men's life-expectancy disadvantage and some equitable ways of responding to it.

Callahan also acknowledges that many elderly people may not have enjoyed all the opportunities that we would associate with a good life. However, he is, once again, insouciant. He says, "More old age is not likely to make up for those deficiencies . . . ; the pattern of such lives, including their deprivations, is not like to change significantly in old age, much less open up radically new opportunities hitherto missing" (Callahan cited in Dixon 1994, 624). This callous observation fails to consider the diversity of people's lives, a diversity that endures even in their last years, and it falsely assumes that all elderly people become inflexible and unable or unwilling to change. It reveals the inherent conservatism of Callahan's apologism, which advocates not just accepting human longevity as it is but also accepting the social conditions that help to determine both the life spans that people achieve and the conditions under which they live. It is hardly radical or excessive to reject such acquiescence and to retort that steps should be taken to modify the social climate and the material conditions in which people of all ages continue to suffer deprivation and in which many may find it difficult to make any changes in their lives.

In addition, we do not yet have a complete and accurate understanding of all the ways in which older persons might be able to take up new opportunities. Our inability to foresee these possibilities is at least partly the result of culturally created limitations on such persons. Indeed, as I pointed out in Chapter 1, to be an "elderly person" is to have an at least partly socially constructed—hence potentially reconstructible—identity. Currently, old age is reified in such a way that it subsumes the elderly person's entire life and also other people's concept of that person. But as Pogrebin states, "None of us wants our age to subsume our entire identity. We don't want to *be* our age, we want to be ourselves" (1996, 33, her emphasis)—and presumably in being ourselves, we could be much more than what our age categories currently predict.

The badness of death may therefore be directly related to the current conditions of one's life, to the opportunities that one may or may not have already enjoyed, as well as to one's future prospects for experience and activities, all of which can be a function of one's social situation. The value of extended life lies in the prospects it offers for further experience and action, and it is a mistake to assume that old people are inherently incapable of benefiting from them.

Instead of deploying the concept of a positive right to life to argue for prolonging human life, Feldman posits an explicitly desert-based theory of longevity. He says that, other things being equal, people deserve more out of life, and, by extension, more *of* life, the more they have put into their life. He gives the example of two young women of approximately the same age with equal abilities and opportunities. One sacrifices, studies, and works diligently to be ready for a career as a scientist, while the other wastes her talents and makes nothing of herself. According to Feldman, if both women die prematurely, although a great injustice would occur in each case, the greater injustice would occur to the would-be scientist "since, by early death, . . . she loses a life in which she has made a greater investment" (1992, 203). One's entitlement to more life is directly proportional to the "investment" that one has made of one's time, talents, and strivings.

The problem is that other things are rarely equal. I don't know whether two young women could have roughly equal abilities and opportunities, or, at least, I don't know how we would ever know that they did. As I've already argued, the circumstances in which people are or are not able to develop and express their talents can vary enormously. What if the one who makes nothing of herself is a member of a racial minority? Has a disability? Is the child of physically or sexually abusive parents? Conditions such as these can affect what we make of ourselves, however good our talents and opportunities may otherwise appear to be. We ought not to take failure to achieve as any de facto evidence of laziness, a disposition to squander talent, or other character flaws. Because there is a fundamental epistemological problem with respect to understanding why some people succeed and others apparently like them do not, and because a variety of social disadvantages may affect people's capacity to achieve, I cannot endorse the Feldman view that one's entitlement to longevity is proportionate to how much one has already put into one's life. In addition, even if we could somehow be quite sure that a failure to achieve is directly the result of a character flaw like laziness, I doubt that the person is less entitled to more life. Western societies do not deny people access to health-care treatments for ailments that may be incurred through "life-style" decisions, such as smoking, drinking, overeating, and the use of illegal drugs. People do not earn the right to live longer based on past accomplishments or lose it through their absence or through bad choices. Rather, it is the prospects for the future that justify both the desire to live longer and the efforts to extend life.

I have assumed that there is a right to life in the negative or liberty sense. The concept of a right to life in the positive, or welfare, sense would be an even more powerful moral instrument on behalf of prolongevitism. It would defeat the notion that people must "earn" longer life, whether through personal "investment," past accomplishments, or demographic characteristics. Because the badness of death is not a mere product of the years one has lived, the right to go on living is not a function of one's age.

But acknowledging the existence of a fully realized right to life in the welfare sense, whether for everyone or for special groups of persons, could be problematic, both for individuals and for communities. In some cases, extending such a right would be counterproductive if prolonging life did not confer any benefits or if the harm it generated for the individual was so high as to overwhelm the benefits (Gillon 1996, 200). Just as significantly, the acknowledgement of a right to life in the welfare sense could entail the exploitation of vast amounts of resources that would have to be devoted to the scientific investigation of aging and ways to prevent it, medical and other forms of health care (not only to prevent illnesses and disabilities but also to combat intrinsic sources of decline), and social-welfare measures to sustain people's lives with reasonable comfort and opportunity in great old age. In its most extreme interpretation, the recognition of a right to life in the welfare sense could devour resources to the extent that it overrode all other priorities.

Hence, because it raises complex ethical and social-policy questions with respect to the employment of social resources and the kinds, amounts, and distribution of human health care, I shall not assume that there is an unconstrained right to life in the welfare sense. Instead, we need to engage in a concrete and practical assessment of the moral, social, and political demands that the adoption of a prolongevist perspective would necessitate. In Chapter 7 I examine the scope of and limitations on possible further entitlements implied by a limited recognition of a welfare right to life and also the role of such a right in the formation and enactment of social policy with respect to prolongevitism.

ADVANCES IN HEALTH CARE AND OTHER CONTRIBUTIONS TO HUMAN WELL-BEING

One more argument for prolongevitism remains, an argument based on some of the alleged beneficial social consequences of extending human lives. In Chapter 2 we saw that Callahan denies that an increase in the average human life span would have positive social consequences. He asserts that an increase in average life span from the low- to the mid-eighties would not "lead to a better family life, greater economic productivity, a richer cultural and scientific life, or a generally higher standard of collective happiness and sense of well-being" (1998, 134). But prolongevists reject this pessimistic assessment and foresee collective as well as individual benefits emerging from increases in human longevity. Gruman (1977, 6), for example, argues that meliorism in general "is an indispensable element in modern society, for a community based on industry, technology, and science must continue to advance or it will face disaster."

Let's examine this argument. Consider the potential economic benefits of prolongevitism: "The option to live a longer life should increase the return on investment in human capital. To the extent that improved health and longevity increase the effective expected working time, there should be increased investment in market-oriented skills, and also a prolongation of the investment period in the life cycle" (Ben-Porath 1991, 98). The longer people live in a healthy state the greater is the chance for them to continue to contribute their labor. In Battin's words, the social contributions made by many elderly people are already "in fact more secure than the still potential contributions of the young" (1987, 321) and provide a sort of track record that promises future potential.

It is further argued that older people have the benefit of years of experience and observation, which enable them to contribute understanding and insights that younger people might not yet be ready to generate.

Gruman (1977, 70) quotes Luigi Cornaro, a prolongevist of the eighteenth century, who regards old age as a time at which "men appear to the best advantage in learning and virtue—two things which can never reach their perfection except with time." Cornaro argues that the most significant works in science and literature have been created in old age. In addition, others say that happy, comfortable old people are moral exemplars as well as sources of optimism and hope for younger people, both in their current lives and in their future prospects:

> A pleasant, comfortable old age, either in an institution or at home, would show the young and middle-aged generations that they have ample time left in life to achieve certain desires and to realize their human potentials. It would teach that life is not meaningless and devoid of quality beyond the age of retirement, that the young and middle-aged need not be greedy and egotistical, rushing to acquire all that they can before life inevitably ends at retirement. (Blasszauer 1995, 127)

According to Gruman (1977, 91), belief in the possibility and desirability of extending human life also contributes specifically to the advancement of science and medicine. So another purported argument for prolongevitism is, he believes, the creation of important developments in health care. Research that is aimed at prolonging people's lives will improve the health status of younger people—for example, through developing a better understanding of nutrition and creating means to prevent or reduce the incidence of serious diseases.[6]

Finally, prolongevists argue that more specific positive benefits, for individuals and for communities, result from having people live longer. Relationships can be continued longer. Friendships need not end early, cut short by death. Individuals can enjoy the company and love of their grandparents, aunts, uncles, and parents for a longer period of their own lives. As Carolyn Rosenthal (2000, 47) remarks, "The longer duration of grandparents' presence in a family ought to create benefits in terms of family cohesion and continuity. It certainly creates the opportunity to be an adult grandchild and for grandparents to have relationships with their grandchildren that extend into the latter's adulthood."

All these claims about the purported beneficial consequences of extending human life appear, uncontroversially, to be true. They acknowledge the many ways in which the adoption of prolongevitism is of potential benefit to everyone within a society, old and young alike. But if taken as the sole justification for prolongevitism, as proof that there should be a policy favoring the prolongation of people's lives just because doing so will potentially benefit more than those who are old, more than just the individuals whose lives are extended, this argument is unconvincing. It takes a purely instrumental view of people, particularly old people. Yet we do not countenance this approach to members of other age groups or to members of other social groupings. We would never say that our society should keep gays or Jews or short people alive for the sake of what they are likely to offer to the rest of society. Indeed, the argument for prolongevitism from social benefits may unwittingly play into the hands of apologists who are anxious about the alleged "burdens" that hordes of old people with long lives will supposedly create. By endorsing social divisions between the old and the not-old, it suggests assessing the wisdom of keeping people alive in terms of costs and benefits to the young and middle-aged and implicitly assumes that younger demographic groups' needs and desires have the most social significance. And *per impossibile* if, in relying on this claim, it turned out that prolonging human life benefited only those elderly persons whose lives were prolonged, the case for prolongevitism would collapse. Such an instrumental approach implies that if it were possible to secure comparable or greater economic, scientific, and social benefits by letting old people die, then it would be justifiable to do so.

Claims about old people's individual contributions are also of doubtful value in the case for prolongevitism. True, ageist ideology encourages the cultural undervaluation of what many elderly people have accomplished, and their work should not be overlooked or underestimated, as it so obviously is in the work of apologists such as Hardwig. But, realistically speaking, there is no necessary relationship between age and the development of wisdom or an increase in social contributions. As I have stressed, some people may have failed to contribute—not necessarily through weaknesses of character but more likely through lack of opportunity or lack of education; some may have been tied all their working lives to jobs that were sheer drudgery yet offered little of social value. Moreover, while the genuine value of individual old people is often denied, there is also a cultural tendency to romanticize in general terms the "wisdom" and experience of those who are elderly.[7] But as I have insisted, elderly people are just as varied as the members of any other group, and therefore it is inappropriate and unfair to require or expect from them the manifestation of exceptional gifts.

On the one had, those who are old do have the advantage of experience; many have learned from it, and, to those willing to listen, they have much to offer. But we should not assign elderly people the role of "social housewives, offering advice that may never be heard, lacking the socio-political status or financial resources to enforce needed changes" (Dixon 1994, 633). Dixon (1994, 616) points out that Callahan allots to elderly people a moral expectation of "finding meaning through self-sacrifice rather than fulfillment of personal needs or exploration of personal identity." This prescription, Dixon says, is similar to traditional gender-role requirements for women. The imputation of such a social function is sheer stereotyping.

On the other hand, some elderly people may not have learned much from their experiences, may not be particularly wise, or may have been so limited in their experiences or restricted and marginalized by their social status that they were unable to learn much. As Lazarus Long, the two thousand-year-old hero of Heinlein's classic *Time Enough for Love*, remarks, "Age does not bring wisdom. Often it merely changes simple stupidity into arrogant conceit. Its only advantage, so far as I have been able to see, is that it spans *change*. A young person sees the world as a still picture, immutable. An old person has had his nose rubbed in changes

and more changes and still more changes so many times that he *knows* it is a moving picture, forever changing" (1973, 19, his emphasis). I don't think we ought to expect elderly people to be paragons, nor need we claim that they are in order to justify extending their lives.

An argument based on the alleged contributions of elderly people comes uncomfortably close to Feldman's desert argument for prolonging life. But the opportunity to live longer is not something that has to be earned. Moreover, it is important to be aware of the ways in which the concept of "contributions" may be gendered and racialized and the ways in which the appeal to individual contributions could, at least individually, work against the best interests of people of color and women of all races. If contributions are understood as career activities, business achievements, or academic, scientific, cultural, or athletic goals reached, then white women and members of both sexes of racial minorities, who have had fewer opportunities, even in the recent past, to participate in mainstream public social life, will have fewer credits (Frances Kamm, cited in Nelson 1996, 58), and their apparent entitlement to live longer will be underestimated.

It is unreasonable and unfair to tie the justification of prolongevitism directly either to past or to potential social contributions of individual elderly people. One important reason for extending people's lives is to give them the opportunities they may not have had earlier in their existence. Those opportunities could include the chance to contribute to their society but need not be confined to it. Nor should the case rest on collective benefits from elderly people as a group—unless those collective benefits also accrue to those who are elderly. There is no reason to uniquely define the value of old people by their contributions to the well-being of members of other groups (Dixon 1994, 632). The argument for prolongevitism should not be made to rest solely on the putative gains for younger people. Defying ageism requires that we acknowledge and accept that prolonging human life benefits primarily those who would otherwise be close to death.

CONCLUSION

In Chapter 2 I showed that the justifications offered for apologism are inadequate. In this chapter I have argued that some but not all of the arguments for prolongevitism are also open to question. So, after evaluating both perspectives, I conclude that prolongevitism is stronger. I advocate prolongevitism because many people in fact want to live longer, because this life is the only one we have, because many old people have been deprived of life's goods, because continuing to live offers the prospect of ongoing opportunities for further experience and action, and because the apologist alternatives to prolongevitism are morally untenable.

Having made the case against apologism and in favor of prolongevitism, I turn next to two groups of questions: a group of metaphysical and ethical questions, and a group of practical policy questions. With regard to the metaphysical and ethical issues, if one agrees that apologism is inadequate and that there are good grounds for extending human life because of the ongoing opportunities for experiencing and doing that greater longevity offers, one is led into difficult questions about just how much life is long enough. If prolonging life is, *ceteris paribus*, desirable, are there any reasonable limits to the length of a good life? How much more life is it desirable to have? Is there an upper limit to the human life span that is compatible with being human? The last is not a question primarily about biology but is rather about what it means to be human in moral and existential terms rather than in physical terms. In Chapters 5 and 6 I explore these questions through an examination of the arguments for and against the desirability for human beings of earth-bound immortality.

The social-policy questions include the following: What are the pragmatic implications of adopting a prolongevist perspective? To what extent can a welfare right to life be recognized? Are there ways of implementing prolongevist values that are both fair and beneficent for the whole culture, that do not entail inappropriate sacrifices from any seg-

ment of the society, and that are consistent with a vision of social justice and improved welfare for everyone? To raise such questions is imperative, for much of the cultural distrust of prolongevitism has arisen from fears of a prolongevist culture run amuck, in which unreasonable and unjustified practices are implemented solely for the sake of extending the human life span beyond any acceptable limits. I explore the pragmatic implications of a reasonable and fair applied prolongevitism in Chapter 7.

FIVE

"From Here to Eternity"

Is It Good to Live Forever?

Immortality is a terrible curse.

> *Simone de Beauvoir,* All Men Are Mortal,
> *quoted in Maggio 1996, 343*

At bottom no one believes in his own death, or, to put the same thing in another way, . . . in the unconscious every one of us is convinced of his own immortality.

> *Sigmund Freud, "Thoughts for the Times on War*
> *and Death," quoted in Enright 1983, 153–154*

If living longer is good, could living forever be even better? Would immortality be a terrible curse or the fulfillment of a legitimate human desire? This chapter and the next are devoted to examining the putative value of human immortality. I don't mean the kind of immortality that is sometimes said to follow on long-lasting accomplishments, such as scientific discoveries or great works of art.[1] And I do not mean the kind of immortality that is said to be achievable by reproducing oneself through one's offspring. Nor do I mean the fragmented immortality that some people promise us through the endurance in the universe of our individual physical particles long after our bodies have disintegrated. Instead, by immortality I mean the absence of any permanent end to individual personal life and the unending and eternal persistence of individual awareness, perception, thought, emotion, and activity through infinite temporal duration.

Now ordinarily, discussions of immortality, whether by philosophers or by theologians, focus on a supposed eternal life in heaven after death here on earth or, more rarely, on a supposedly very long (and sometimes eternal) life lived through successive deaths and subsequent reincarnations within new bodies. These discussions are directed at such questions as whether the postulation of those forms of survival is conceptually coherent, whether there is evidence for them (e.g., Penelhum 1982), and what the purpose and function of immortality might be in relationship to finite life here on earth (Perrett 1986). Most discussions simply assume the value of living forever and take for granted that prolonging one's existence is desirable. Indeed, the prevalence of belief in an afterlife, to some degree as a theme within the history of philosophy but even more as an incontrovertible tenet within religions such as Christianity and Islam and within popular culture at large, gives a clear indication of the apparently unquestionable attractiveness of immortality. As I suggested in Chapter 2, belief in an eternal afterlife probably helped persons living in earlier centuries, especially in medieval times, to be almost indifferent to greater longevity here on earth.

Debates about the possibility and, more relevantly still, the value of immortality are closely connected to debates about human longevity. Apologism accepts old age and death as inevitable occurrences within human life and, while not attempting to change them, tries to provide satisfactory explanations for them (Gruman 1977, 10). But if the standard justifications for apologism are inadequate, and a case can be made for prolongevitism, one is led into difficult questions about just how long a life is enough. As Roy Perrett (1986, 222) puts it, "Most people consider their lives worth living: they do not contemplate suicide, but rather attempt to prolong their lives (provided, of course, that conditions do not degenerate too badly). Nor do they generally regret having been born. If their lives are valuable to them in this way, would not the endless extension of them also have value?" Given a quality of life that is at least "comparable with the quality of life exhibited by an ordinary mortal life that is considered worthwhile by the person living it" (Perrett 1986, 222–223), would there ever come a point at which death would be morally and psychologically acceptable or at which we could say we have had enough? Or would it be the case that, as Stephen Clark (1995, 15) puts it, "if there is no amount of something that we can recognize to be 'enough,' then no amount of it will fill our need"?[2] Are we led, inexorably, to a desire to be immortal?

The desire for immortality is, I would argue, a form of prolongevitism. The prolongevist seeks "not merely an increase in time *per se* but an extension of the healthy and productive period of life" (Gruman 1977, 8). The desire for immortality is the expression of prolongevitism taken to its limit. But with respect to the connection between prolongevitism and immortality there appears to be an axiological double bind.[3] On the one hand, a life that has no limit, a life of immortality, seems not to be a recognizably human life (Williams 1975). Many philosophers argue that our limits and limitations—material, temporal, and psychological—help to make us human, in the moral and social sense. On the other hand, if a person is reasonably healthy, both mentally and physically, then, given the previous arguments against apologism, no definite length of life will necessarily or inevitably be enough. *Ceteris paribus*, barring serious, debilitating, degenerative illness, there is no good reason, in principle, to regard a finite life of any particular length as a good thing. As Williams (1975, 417) puts it:

> But now—if death, other things being equal, is a misfortune; and a longer life is better than a shorter life; and we reject the Lucretian argument that it does not matter when one dies; then it looks as though—other things always being equal—death is at any time an evil, and it is always better to live than die. . . . It looks as though it would be not only always better to live, but better to live always, that is, never to die.

Because of this conceptual link with issues concerning human longevity, I wish, by contrast with traditional investigations about the possibility of immortality as an eternal life lived in heaven after death (or through successive reincarnations in different bodies after death), to examine the concept of immortality defined as the unending and eternal persistence of individual personal awareness, perception, thought, emotion, and activity through infinite temporal duration within human life on earth. I am therefore not concerned with the lengthy history of speculation about the existence of an afterlife in heaven.[4] Moreover, my main question is not whether immortality within present human existence is possible and attainable. Obviously it is not, or at least not yet,[5] although research devoted to the cessation of natural aging, the prevention and cure of diseases, and the creation of therapies for regenerating or replacing damaged body parts continues (Momeyer 1988, 30). Indeed, in an article on New Year's Day, 2000, science-fiction writer Spider Robinson predicts a future a thousand years hence in which all persons are both "immortal and invulnerable" (2000, M9). Instead, my main question is the speculative and highly theoretical one of whether immortality in our earthly lives would be desirable—whether, that is, immortality is conceivably a good thing to have even if it is not possible to have it.

Relatively few debates in the philosophical literature concern themselves with the value itself of immortality. Yet the issue is worth exploring— first, for its own sake, because of its status as a cultural and religious shibboleth; second, because the inadequacy of the arguments in favor of apologism appears to necessitate its consideration; and, third, because an assessment of the arguments about the desirability of immortality may have additional implications for our understanding of the value of human longevity. Finally, an inquiry into the putative value of immortality may have consequences for how we live our lives now, for it raises fundamental questions about what gives meaning and value to human life even in its current mortal form.[6]

Assessing the value of immortality requires a tremendous exercise in imagination. Although immortality plays an apparently straightforward part in the religions and mythologies of many cultures, its meaning and value are seldom described in detail. Literature, especially science fiction (see Clark 1995), provides us with depictions of the possible nature and characteristics of a life of immortality on earth. I shall make use of several imaginary accounts of immortal life in order to provide a more vivid picture of the possibilities.

BASIC ASSUMPTIONS

Some objections to immortality seem to be based not on the nature of unending life itself but rather on such considerations as the conditions under which immortality is achieved or the impossibility of surrendering immortality once it is achieved. I think that such objections simply miss the central questions about the value of immortality itself. For purposes of evaluating immortality, therefore, I make the following five explicit assumptions.

First, in a world where immortality was possible, people would not be born immortal. Rather, they would have the opportunity of achieving immortality at some point during their life through some recognized medical process, operation, or formula. Thus, for any given individual, immortality would not be inevitable and unavoidable; it would be imposed neither by circumstances of birth nor by parental or societal fiat before one was able to make an informed and meaningful choice about the procedure. One would always have the chance to make a reasoned decision as to whether to become immortal. Hence, any objection to immortality on the grounds that it was not freely chosen would be irrelevant to this discussion.

Second, people would know they were immortal, or, at least, having chosen (by some mechanism) the immortality option, they would have good grounds for believing they were immortal and could assess its desirability in a realistic way. So I set aside, simply through stipulation, Rosenberg's claim that a person who possessed "corporeal immortality, the complete freedom from death," probably could never know that he actually possessed it. According to Rosenberg, although such a person could of course know that he had lived for thousands of years without dying, it is more difficult to see how he could know that he could not die, "for it is not obvious what might empirically differentiate such actual immortality from, for example, an extraordinary (but still bounded and finite) lifespan of, say, one or two million years" (1983, 202). I agree that, in the absence of some special mechanism to bring about immortality, no one could know for sure that he or she was immortal, although as the life got longer, the predisposition to believe it would surely grow; so I simply stipulate that the person would know his or her immortal status by virtue of having deliberately chosen it.[7]

Third, I also assume that if immortality for human beings were possible, everyone would have the opportunity to opt for it. This stipulation has two consequences. First, on a prudential level, it would have the effect of obviating the envy and resentment that might otherwise be directed by mortals at the immortal. If it were reserved for the privileged, then the immortal few would always have to live under threat of attack from the mortal majority. As the robot hero says in Isaac Asimov and Robert Silverberg's science-fiction novel, *The Positronic Man*,[8] "[Human beings] would never be able to tolerate the idea of an immortal human being, since their own mortality is endurable only so long as they know it's universal. Allow one person to be exempted from death and everyone else feels victimized in the worst way" (1995, 283–284). Second, on a moral level, this stipulation means that immortality would not be limited, in principle, either only to persons of a certain physical type, talent, or capacity, or only to persons belonging to certain elite groups. As Momeyer (1988, 39) points out, "It is impossible to imagine what criteria could be used to identify some among us as deserving of endless life or what the compensating benefits for mortals left behind would be." Despite Clark's ready answer, "Why should society agree to make everyone immortal, however stupid, dissolute or ill-willed they were?" (1995, 58–59), I agree that finding criteria for awarding immortality would be tremendously problematic. At least if immortality were an open option, then although it is not clear how many would choose it, it would not be confined to the privileged.[9] Hence, an objection to immortality on the grounds that it either would occasion envy and resentment or would be inherently unfair would be irrelevant.

Fourth, individuals who chose immortality would be reasonably healthy and energetic. For them, the elimination of death would also mean the elimination of aging, at least those forms of aging that involved increasing weakness, physical and mental deterioration, the onset of disabilities, and vulnerability to illness. Hence, any objection to immortality on the grounds that one would still be subject to the worst effects of extreme old age would be obviated.

Fifth, I assume that, having attained immortality, people would still have the opportunity to opt out of it. I am therefore setting aside a suggestion, made by Samantha Brennan (2001, 734), that the problem with immortality, as commonly understood, is the absence of autonomy to end one's life. Nothing inherent in the concept of immortality entails that one would lack the option to end one's life whenever it became advisable to do so. Thus Hunter Steele says that we must distinguish between what he calls necessary and contingent body-bound immortality. In necessary body-bound immortality, the individual would and could never die, no matter how much he might want to. But, says Steele (1976, 426), "only some indestructible Superman" or some other implausible being could have this characteristic, and so contingent body-bound immortality is more believable.

Brennan (personal communication, 1999) suggests that if the concept of immortality were to include the possibility of ceasing to be immortal, then it would imply that the immortal person could be a possible target of murder:

> If we define immortality as living as long as one chooses, it's hard to imagine what would constitute the conditions under which one could end one's own life which couldn't also be used against one. Suppose you take an immortality elixir every day as long as you choose to go on living. Murder remains a possibility as long as someone could steal the drug or otherwise prevent you from taking it.

And so [a] new concept [of immortality] might have to allow for
the end of life both by one's own hand or those of others.

I don't think this implication is a problem. The notion of immortality in
which I am interested is not a form of everlasting life that would make
the individual literally bullet-proof but rather a form, most closely connected to the prolongation of mortal life sought by prolongevists, that
would give an ongoing and permanent exemption, subject to autonomous
revocation, both from death and from the otherwise inevitable decline
in and deterioration of one's general health and well-being and one's physical and mental capacities.[10] The immortal individual might still die,
through deliberate intent on her own part or someone else's, but her death
would no longer be inevitable simply by virtue of being human.[11]

Nussbaum (1994, 227) argues that immortality makes the virtue of
courage impossible, "for courage consists in acting and reacting in the
face of death and the risk of death. A being who cannot take that risk
cannot have that virtue." My version of immortality, in which death is
no longer inevitable but is still possible, would allow courage, in Nussbaum's sense, to be an achievable virtue. (In any case, many aspects of
life do not entail the risk of death but still provide the opportunity for
exercising courage.)

However, it might be argued that this stipulation has a problematic
consequence for the lived experience of being immortal. The immortal's
vulnerability would surely make her ultracareful and cautious, for a mis-
step could mean not just the loss of finite life but, more significantly, the
loss of eternal life. For this reason, the immortal would be prevented from
living life to the fullest; she would always tend to hold back from many
activities out of fear. She would be less willing to take risks or to sacrifice
herself, for example in the interests of a moral cause (Sue Donaldson,
personal communication, 2000). I have two responses to this objection.
First, as I already remarked, I do not imagine immortals as superhuman,
invulnerable beings. They are human beings who happen to have the po-

tential to live forever. So individuals such as these would not be totally different from human beings as they are now. Although the immortal's loss at death is infinite, both the mortal and the immortal human being have a comparable vulnerability to sudden death. Second, consider the situation of human beings now. As mortals we each have only one life, it is quite short, and, in losing it, we lose everything. Fear of losing one's life encourages people to circumvent most serious risks and to avoid being reckless, yet most of us are not inhibited by this fear from living life fully. And some people are also able to take risks and even to sacrifice their life. (We may be inhibited by material want and lack of opportunity, but that is another issue.) I don't believe the situation of the immortal would be much different, for like the mortal she would quite likely shun death-threatening activities, yet, unless she suffered from a serious personality disorder, having chosen eternal life, she would surely be motivated to take advantage of the prospects it offered.

The proviso that the immortal could still die by deliberate intent also takes care of a worry expressed by Clark. He claims, "In a world where no one could be required to keep their word [by threat of death], no words are more than wind" (1995, 56). Although I'm not at all convinced, as Clark seems to be, that people's only motive for abiding by the law, keeping their word, and building close human relationships is ultimately the fear of death, if such a fear does play a significant civilizing role, then it would still be present in a society of immortals who had the potential to live forever but could nonetheless be killed.

The immortal can revoke her status by dying, but should she also be endowed with the additional autonomous capacity to return to the status of an ordinary mortal? Some tales of immortality offer this possibility by making immortality contingent on the repeated consumption of an immortality potion (Čapek [1922] 1990). If the individual chooses not to consume the potion, she thereby revokes her immortal status and will eventually die. But this arrangement detracts from much of the momentousness of the decision to become immortal. In effect, by drinking the potion, the individual is deciding to prolong her life for only a period of time, with the option of becoming mortal whenever she decides not to drink it.[12] In effect, then, her normative decision is not about the value of immortality itself but rather about the value of greater and greater longevity. Because this condition would change the question in which I am interested, I do not add it to my stipulations about the circumstances in which immortality is acquired.

Given all these conditions, would it be good to be immortal here on earth? I used to be convinced that it would. But my examination of this issue has shown me that it is much more complex than I had previously recognized. In this chapter and the next I examine the main arguments intended to show that immortality would be a bad condition for human beings. Not all reasons for calling the value of immortality into question are equal; some are stronger than others.

THE RESOURCE LIMITS OF THE PLANET

Some obvious objections to the desirability of immortality concern practical obstacles and are founded on the material limitations of the earth's resources. The problems of overpopulation and the resource constraints of the planet constitute an argument against the value of immortality from a collective rather than an individual perspective. The apologist argument against the extension of human existence that invokes the "rhythm of life" is relevant to assessing the value of immortality, and in this context it is far more convincing than when applied to a finite life. Nuland writes:

> Mankind cannot afford to destroy the balance [of nature]—the economy, if you will—by tinkering with one of its most essential elements, which is the constant renewal within individual species and the invigoration that accompanies it. For plants and animals, renewal requires that death precede it so that the weary may be replaced by the vigorous. This is what is meant by the cycles of nature. There is nothing pathological or sick about the sequence— in fact, it is the antithesis of sick. (Nuland 1994, 58)

Though not a Christian himself, Nuland (1994, 267) uses New Testament language to suggest that each of us possesses the "miracle of life" because "trillions upon trillions of living things have prepared the way for us and then have died—in a sense, for us. We die, in turn, so that others may live." This ongoing pattern of creation, death, and renewal enables the generation and development of entities and forms of life that would not otherwise exist.

The "burden" argument commonly used against the finite prolongation of human life also arises in spades with respect to immortality. Assuming that a substantial number of people, though perhaps not everyone, would choose everlasting life, then unless we also assume that people who live forever would be intelligent enough to figure out how, in material and social terms, to accommodate the needs and wants of an immortal population, the planet would be burdened with overpowering resource depletion, pollution, and waste generation occasioned by the permanent survival requirements of the immortal population. How could societies handle the never-ending requirements of immortals, including food, shelter, ongoing education, health care (immortals are stipulated not to die and not to age, but they are still likely to have medical needs), social support, pensions, insurance, and employment?[13]

Woods suggests that the overpopulation burden includes costs not only to existing human beings (and I would add all the nonhuman planetary life as well) but also to possible persons, those who would exist if immortal individuals had not exhausted resources. When the "rhythm of life" is interrupted, countless persons will not be brought into being. Woods (1978, 128) therefore posits that an immortal population could take one of three possible paths with respect to human reproduction.

First, if immortals remained young in physiological terms, they might reproduce forever, thus exacerbating indefinitely the resource burden that they already constitute. A culture of immortals could simply permit the population to increase "with the certain consequence that the general life support system would fail" (Woods 1978, 128). Admittedly, human beings can be obtuse when it comes to environmental and long-term survival issues. But simply letting the population increase seems to be an implausible choice for an immortal population, who of necessity would have to eschew any short-term points of view. Unrestricted population growth would be self-defeating: no one or almost no one would survive. Indeed, Momeyer (1988, 36) believes that such a situation would provoke an "onslaught of violent death" in a frantic if irrational attempt to curtail population growth. Second, and alternatively, according to Woods (1978, 128), in a culture of immortals, "pregnancy would need to be outlawed, perhaps made a capital offence in order to offset population increases." Thinking along similar lines, Harris (2000, 59) remarks that "society might be tempted to offer people life-prolonging therapies only on condition that they did not reproduce, except perhaps posthumously, or that they agreed if they did reproduce to forfeit their right to subsequent therapies."

Singer (1991, 136) also expresses worries about "the loss to our species of the spontaneity which comes from the renewal built into the cycle of generations; and the loss to the possible future generations who will not come into existence—or not in the same numbers—if the present generation continues indefinitely." Writing not about the elimination of births but about their curtailment, Singer urges prolongevists to consider the interests of future generations and points out that what those interests are, and, indeed, what the identity of members of those future generations will be, depends on actions we take in the present. If we extend human lives significantly and also cut back on the number of births in order to conserve resources, then the members of future generations will be significantly different than they would have been if we had not extended human lives (Singer 1991, 141–144). He urges that the interests of people to be born in 2088 should count equally with the interests of those born in 1988, insofar as we can tell what their interests are. "Perhaps what we should do is be guided by concern for what will lead to the greatest total amount of happiness, or welfare, over time" (144). He allows a "discount for uncertainty" (143)—that is, if we know we can create great benefit in the present by doing A and merely think we might create great benefit a century hence by doing B, we should do A.

I accept part but not all of this argument, for I doubt that we have a moral responsibility to count the interests of people in the future equally with those of people in the present. I agree that those interests must count. But just as I have more of an obligation to my own children than to my neighbor's children, so too I have more of an obligation to members of current and near generations than to members of far off ones. The reason is founded partly on emotional and reciprocal bonds: just as we usually have far stronger emotional and reciprocal connections with our own children than with other people's children, we are also more likely to care for and be morally indebted to members of current and near-future generations—because we know them, interact with them, and in some cases live with them—than to members of distant generations, whom we will never know. As significantly, there are serious epistemological problems in knowing what will serve the interests of members of far-off generations. Just as I know very well what is good for my own children but am less likely to know what is good for my neighbor's children, so also I am more likely to understand the interests of near-future generations than those of generations in the distant future. In addition, we are more likely to be effective and less prone to error if we care, plan, and provide for near generations as best we can and trust the judgments of more future people to care for their generations.

Although I deny that we have obligations to members of distant generations that are equal to our obligations to members of existing and near-future generations, I entirely agree that if pregnancy were "outlawed" and births ceased altogether, the human population would incur serious losses. Indeed, Momeyer (1988, 36) thinks that if two of the "basic facts" of life, birth and death, were eliminated, we would be left with "only copulation available as a central experience." This rather extravagant claim seems both to underestimate the number of "central experiences" to be found in human life and perhaps (given the worthwhile lives of individuals who choose to be celibate) to overestimate the significance of sexual experience. Nonetheless, it is hard to see that making pregnancy a capital offence could be justifiable, and certainly denying to everyone the right and opportunity to reproduce is an enormous privation. It is a cost not only to individuals themselves, who would be denied experiences such as pregnancy, breastfeeding, and the rearing of children, but also to the culture as a whole, which would suffer a staggering loss of relationships and interactions with babies and children and the invigoration and renewal provided by the presence of young people. In such a world, the immortals would be like parasites; they would have benefited from a system that gave them the love and care of their parents and the education afforded by their teachers, and yet they would seek to deny these benefits to future human beings (Nussbaum 1994, 225). And it would seem especially unfair to mortals if they were expected to give up procreation because of the needs generated by immortals.

It might be argued that the social costs incurred by the potential absence of death for part or all of a population would necessitate desperate measures, including ultimately the imposition of limits on the right to continue living. Woods (1978, 128) claims that if the route of making pregnancy illegal were to be rejected, it would have to be because "the right to reproduce outweighs even the right to live beyond a certain fixed number of years." So a third possibility for handling the burdens of an immortal population, according to Woods, is to set "some definite upper limit on the duration of one's right to live." The argument for this alternative is that indefinitely long life "would be insupportably selfish, since it would occasion the need to prevent the conception of persons who otherwise would be allowed to come into being." Woods claims that this approach accords the right to live to "possibilia, the as yet *unconceived*" (1978, 128, his emphasis). In such an approach, "another's merely possible personhood is enough to bring about the lapse of the right of an actual person to be kept in being" (128):

> The whole thrust of such a view would seem to be that our very immortality is not morally sufficient cause to discontinue repro-

duction, that in a contest between sterile immortality and fertile
mortality, the course of personal annihilation would win out. . . .
It implies that something that is good to have is not good to have
for unlimitedly long, and is definitely bad to have unlimitedly if it
would seriously deprive others, even the merely possible and totally
non-existent "others." The metaphysics of the position is striking:
it implies rights for the utterly non-existent, that is, for "objects"
which lack all actuality of any sort or degree.

However, contra Woods, the reason for favoring "fertile mortality"
over "sterile immortality" may not necessarily be the rather implausible
attribution of rights to nonexistent, merely possible beings. Indeed, I cannot see why the putative rights of merely possible beings should trump
the actual rights of already-existing beings. Nor is it clear why the right
to reproduce would trump the right to go on living, and Woods offers
no argument to support such a claim. Instead, it would be better to argue against the outlawing of reproduction on the basis I mentioned earlier of the loss, occasioned by the immortality of some individuals, to existing people, who would no longer possess an exercisable right to
reproduce and would no longer benefit from the arrival of and experience of being with new human beings.

But even if reproduction ought not to be outlawed, it is hard to see
that the adoption of the alternative, limiting the amount of time that
people are permitted to live, is justified. Many of the moral problems cited
in my discussion of the concept of a duty to die would arise under these
circumstances. At what age would people be compelled to give up their
lives, and how would we choose that age? How would otherwise healthy
people be persuaded or forced to end their lives? Would they have to be
killed? There's a danger that the landmark of being "too old" could be
moved earlier and earlier in human life, and the accusation of being a
"burden" on the fertile young could be used to exterminate elderly people
with impunity. The notion that one could, at some age only arbitrarily
related to one's own life projects, lose one's liberty right to life or that it

would be trumped by other persons' right to reproduce or by the cultural need for the birth of young people would constitute a serious moral threat to older individuals' happiness, security, and autonomy; it would create terror and anxiety among aging persons. Aging people have no individual obligation to die simply to make room for new human beings. As Woods (1978, 130) himself concludes, "None of us, severally or jointly, need feel obliged to pay with our lives for the consequences of an out-of-control population." One need not sacrifice one's own life for the sake of others' possible lives or even for others' reproductive opportunities. Unless he constitutes an irrevocable mortal danger, no person loses his liberty right to life because of a supposed right to acquire life on the part of possible beings.

At the same time, the overwhelming problem of resource depletion and social burden may obviate any legitimate claim to justifying immortality. The assessment of problems in dealing with the demands of an immortal population is a sobering exercise in the realities that lie behind the idealization of infinite life. Resorting to any of Woods's alternatives might be avoided if the opportunity for becoming immortal were confined to a select few. The rest of the population would then live out their finite lives as human beings now do. Such a solution allows some special few to be exempt from the fate of the many. However, the problem of determining who should have the privilege of immortality (if it is indeed a privilege), the clear implication of unfairness, and the practical challenges of policing access and mitigating jealousy, anger, resentment, and fear on the part of the nonmortal population all serve to rule out allowing access to immortality to only a select few, as I suggested in my original stipulations. And it is probably too much to expect that immortals would freely choose to abandon their immortality—even if, as Clark (1995, 16) claims, "virtuous immortals must give some weight to the thought that 'it's someone else's turn.'"

The potential population burdens and resource costs of immortality, themselves possibly infinite in nature, may be sufficient to rule immortality out as in any way a tenable goal for a society. The only possible way around this problem that I can imagine would be the migration of immortal human beings to other planets, perhaps planets in other solar systems; the burden that they would pose here on earth would thus be relieved. However, the argument from burdens to society is not sufficient to show that immortality is undesirable from the point of view of an individual, for I, as an immortal, might be able to avoid suffering from the worst depredations of planetary overpopulation. Or, possibly, so few individuals would choose immortality that they would not necessarily overburden the world's resources.

I therefore now turn to the nature and limits of the value of unending life from the point of view of the individual. Do I, as an individual, have good reasons for rejecting earthly immortality? The strongest and most interesting arguments against immortality are based on certain views about what makes a human life worth living, about what it means to be a human being, and ultimately about the nature and boundaries of human identity. So it is to these questions that I turn.

THE LOSS OF ALL ONE KNOWS

From the point of view of an individual, one possible drawback of immortality might be the prospect of being the only one who chooses it. Immortality, it might be argued, is undesirable unless a substantial number of one's friends and relatives also acquire it. What would be the attraction of living in a world where one knew and was attached to absolutely no one whose situation was comparable to one's own? Many people with whom I have raised questions about immortality argue that it would be an undesirable condition if it meant that one outlived all one's relatives and friends or, in other words, if almost no one else about whom one cared were to choose immortality.[14] Thus Momeyer predicts that the immortal individual would encounter "insuperable barriers to sustaining the kinds of human relationships that make life worthwhile and meaningful." Immortal parents would have to see their mortal children grow up, age, and die. Inevitably the relationships of an immortal with mortals would be temporary and, relative to the immortal's life, all too brief; immortals might find it difficult, perhaps impossible, to be open with their mortal friends (Momeyer 1988, 38). They could also experience enormous and repeated grief at the death of any mortal persons with whom they develop a relationship. Clark (1995, 13) writes, "Maybe immortals must keep company especially with each other: mortal mayflies could not hold their attention long. . . . Would they cultivate mere mortals to occupy familiar slots, surrounding themselves with good examples of a type they once knew well? Would they notice which individuals fulfilled those roles, or would they care?" He predicts that people who "cannot conceive of an ending" "are likely to think the rest of us of little importance; they may have little conception of a world that is not theirs, nor even of their own selves within the world" (61). He also suggests that the immortal person might have difficulties constantly learning new languages and descendents of existing languages in order to be able to communicate with new generations (13). To these problems we could add the challenges of keeping up with enormous technological innovations and powerful cultural transformation forever.[15] In addition, just as aging people even now can be overcome with sadness as they reflect on their past, the immortal could suffer from intense nostalgia. Because of the quantity and quality of change immortals would witness as their past gets longer and longer, they could experience longing and regret for a historical past that is gone forever.[16]

A novel for young people entitled *Tuck Everlasting* (Babbitt 1975)[17] depicts some of these problems. A family of four become immortal after unknowingly drinking from a spring that bestows eternal life. Their subsequent existence is a challenge for them, as they outlive all their other relatives and friends. Convinced of the undesirability of immortality and hence committed to keeping the existence of the spring a secret, the family members are driven to a peripatetic life in which they are compelled to move on before raising the suspicions of their neighbors about their failure to age. Unable to make permanent friends, possessing no other immortal relatives, and having only each other for eternity, they are lonely, isolated, and apparently without goals.

However, this objection to immortality is not convincing. I grant that it would be desirable for most if not all of one's friends and family to choose immortality, and I have assumed that immortality, if possible, would be available to all who wanted it. Why should we suppose that no one else would choose immortality? Although it certainly might not be attractive to everyone, we cannot assume, a priori, that no one would find immortality worth choosing. So if we are to imagine that immortality is possible and available, we must imagine it for a group of people, maybe even a large group. Then the immortal individuals would not have the pain of seeing everyone they loved die. (Of course, they might then encounter the further problem—envisaged by Clark (1995, 13)—that "immortals [could] be the worst company of all, with thousands of years to find each other's habits more exasperating.")

If, however, none of one's near and dear ones chose immortality, it would be painful indeed to see one's existing relatives and friends all die. Yet as Momeyer (1988, 38) points out, even in this life most of us experience serious losses through deaths, departures, and divorces. The experiences of the immortal would simply be a larger and more prolonged version of what even today many very long-living people go through anyway when they live to see virtually everyone of their own generation die. Such individuals even now also have to adjust and adapt to technological change, cultural evolution, and regret for the past. Many do so successfully. Some people might not find these costs too high for eternal life.

Moreover, if most or all of the immortal individual's family and friends did not also choose immortality, the experience of outliving all one's friends and relatives might not be all that different from the experiences of a person who is a sole immigrant to a land where he has no loved ones and no way of communicating at all with those back home, indeed a situation similar to that of some of the immigrants to North America one or two centuries ago. Such a situation of loss of connection, cultural discontinuity, new languages, and radical change is hard but not necessarily unbearable. We know that human beings have dealt with it in often positive ways. And we also know that the hardships are at least partly compensated for by the new opportunities gained.

Finally, the argument that immortality would be unbearable if it involved outliving all one's relatives and friends makes two questionable assumptions. First, it makes the ageist assumption that as a person ages, she is not capable of making new friends and forming relationships with people who are considerably younger than she. But there is no insuperable reason why a person of ninety cannot form a friendship with a person of forty or twenty. Second, it also assumes that the immortal person's mortal relatives all die out and do not reproduce themselves. It would be sad if the immortal person were to outlive her own children, not by virtue of their premature death but by virtue of her living forever while they (by choice) do not. But possibly they or her nieces and nephews or her first cousins once removed would have children and grandchildren and great-grandchildren with whom she could have close bonds. For all these reasons, it seems highly improbable that the immortal would inevitably outlive all her friends and relatives, and it is by no means inevitable that she would find impossible or unbearable the personal and social adaptation demanded by living through vast generations.

THE PROBLEM OF BOREDOM

> Millions long for immortality who don't know what
> to do with themselves on a rainy Sunday afternoon.
> *Susan Ertz, quoted in Maggio 1996, 344*

Still, the anxiety about outliving all one's friends and relatives may well be related to another worry frequently expressed about immortality: that it would be monumentally boring. This worry takes the Lucretian and Epicurean argument against greater longevity and applies it to immortality. Certainly the conventional theistic pictures of life in everlasting paradise encourage us to have this fear. Grace Jantzen (1994, 267) writes, "A paradise of sensuous delights would become boring; it would in the long run be pointless and utterly unfulfilling. . . . On this view survival is tedious simply because there is no progress, no point to the continued existence except the satisfaction of hedonistic desires." John Donnelly (1994, 304) suggests that one of the main challenges of living forever would be that "our desires, wants, needs, interests, etc., are inherently exhaustible, and life in heaven would prove intolerable in the long run." The result is boredom: "a boredom connected with the fact that everything that could happen and make sense to one particular human being . . . ha[s] already happened" (Williams 1975, 418).

In his arguments against the desirability of immortality, Williams draws on an opera by Leoš Janáček that is based on a play by Karel Čapek entitled *The Makropulos Secret* ([1922] 1990). The play tells the story of a woman named Elina Makropulos whose father, a court physician, gives her an elixir to enable her to prolong her life for three hundred years. In effect, provided she takes the elixir at approximately three-hundred-year intervals, she can be immortal. In the operatic version of the play that is used by Williams, Elina is depicted as being forty-two and as having been forty-two for three hundred years.[18] According to Williams, in order for Elina to be the same person throughout those centuries, her character must remain much the same. Then, over the decades, except for "some changes of style to suit the passing centuries" (Williams 1975, 418), she simply accumulates memories of earlier times. After a while, given what her character is, she tends to have much the same experiences and the same relationships and hence faces the problem of eternal boredom. Čapek's Elina describes her life:

> Boredom. No, it isn't even boredom. It is . . . it is . . . oh, you people, you have no name for it. . . . Everything is so pointless, so empty, so meaningless. . . . One finds out that one cannot believe in anything. Anything. And from that comes this cold emptiness. . . . And no one can love for 300 years—it cannot last. And then everything tires one. It tires one to be good, it tires one to be bad. The earth itself tires one. (Čapek [1922] 1990, 173–174)

Another character, Gregor, describes Elina as "cold like a knife. As if you'd come out of a grave" (145).

Williams (1975, 424) suggests that boredom within a finite lifetime is tolerable only if it is part of some greater project.[19] He assumes that an immortal person would run out of short-term objectives and could have no indefinitely long-term goal, no "categorical" desires that existed independently of the mere desire to continue to survive. Victor Frankl amplifies our picture of the apparently meaningless life of the immortal by arguing, "If we were immortal, we could legitimately postpone every action forever. It would be of no consequence whether or not we did a thing now; every act might just as well be done tomorrow or the day after or a year from now or ten years hence" (quoted in Nozick 1981, 579). Nuland (1994, 87) says, "The fact that there is [now] a limited right time to do the rewarding things in our lives is what creates urgency to do them. Otherwise, we might stagnate in procrastination." Such a person, then, has no good reason to do anything at any particular point; he simply exists from day to day.

The result, according to Williams (1975, 423), is that "boredom, as sometimes in more ordinary circumstances, would be not just a tiresome effect, but a reaction almost perceptual in character to the poverty of one's relation to the environment." What this means, I believe, is that the experience of immortality would be analogous to the experience of severe insomnia, in which, having been awake for seemingly endless hours without respite, one feels tired of being aware and exhausted by being oneself and wants only the nothingness of unconsciousness that is afforded, temporarily, by deep sleep. From the point of view of the immortal, then, the only respite from something like an eternity of insomnia could be the permanent nonconsciousness of death.

In response to this worry, one cannot merely stipulate that beings endowed with immortality would necessarily be so different from mortals that they would never experience boredom,[20] for what we are imagining here are individuals who are human in every respect except longevity.

Nevertheless, there are at least three reasons for thinking that Williams may be too pessimistic in his assumptions about the inevitable boredom of immortality. First, Steele (1976, 425) suggests that we should distinguish between "(a) being bored at some points during eternity, and (b) eternal boredom." Whereas Williams insists that for the immortal individual boredom must be unthinkable, Steele argues that it would be enough that our boring moments "not exceed a certain proportion." Because, in our present finite existence, we don't demand that we never be bored, we should not expect it of eternal life either. Says Steele (1976, 426), "If a reasonably normal and happy man were offered an eternal existence in which he would be no more bored, proportionally, than he ever had been, would he not accept with alacrity? I am convinced that he would."

Second, boredom is not a necessary and inevitable result of the repetition of experiences. Williams appears to acknowledge this point, indirectly, when he comments that the sole condition under which an immortal might conceivably be able to avoid impending boredom would be if he were to have an "impoverishment" of consciousness, for, Williams claims, "not being bored can be a sign of not noticing, or not reflecting, enough." A person in this state lacks the "consciousness which would have brought discontent by reminding him of other times, other interests, other possibilities" (Williams 1975, 423).

This description of the absence of boredom certainly makes sense when applied to nonhuman animals. A dog, for example, wakes up each morning with apparent eagerness and enthusiasm. As on every other day, he is excited about the prospect of having breakfast and going for a walk, two of the most pleasurable activities in his life. The fact that he has had breakfast and a walk every previous day of his life and is likely to have them on every future day until he is too ill to move in no way detracts from his enjoyment. Although he has both memories and the capacity to anticipate upcoming activities, the dog's needs, desires, and interests are fairly basic and immediate, and he does not have a sense of the past or the future as a cumulative and boring repetition that fails to challenge him intellectually and emotionally. A dog can experience boredom, but such boredom is, I believe, occasioned by a protracted lack of stimulation within a limited present-time context. For the dog, provided he is reasonably well loved and cared for, there is no such thing as being bored by his life, and if he could awake every day with the prospect of breakfast and a walk, he could probably be happy to go on awaking every day for eternity.[21] The example of the dog shows, at least in the case of nonhuman species, that Williams's belief that the concept of a "reasonably happy" case of "body-bound immortality" (to use Steele's term; 1976, 425) could not possibly be instantiated is false.

Might a human being enjoy the same sort of immunity from boredom in the repetition of certain experiences that nonhuman animals possess? Momeyer (1988, 19) suggests, "Consider satisfaction of the basic biological drives: so long as appetite remains strong, food and sexual union remain satisfying. It is in the very nature of such desires that they are self-renewing, never once and for all satiated and abandoned." So some experiences, at least those related to fundamental biological drives, could be repeated indefinitely without boredom's being the inevitable outcome. And, contrary to Frankl, we would have urgent physiological reasons for seeking them out and not postponing their pursuit indefinitely.

Under certain circumstances members of our own species are also capable of enjoying the same sorts of intellectual, aesthetic, or recreational activities over and over again, provided that the activities are themselves somewhat varied and one has the choice of moving from one activity to another. So, for example, an individual might enjoy watching hockey games—not the same hockey game, of course, but games involving different teams and different players—over and over again, with no foreseeable end to the enjoyment. Another individual might enjoy listening to many genres of music without ever becoming bored and might return repeatedly to favorite recordings with clear pleasure. Goods such as spectator sports and appreciation of the arts are not like assets that get exhausted through being consumed but are more like renewable resources, to whose enjoyment one can return again and again. So although the immortal person certainly could postpone doing things, he need not do so and in some cases cannot do so, and he might also return to certain activities again and again simply because he likes them. Moreover, the finite nature of human beings means that we often neither fully absorb a present experience nor perfectly remember previous experiences, and for this reason some people can, for example, listen to a piece of music again and again without being bored by it.[22]

Now it is not clear whether our limitations as human beings and our ability to return to the same activities over and over would, in and by themselves, be sufficient to rescue an immortal human being of ordinary intelligence and perspicuity from the tedium of eternal boredom. (Individuals suffering from certain sorts of senility can always be content with repeating an activity over and over again. Because of the failure of their memory and intellect, the activity continues to retain the original enjoyment it held for them. But such a life would likely seem pointless to those without such impairments.)[23] Williams is correct that because of the human facility for the development of new interests and for intellectual and psychological growth, human beings also have a fairly ready capacity for becoming bored in the absence of opportunities for such growth. Moreover, as George Harris observes, "There are many clear values that death would come as a blow to if death came too soon *and* that it would not come as a blow to if things went on forever" (1997, 91, his emphasis). He gives examples ranging from love of one's children to engaging in philosophical thought. We may value and enjoy them within the constraints of a finite life but without believing that they would suffice for eternity. In addition, individuals have a deep and developed awareness of past events and future possibilities, and so they can easily choose to compare their present situation with other possible situations and hence be insufficiently stimulated by an impoverished environment.

So I am not entirely convinced that the mere repetition of certain categories of activities, however pleasurable they may once have been, would not result in stultifying boredom during a lifetime of eternity. But what is especially interesting to me is that different individuals argue on different sides of this thesis with equal intensity. While some philosophers, like Williams, are deeply certain that an eternity of repetition of experiences would be so stultifying as to make death the only solution, others, like Momeyer, are equally deeply certain that a meaningful and mostly happy eternal life could include a great deal of repeated experience. This fundamental disagreement suggests the existence of deeper differences between the two sides. I return to this idea in Chapter 6.

A third reason for believing that potential boredom could be assuaged or avoided is that in the immortal state the individual has "all the time in the world" not only to return to previous interests and to re-create former pastimes but also to construct and explore new possibilities for both growth and entertainment. As Jantzen suggests:

> Death is sometimes seen as evil because it means the curtailment
> of projects; immortality would be required to give significance to
> life because it would allow those projects to be meaningfully contin-
> ued. Of course, most of our projects would not require all eternity
> to complete. But even in this life, one enterprise leads to another,
> and provided endless progress were possible, we might pursue an
> endless series of challenging and absorbing tasks, each one develop-
> ing into another, without any risk of boredom. (Jantzen 1994, 267)

In an eternal existence repetition of some experiences would probably be inevitable, but no individual would be confined to such repetition. On the contrary, part of the potential value of immortality lies in the prospects it offers for exploring new activities, creating new relationships, and generating new projects.[24] Even Harris's view that the love of family members or engagement in philosophy is exhaustible is not entirely convincing, for if people can grow and change through a process of self-transformation, as I argue in the next chapter, and if philosophy develops and evolves through the contribution of many different thinkers, then it is unclear why their attractions must, in principle, eventually be used up. Nussbaum (1994, 226) goes so far as to suggest that our mortality, our sense that opportunities are finite, is "a constitutive factor in all valuable things' having for us the value that in fact they have," including many of the virtues, like courage, justice, and moderation, and most personal, family, and social relationships. But her argument is founded on the concept of immortality that is attributed to the Homeric gods, curiously unchanging beings who cannot die, cannot take risks, and apparently cannot choose to make radical transformations in their life story. I see no reason to build such artificial conditions into our concept of immortality.

The belief that death, or at least the prospect of death, is necessary to give meaning to human existence elevates personal extinction over personal projects in a way that ignores the real significance we attribute to human lives. Certainly, we remember outstanding human beings not because they died or even because their dying gave meaning to their life but largely because of the projects, relationships, and activities they engaged in while alive. Infinite life would seemingly provide the potential for an indefinite number of projects, all of which could come to fruition. Pogrebin (1996, 303) says, "The reason I will always fear death is my passion for life, and the reason I will never have enough time is that I cannot have forever." Vitek, a character in Čapek's play, explains the advantages of immortal life over mortal life:

> Just think: the human soul, the thirst for knowledge, the intellect,
> the work, love, creativity, everything! My God, what can a man do
> in a mere sixty years of life? How much can he enjoy? How much
> can he learn? He can't even harvest the fruit from the tree he plants.
> He never learns what his ancestors knew. He dies before he begins
> to live! God in Heaven, we live so briefly! . . . We don't have time
> for happiness, or even thinking. We don't have time for anything but
> this eternal scratching for a piece of bread. We never see anything—
> not even ourselves. We are just fragments of something else. . . .
> Man has never accepted this animal part of life. He cannot accept
> it because it is too unjust to live for such a short time. A man should
> be a little more than a turtle or a raven. A man needs more time to
> live. (Čapek [1922] 1990, 168)

And there may be many open-ended projects by virtue of which the potential boredom of eternal life could be avoided. In commenting on the same fictional case that worries Williams, Donnelly writes, "The heavenly environment offers tasks, purposes, etc., as one strives for greater participation in the divine life. Elina became bored by the endless pursuit of *finite* pursuits, but the *visio Dei* offers *infinite* variety for imaginative, creative personal involvement" (1994, 309, his emphasis) and "to develop ourselves, to acquire knowledge, to pursue various leisurely activities in a congenial atmosphere" (318). I don't see why a location in heaven is necessary for participation in most of these activities. The pursuit of artistic, scientific, athletic, or intellectual development could just as well occupy us during earthly immortality. Is it so far-fetched to suppose that a deep understanding of this infinite universe would take an eternity? Another example of an unending and boredom-defying activity is the quest for wisdom or enlightenment. In many traditions, the fulfillment of that quest is thought to require many lifetimes. An immortal life on earth appears to provide the opportunity for taking seriously the pursuit of satori.

Some philosophers have suggested that moral improvement is another potential antidote to boredom (Jantzen 1994, 270). According to Donnelly (1994, 312), "The counsel, command, or ideal 'to be perfect as your heavenly Father is perfect' is an endless task that the Christian is progressively engaged in, both here on earth and in Heaven." Yet this quest need not be framed as part of a Christian or other religious ideology. Instead it could be understood as the search for ethical insight, for an understanding of others' needs and propensities, for a sense of unity with other beings, and for deepening as a moral person. I am not taking the Kantian position that morality requires immortality as a postulate of practical reason or that belief in immortality is justified on that basis. But I am saying that the process of moral growth is one that (for some of us at least!) might well be limitless, and it therefore appears to afford one possible and challenging task for the immortal life.

It might be objected that, in a world where human beings are immortal, there could be no such thing as helping people; they would need no help. Hence, a central component of moral behavior and values would be rendered otiose. But I don't think that view is correct. First, according to my stipulation, not everyone would necessarily choose to be immortal, and any mortals living among immortals would probably continue to need all the various forms of assistance and support that we need now. Second, even for immortals, the absence of death does not mean the absence of other needs. According to my stipulations, such persons would still possess ordinary biological needs for food, shelter, clothing, and sex, and would still be vulnerable to accidental death or deliberate murder and might need protection therefrom. But, in addition, and more important, they would still have needs for friendship, education, love, care, mentoring, guidance, encouragement, and moral exemplars, and offering these to people is, in my view, a crucial part of living the moral life. So immortals would find plenty of opportunities for moral growth through human interactions much like those we have now.

With respect to this agenda, Antony Flew (1967, 148) complains that human beings would be engaged in an endless and frustrating moral practice according to which we would "forever approach asymptotically [an] eternally unattainable ideal." Yet such a program should not be regarded, a priori, as unappealing and unacceptable, for we know from ordinary experience that in many human pursuits, physical, artistic, and intellectual, one can get better and better, approaching but never achieving perfection. For example, most persons who take up playing the violin in adulthood have no expectation of achieving perfect virtuosity but, if they are sufficiently motivated, simply hope to become more and more proficient.

Perhaps I am being naïve or hopelessly optimistic, not about the possibility of projects where endless improvement is possible but rather about the prospect of individuals' adopting such tasks. In contemplating the potential value of immortality, we may need to take into account the meaning of eternal life for those who are nasty, mean-spirited, cruel, or just plain insensitive. Clark (1995, 20) writes, "The wish to be immortal, if it is to be rational, must be a wish to merit, or be capable of, such immortality. It would be a disastrous idea for the wicked, including the 'ordinarily wicked' (which is most of us)." Although I don't agree that the only rational desire for immortality is also a desire to merit immortality, I agree about the potential for disaster if so-called wicked persons attain immortality. With all eternity in which to meddle, the truly evil person could devote his time to actualizing all his potential to hurt and harm. I acknowledge that this is a horrible prospect. (Such persons, however, would likely not be bored!) My point here is just that a view like that of Williams assumes far too hastily that any immortal individual, of whatever moral caliber, would inevitably and easily become bored. Those for whom moral integrity matters would find more than adequate challenges. And pursuing the goal of moral maturation need not be experienced as stultifying.[25]

INTERIM CONCLUSION

Taken to its logical limit, prolongevitism leads to a quest for immortality, the endless persistence of individual human consciousness within life on earth. To examine the putative value of immortality, I defined it so as to preclude objections based on the conditions under which it is achieved or the impossibility of surrendering it. The resource limits of the planet provide a definitive argument against making immortality a tenable social goal. However, from the point of view of an individual, some of the usual arguments against seeking immortality are less convincing. An immortal person would not inevitably lose everyone she knows and loves, and even if she did, contemporary and historical evidence indicates that people are able to handle such a situation. Moreover, the charge that immortality would inevitably be boring carries weight only if one assumes that individuals can get no pleasure from the infinite repetition of some activities or that, during an eternal lifetime, human beings cannot take on an indefinite number of relationships and projects. Instead, I have argued that, given the prospect of engagement in certain sorts of open-

ended activities—artistic, scientific, intellectual, moral, and spiritual—
the potential for indefeasible boredom may not, after all, be an unavoidable impediment to the desirability of immortality. This is not to say that
immortal boredom is impossible, but the defenders of this view of immortality have not shown that it is inevitable and unavoidable. In the next
chapter I evaluate some further arguments against the desirability of immortality and explore the idea of self-transformation as a possible answer to them.

SIX

"The Death of Death"
Immortality, Identity, and Selfhood

In Chapter 5 we saw that two of the most frequent arguments against personal immortality—the loss of all one knows and the problem of boredom—are inadequate to establish that personal immortality cannot reasonably be considered desirable. In this chapter I show that exploring the value of immortality and its possible drawbacks leads inexorably to fundamental questions about personal identity. I argue that two key concepts of being a person or self underlie debates about whether immortality is desirable and that which kind of person one chooses to be is related to whether one regards immortality as desirable.

PRESERVING PERSONAL IDENTITY

Rosenberg (1983, 203) writes that accounts of immortality that depict it as "bleak and burdensome" and emphasize that living forever would be unutterably boring are "embodiments of a certain pessimism about human potentialities." Although he does not further develop this idea, I believe he is correct to situate worries about the tedium of immortality in skepticism about what human beings are and are capable of. Indeed, objections to both the possibility and the desirability of immortality have frequently been made on grounds that immortality is incompatible with identity—both in general terms, that immortality is incompatible with being a member of the species *Homo sapiens*, and specifically, that one cannot continue to be the person one is if one is immortal. Thus, with respect to species identity, John Macquarrie writes, "People usually want to postpone death, but death and temporal finitude are so much a constitutive part of humanity that an unending human life would be a monstrosity" (Macquarrie 1972, 197).[1] As for specific personal identity, Williams insists, "it should clearly be *me* who lives for ever" (1975, 420, his emphasis). Moreover, "the state in which I survive should be one which, to me looking forward, will be adequately related, in the life it presents, to those aims which I now have in wanting to survive at all" (420). Williams believes that the state of immortality cannot fulfill these conditions. Might there therefore be, as Ariès suggests, "a permanent relationship between one's idea of death and one's idea of oneself" (1974, 106)?

In *Tuck Everlasting* the father, Mr. Tuck, describes the family's immortal situation in a way that implies Ariès may be correct:

> Dying's part of the wheel, right there next to being born. You can't pick out the pieces you like and leave the rest. Being part of the whole thing, that's the blessing. But it's passing us by, us Tucks. Living's heavy work, but off to one side, the way *we* are, it's useless, too. It don't make sense. If I knowed how to climb back on the wheel I'd do it in a minute. You can't have living without dying. So you can't call it living, what we got. We just *are*, we just *be*, like rocks beside the road. . . . I want to grow again . . . and change. And if that means I got to move on at the end of it, then I want that, too. (Babbitt 1975, 63–64, her emphasis)

Questions with respect to the sheer possibility of preserving personal and species identity are generated, I think, as a result of attempts to show that immortality need not be endlessly boring. For example, in his depiction of the rewards of immortality (passed in heaven, but his point would apply to earthly immortality too), Donnelly (1994, 316) imagines that in an immortal state a person could remain the same physical and phenomenal age but would gradually evolve and develop in intellect, moral capacity, and personality: "A person . . . could be 33 going on a thousand-plus years. His or her intelligence and ethico-religious personality might increase, but the body would not age. A person need not then noumenally think of themselves as 33, but phenomenally they would present that physical appearance."

But Williams (1975, 418) regards this sort of picture as problematic, for he believes that in order for immortality to be desirable to me, as an individual, it must be *my* immortality—that is, it must enable me to maintain the same character and remain "much the same sort of person." This requirement then places a de facto limit on the experiences that I can have and the amount of development I can undergo, for beyond a certain point new experiences and further development would change me so utterly as to make me literally no longer the same person. The only alternative, according to Williams (1975, 418–419), is that new experiences would have to happen without changing the immortal person's personality, with the result that such a person inevitably must become "cold, withdrawn, . . . frozen," as Elina is.[2] Thus the very possibilities of learning, moral development, and the acquisition of wisdom, which I've argued would have the potential to stave off boredom or psychological dormancy, ensure, according to Williams, that one just cannot remain the same person if one is immortal. The identity requirement is unsatisfied. Over great reaches of time, future states of the immortal me would have no relationship to "aims I now have in wanting to survive." Williams argues that if we could know that this is so, then we would have no way of judging whether such a future is desirable. If we imagine the demise, in our immortal future, of our present character and desires, then we have nothing by which to judge that future desirable, whereas if we imagine that our character and desires are maintained, then we are able to assess the desirability only of a near, never of a remote, future time (Williams 1975, 421).[3]

Is this argument successful? Given that personality changes usually take place gradually, over a period of time, and that sudden discontinuities in the evolution of character are not inevitable, it is difficult to see why an individual who is eternally developing and changing in character and intellect would necessarily cease to be the same person who survives forever. Moreover, even the large changes in personality and intellect that would presumably evolve over vast eons of time need not be incompatible with the ongoing identity of the immortal individual. Williams (1975, 419) believes that one's character cannot remain fixed throughout "an endless series of very various experiences." His mistake lies in regarding this absence of fixity as incompatible with the preservation and prolongation of one's identity. Consider that, even in our present nonmortal circumstances, a person can rationally desire not to be himself or, to put it less paradoxically and more positively, can rationally desire to undergo personal transformation and thereby become, relative to his old self, a "new person."[4]

To at least a limited degree, becoming a new person or new self is just what someone aspires to if she joins Alcoholics Anonymous or a religious order, if she survives a serious accident or illness or near-death experience and as a result seeks to change her life, if she takes on a new role such as raising children, or if she sincerely vows to give up a criminal or drug-addicted past. She cannot necessarily foresee what she will become, many years hence, or the extent of the changes in her personality once her aspirations for change have been realized; yet it is not unreasonable in circumstances such as these for her to seek personal transformation. At the same time, in being transformed, she does not cease to be herself. Just as extensive international travel or several years of intensive education or undergoing a religious or moral or intellectual conversion or raising children or suffering a severe illness or disability can transform one's personality while one yet remains the same person, we have to imagine that the immortal person undergoes continuing personality change, growth, and development of these kinds without losing her identity or the continuity that enables her to understand herself as one being.

The desire for personal transformation need not, by the way, be a body-hating perspective involving renunciation of physical urges and desires; nor need it presuppose an unnecessarily or unsoundly dualistic view of the self. Because to be a person is to be at once and inextricably both a biological entity and an individual with a mental, moral, and social life, experiences of personal transformation often have concomitant effects on one's nature as a physical being. In aspiring to be another self, a person could be aspiring to be someone who uses her body differently—for example, as an athlete—or develops her talents more effectively.

I wonder whether Williams's insistence on the importance to identity of what he calls "constancy of character" (1975, 418), his assertion that the prospective immortal's future life, however far distant, should always be something she can in the present conceivably foresee, desire, and hope for, and his conclusion that the failure to meet these conditions creates an insuperable barrier to the desirability of immortality reflect a lack of imagination about the range of life's possibilities. Does Williams have difficulty believing that any life other than the one that he has actually chosen to lead could possibly be satisfactory and desirable to him? If so, then his argument may simply be a reflection of his own particular preferences. On the contrary, I would guess that most people can imagine several lives, quite different from their present ones, that they would have greatly enjoyed and flourished in if they had had many more years in which to develop them and the opportunity to choose them. Williams might argue that these alternate lives are probably not entirely unrelated to one's personal history and present life, and, indeed, what any one individual can and will ever regard, at any particular time, as a desirable transformation of self may well have some limits. But with all the time in the world the limits on what would constitute, for any given person, an attractive life are likely to be broad. I also concede that some people's hopes and ambitions may be far narrower and that they may aspire to have only one sort of life. My argument seeks only to show, first, that the desire for self-transformation is a recognizable phenomenon among at least some people. Second, such a desire and its possible fulfillment appear to provide a means for imagining a form of immortal life that does not fall victim to the insidious boredom evident in the fictional Elina and necessarily endemic, according to Williams, to all immortal lives, and that at the same time preserves personal identity in the immortal individual.

If one's current self can rationally aspire to become one's self 2, which can then aspire to become one's self 3, and so on indefinitely, then Williams's identity argument against the desirability of immortality is less convincing. In wanting to be immortal, an individual could, in effect, be wanting to undergo a series of transformations of self, a series that will be indefinitely long. In what way, then, does the person herself persist throughout these transformations? Only insofar as each transformed self is desired and actively sought by the previous one, so that the transformed self grows out of the previous self, is causally generated by the previous self, and can be understood as a continuation of the characteristics of the previous self (Nozick 1981, 35). Each finite version of oneself generates the next transformed (but still finite) version of oneself. In this way, the future experiences that one has as a transformed self can be anticipated as being as much one's own as would be the future experiences that one would have had if one had not gone through the process of transformation.[5]

It might be argued that some transformative events and stages in human life, especially those that are ordinarily considered permanent and lifelong, would lose their value if life were unending.[6] For example, the prospect of taking on a new role as a marital partner "for life" would be so different for an immortal than for those with finite life spans that it would perhaps be undesirable. I don't believe, however, that this observation shows that all personal transformations of the sort I have cited above are meaningful only if they occur within a finite life span. Religious and spiritual conversions, to take an obvious example, are often perceived by those to whom they occur as being transformations that will endure past death and into a life everlasting with God. Being (believed to be) situated within an eternal time frame makes them no less significant to the individual. Now it may be that a particular transformation could not last forever or that it would inevitably lose its freshness and compelling nature. But that fact alone does not make transformations meaningless within an immortal life; it just shows that they have limits. And it may be that in some cases one would seek out a transformation in good faith, believing it to be lifelong, and subsequently decide that it should be superseded. Such a decision in no way compromises the value and meaningfulness of the original transformation. Perhaps immortal persons would undergo a large, possibly indefinitely large, number of transformations. The possibility of such personal transformations appears to provide a means by which an immortal life might remain desirable and challenging, while personal and species identity was preserved.

CHRONOLOGICAL AGE AND PHYSICAL LIMITATIONS

But we have not yet cleared all the potential impediments to the desirability of immortality. A possibly more difficult problem comes to light if we ask what age one would be as an immortal. Williams (1975, 418) writes, "If one pictures living as an embodied person in the world rather as it is, it will be a question, and not so trivial as may seem, of what age one eternally is."

Would one simply be whatever is the sum of the years one has lived so far—419, 5,371, or 10,869? As Raymond Martin (1994, 362) says in another context, "Our conventions, which were formed to apply to cases that arise in normal circumstances, underdetermine what we should say about . . . extraordinary examples." In *Gulliver's Travels*, Jonathan Swift settles the question by making his immortals, the Struldbruggs, exactly as old as the chronological duration of their existence. An immortal who has lived for eighty years would be eighty; one who has lived for eight hundred years would be eight hundred. The horrible consequence, as Swift depicts it, is that these individuals' bodies continue to age and deteriorate throughout the years, so that eventually they lose all their physical capacities, their health, their memory, and their intellect, and exist in a state of extreme misery (as summarized in Enright 1983, 160–161). On the basis of his observation of the sufferings of these people Gulliver's "appetite for perpetuity of life" is, not surprisingly, destroyed.

But if we assume, as I stipulated at the beginning of Chapter 5, that eternal life does not necessitate eternal aging, the question remains what age the immortal would be. Williams answers it by assuming that the age at which one becomes immortal is the age one remains forever. Thus, in his discussion of Čapek's Elina, who becomes immortal (in the operatic version of the story) at the age of forty-two, Williams assumes that she remains forty-two for each of the next three hundred years.

This assumption is puzzling. What could the phrase *aged forty-two* mean within the context of an immortal life? Obviously, it could no longer denote the condition of having lived for forty-two years. Perhaps what Williams intends to convey by saying that Elina is always forty-two is just that she remains fixed, developmentally, at that age. In psychological terms, she does not change, for otherwise, according to Williams, she could not be the same person. In *Tuck Everlasting*, that is precisely Jesse Tuck's problem. As his mother describes him, "Jesse now, *he* don't ever seem too settled in himself. Course, he's young" (Babbitt 1975, 53, her emphasis). The irony of her statement is that Jesse at this point has lived for 104 years. Yet he remains, developmentally, seventeen, the age at which he acquired immortality.

But the assumption that immortality would necessitate the absence of further development is precisely the assumption to which I alluded in my discussion in Chapter 5 of boredom as an alleged problem for immortality, and it is ill founded. There is no conceptual reason to believe that immortality means fixation at one stage in life. Because immortality would provide unlimited opportunities for personal growth, development, learning, thought, and experience, it seems inappropriate to think of Elina and Jesse as necessarily remaining the same age—at least not the same psychological or developmental age. Whatever physical condition each may enjoy, the phenomenological state of the immortal being could not remain identical to that of any comparable age that is now associated with that physical condition.

One possible alternative to immortals' remaining forever the same age is suggested by Steele (1976, 425): "Instead of imagining a person living eternally at the age of 42, we can imagine him living eternally between any two desired ages; say between 16 and 60." Steele's meaning is ambiguous. He may mean that the person would not be any specific age but would possess the physical, mental, and psychological characteristics of a person no younger than sixteen and no older than sixty. But since this age range encompasses a broad range of experience, maturation, and abilities, it is difficult to know what characteristics the individual would have.

Alternatively, Steele may mean that all the stages between sixteen and sixty would last forever. Yet such an alternative cannot obviate the problem of chronological age that is generated by immortality. The immortal person couldn't be each age for an infinite amount of time because then he would never get to the next age. But suppose that the immortal exists at each age for a finite amount of time. As Vitek, the character in Čapek's play, describes it, "Fifty years to be a child and a student, fifty years to understand the world, a hundred years to work and be useful, then a hundred years to be wise and understanding, to rule, to teach and give example!" (Čapek [1922] 1990, 169). In this case the immortal would sooner or later exhaust possible chronological stages, at least exhaust those ages that human beings at present can be and that we understand as plausible human stages. What would it mean to be moving, however slowly, through age 1,002 or 19,433? Our understanding of normal human development provides no idea. The problem of biological age is even more puzzling if we imagine individuals being immortal from the start of their existence. Presumably immortality as a one-month-old, a two-year-old, or even a nine-year-old is not the state that would-be immortals are seeking. Instead, most depictions of immortality assume that an immortal being would age like a normal human being through infancy, childhood, puberty, and adolescence, and then come to permanent biological rest somewhere within the adult years.

As I pointed out in Chapter 2, if their life were greatly prolonged, most people would legitimately prefer to live it in a state of health and reasonable comfort. This desire helps to explain the motivation behind traditional searches for the mythical "fountain of youth." People do not literally want to be fixated at a youthful stage of life; rather, correctly or incorrectly, they associate youth with health, capacity, and vigor, while they associate old age with illness, disability, and weakness. Therefore, if they could choose, potential immortals would likely decide to remain fixed at some relatively healthy physical stage.[7] From this point of view it is not implausible to stipulate that Elina would remain forty-two in terms of the physical condition of her body. Even so, it seems arbitrary to assume that she would remain the age at which she happened to become immortal because there would seem to be nothing compelling about the physical condition associated with that age. Perhaps she could gradually develop as a physical being rather than decay, as is the reality for mortals. Perhaps she could gradually become stronger, healthier, more flexible, more coordinated, more nimble, and more skilled in physical activities. Rather than remaining forty-two, perhaps Elina could be revitalized to become the physical equivalent of an earlier age.

So I imagine Elina, then, not as a cold and desperately bored eternal forty-two-year-old woman, as she is in Čapek's play, but instead as a revitalized immortal with all the potential for growth and transformation that her eternal state will allow. But, in imagining this woman, I may finally be reaching some genuine obstacles to the desirability of immortality, for an immortal person is a being unlimited in one crucial respect— length of life—but not in others. Although the brain is not a mere vessel that can be filled completely full, and the body is not a mere machine that can be worn out, nonetheless, because we are material entities, there are limits on what is possible for individuals. Some kinds of behaviors and activities are simply beyond the capabilities of certain individuals. Given the kind of body and the kind of abilities a person has, she may never become a gymnast or may never be able to understand nuclear physics—even if she has all the time in the world. As a finite physical being, an immortal person does not possess infinite physical capacities.

Our limits, as material beings, might generate certain psychological and social dangers. Our finite nature as physical beings could be difficult to reconcile with our infinite temporal nature.

> Wouldn't we become obsessed with the fact of the natural lottery of talents/looks/abilities/temperament etc.? It's hard enough in our limited lives to accept our place in the natural lottery. But since our lives are so limited, we can at least try to focus on the things we can do, since we are unlikely to exhaust the possibilities. And in a short lifetime, we have a sense that there's no point wasting time in envy of others, or bitterness about the unfairness of natural allotments. But if we were immortal, I think we might become extremely bitter about our limitations, or any unchosen inequalities amongst people. We would have endless time to fret about being less attractive than average, or not having been blessed with a sunny temperament, or a talent for playing the violin. (Sue Donaldson, personal communication, 2000)

Although some of these physical, physiological, and psychological conditions would be open to amendment and improvement through genetic engineering, I think Donaldson is right about this sort of danger. At least some individuals could feel envy of more gifted others, resentment of their abilities, and discouragement and anger about the limitations that nature arbitrarily imposed.

But there is a greater problem. At some point, possibly after three hundred years but also possibly much later, the immortal person would have fully exploited all the capacities of his brain and body. He would arrive at a stage where his finite brain could not encompass any more and his finite body could not do or feel any more than they had already. In other words, the immortal's physical limitations would eventually place insuperable boundaries on his life prospects. Consider the fate of the central character in Chapter 10 of Barnes's *A History of the World in 10½ Chapters*. After becoming immortal in heaven, the hero is finally free to do all the things he has wanted to do and for as long as possible. Golf is one of them. But eventually, after centuries of play, during which he gets better and better at it, the story's hero finds that golf "gets used up." The character has become a superbly good golfer and no more improvements are even imaginable, for he is able to get around any golf course in the minimum number of strokes possible. We can imagine that even if constant practice did not make him a perfect golfer, he would still, eventually, reach the outer limits of his golf proficiency and thereby find that the sport was "used up." When it is suggested to him that he move on to try other sports, he responds, wisely, "They'd get used up too" (Barnes 1989, 296).

I am not here adopting Williams's view that constancy of character eventually dooms the immortal to boredom. As I have already argued, constancy of character is not a necessary component of immortality. Instead, because of the body's finitude, the body's constancy, so to speak, the immortal would eventually exhaust the capacities to do, to learn, and to experience new things that were within the scope of his particular body. Although the repetition of old familiar activities would still be possible for the immortal, the problem is that even if he had extraordinary abilities and intelligence, every activity he undertook would eventually be "used up." At that point, Barnes's story predicts, immortality would no longer be desirable for such a person, and he would feel ready to die. He would die without regrets about unfinished business, unexplored opportunities, unrealized potential, or undeveloped talents, secure in the understanding that, for him, the phrase "been there, done that" truly applied.[8]

Some very elderly people apparently feel "ready to die" for something like this reason: they believe they have done all that they could manage and hope for. Not everyone reaches this stage, but some at least do seem to attain before death a sense of fulfilled potential. However, many other people die far too soon. An important reason for resisting death and for mourning an early demise is that usually the deceased person could have learned and experienced and done so much but never had time to. So a much longer life than we have now would be good for most people. But because human beings are finite material entities and our capacities are not unlimited, unending life could become undesirable as we "use up" our physical potential.

But there is an important objection to this argument that the body's limitations would eventually doom the desirability of immortality. Current and prospective research, as well as some science-fiction stories, suggests that perhaps we should not too hastily assume that the human body must necessarily have limited capacities, especially in an immortal person. As organ replacement, using biological organs (donated or cloned) and synthetic substitutes, becomes both more pervasive and more successful, and as gene splicing fights off the aging process, perhaps we can foresee a day when the replacement or regeneration of body parts is routine, and our physical capacities are thereby enormously enhanced. Perhaps also we should contemplate the possibility of replacing an individual's body parts not with a succession of qualitatively identical or similar parts but rather with a succession of different and possibly superior organs. If we imagine a future in which body technologies are far advanced, then the material environments created would allow one to select new body parts or additions in order to become the painter or basketball star one always wanted to be. Thus the human being would achieve eternal life as a cyborg.[9]

But even if I can fairly readily imagine the immortal's getting a new arm or a new heart when the old ones are worn out and nonfunctioning—even if, that is, parts of the body can be renewed and replaced—the brain seems not to be replaceable, and perhaps therein lie the limits of our mortality. As Clark (1995, 31) expresses it, "Neurological decay would make our lives not worth living long before the rest of our carefully coddled bodies had worn out. Other organs, if they do wear out, can be replaced; if our brain is replaced it is not clear that anything else could take on the job of sustaining our own selfhood." Moreover, the brain cannot merely be increased in size. According to Ian Pearson (2000, 1), "The brain is limited in size by a variety of biological constraints. Even if there were more space available, it could not be made much more efficient by making it larger, because of the need for cooling, energy and oxygen supply taking up ever more space and making distances between processors larger." So the finite nature of the human brain, its exhaustibility no matter how developed medicine may become, seems to spell the end of hopes for immortality and a limit to the desirability of a very long life. As Asimov and Silverberg say in *The Positronic Man*, "What matters is that organic human brain cells die. *Must* die. There's no way of avoiding it. Every other organ in the body can be maintained or replaced by an artificial substitute, but the brain can't be replaced at all, not without changing and therefore killing the personality. And the organic brain must eventually die" (1995, 283, their emphasis). When one's brain dies or ceases to have any higher functions, one's identity ceases to persist; thus a desirable form of immortality—for the individual that one is, no matter how many personal transformations one may have experienced during one's brain's existence—is impossible.

The brain, like all material objects, may not last for eternity, but, contra Asimov and Silverberg, might it be replaced? Could that which the brain contains or enables or makes possible be made to endure? Even if the brain were to inevitably decay or die, perhaps one's individual personal awareness might be perpetuated via entirely artificial means. Already, in fact, at least one such mode of immortality has been suggested. A sophisticated computer could make a duplicate of the brain (Pearson 2000, 1): "On the computer side, neural networks are already the routine approach to many problems and are based on many of the same principles that neurons in the brain use. As this field develops, we will be able eventually to make a good emulation of biological neurons. As it develops further, it ought to be possible on a sufficiently sophisticated computer to make a full emulation of a whole brain."

Would this breakthrough offer us, as claimed, a desirable form of potential immortality? Preservation within a computer, whatever it may offer to the vanity of self-memorialization through the conservation of past experiences, does not appear to constitute immortality in the sense of unending life. Containment within a computer hardly provides the kinds of opportunities for ongoing human experience and activity that are associated with being a person. Unless the computerized record is subsequently implanted in a machine in such a way as to produce a self-conscious and self-determining robot (Pearson 2000), the computer record alone does not provide us with any prospect of true immortality.[10] So we seem to be faced either with a form of pseudosurvival in a computer, which records our brain patterns but does not permit ongoing bodily existence, or with the eventual death of the brain and hence the termination of one's personal identity.

However, Martin offers another possibility. In his defense of a limited version of reincarnation Martin (1994, 346) suggests, "For many people the preservation of personal identity does not matter primarily in survival." "One might survive as someone else whose existence one values as much as one's own" (346), inasmuch as one could anticipate and desire the future experiences of that someone else in the same way that one now, as a mortal being, anticipates and desires one's own future experiences. In making this claim, Martin has in mind some thought experiments generated within philosophical debates about the basis for personal identity. He mentions David Wiggins's example of the amoebalike fission of one individual into two (Wiggins 1967, 37–38) and Sydney Shoemaker's example of the division of an individual's brain into two functioning halves and the transplantation of each half into each of two bodies that are qualitatively identical to that of the original individual (cited in Martin 1994, 346). Another such thought experiment is Derek Parfit's (1984) teleporter, which transports a person to Mars using a "Scanner." The Scanner destroys the person's brain and body while at the same time recording all the conditions of the person's cells. The message is beamed to Mars by radio, where a "Replicator" creates, out of new matter, a brain and body exactly like that of the original person.[11] Martin (1994, 363) also notes Shoemaker's idea concerning "an environmentally polluted society of the technologically distant future in which people, to keep from getting very sick, have to replace their bodies every several years with qualitatively identical ones"—presumably through the transfer to the cloned body of all the individual's memories and experientially derived habits and predispositions.[12] Indeed, according to Robinson, who takes the prospect of cloned cyber-immortality a giant step further, around 2200 human beings will become "permanent ongoing depositors in the Memory Bank." "If [a person] is ever creative enough to somehow explode her head, the Bank will grow a clone from her stored DNA and decant into its skull all her memories up to the moment of death. She will resume her life almost uninterrupted, death having been a brief nuisance" (2000, M9). In this way, computer-facilitated psychological continuity would be paired with a cloned body.

But now we need to ask whether the prospect of creating replacements such as these would be adequate to make immortality feasible and desirable. What Wiggins's, Shoemaker's, Parfit's, and Robinson's imaginary examples have in common is that in each story the newly created individuals, although they are replicas of their originals, are not numerically identical to or even spatiotemporally continuous with the individuals from whom they were generated. So in that sense the original individual's personal identity is not preserved. Yet Parfit (1984) argues that we "ought to regard having a Replica as being about as good as ordinary survival" (201), for "personal identity is not what matters" (255, emphasis in original removed). And Martin (1994, 362) suggests that even though "a great deal (quantitatively) may have been lost" in these sorts of transformations, nonetheless what is lost may be trivial from the vantage point of the concern for meaningful personal survival. He argues that all these forms of replication facilitate the persistence of what he calls the survivor's "psychology"—his or her "beliefs, memories, intentions, personality, and so on" (362) within another distinct body—and this conservation of individual psychology should be highly valued by the person seeking survival even if it does not involve numerical identity or spatiotemporal continuity.

Provided they would not necessitate a stultifying sameness of character that would make impossible what I earlier called personal transformation, I agree that these replicas give us a means by which we can imagine a form of life indefinitely prolonged through the preservation and transfer of the individual's psychology from one body to another. Although the replica is not spatiotemporally continuous with the original person, in the absence of such continuity the replica provides as good a form of survival as one could hope for. However, in these thought experiments it is still not clear whether such a form of immortality would be desirable, for the replicas, if each one were qualitatively identical to or even just qualitatively similar to the original body, would, by virtue of their finite physical capacities, still place absolute limits, at least eventually, on the range of what persons could learn, do, and experience. Because the immortal would be in all respects except longevity a finite physical being, even with all the enhancements science could provide, his material limitations would eventually ensure that he would reach the limits of his capacities. In the long run, the confines of the finite replica brains in finite replica bodies would be reached. Talents and activities would be used up. The only potential saving grace would be the enjoyment of the repetition of various experiences.

In order to stave off the point at which one's capacities are exhausted and only repetition is possible, perhaps we should simply imagine that the physical capacities of the immortal are increased gradually and indefinitely. Perhaps there need be no limits; the immortal's body would be endowed with more and more material improvements to facilitate the acquisition of greater and greater abilities and talents.[13] Perhaps this lack of limits would be made possible through the much-touted development of nanotechnology, in which molecule-sized robots would repair, rebuild, replace, and enhance parts of the human body indefinitely (Holt 1999, 76).

It is difficult to know what to say in response to this suggestion. I may be reaching the limits of my own capacity meaningfully to imagine a state of immortality. I'm inclined to say that even if it were possible to make replacements of parts of the brain, given all eternity, it seems implausible that an immortal individual could receive finite brain replacements sufficiently like her own to enable her to maintain at least some minimal continuity as a person while also affording an open-ended range of possible experiences, thoughts, and feelings. To go beyond those limits would, I suspect, require having a qualitatively different brain and thus becoming a new person. Indeed, Robinson claims that, after centuries of existence and the sequential assumption of many different personalities, the immortal person of the future will tend to outgrow any "sentimental attachment" to her original personality (2000, M9)—and perhaps she would also "outgrow" any metaphysical or moral preferences for the preservation of her selfhood. Because of the ongoing need for expanding and developing the physical body, the cost of immortality could be the loss of any fragment or aspect of one's enduring personal identity.

In the end, sustaining an eternal life and avoiding the prospect of "using up" all one's capabilities appears to require the possession of a body and a brain with capacities that are in principle unlimited. Thus, to be immortal and never run out of the potential for novelty may require giving up the attachment to being human. Could it nonetheless make sense, in these conditions, to want to be immortal? Only if it makes sense to want to be a god, or at least godlike, for in effect, one would have to be godlike if one were to live forever and not be limited by one's material being. In becoming godlike, I submit, one ceases altogether to be the human person one was.

Historically, the cultural ideal of immortality has, not coincidentally, most readily and comfortably been allied with the idea of an afterlife lived with God. Theists can all too easily claim that God's omnipotence, not human cunning, makes our human immortality possible. However, the appeal to God's infinite capacities is just a way of dodging the very real conceptual question of how a material being with a perdurable personal identity could avoid the limitations imposed by her own finitude.[14]

I conclude that the limitations of the physical body, and especially the brain, combined with the desire not to be limited by that body, raise the most difficult questions about the appeal of immortality. Whatever science offers, a time might come when most human beings, no matter how desirous of a long life, could accurately say, "I have done and achieved all that is possible for me in this life."

At this point in the analysis what I called, at the beginning of the previous chapter, the axiological double bind appears to have no simple resolution. My investigation so far suggests that a life that has no limit, a life that would not entail the prospect of exhausting one's capacities, may not be a recognizably human life because it appears to require both the loss of personal identity and the attainment of godlike abilities. Yet a person who is reasonably healthy, both mentally and physically, has no good reason to regard a finite life of any particular length as a good thing.

WHAT KIND OF SELF?

There is one possible and important exception to my conclusion about the undesirability of immortality. Although some persons, like Barnes's golf-playing hero, would grow tired of endless life because everything they did would eventually be "used up," others are convinced that a meaningful and mostly happy life, eternal or not, does not require constant new achievements and accomplishments. They think that an individual who reached the outer boundaries of talent development and exploitation of finite abilities might nevertheless still find pleasure and solace in the sheer variety of repeated experience attainable within the confines of his or her finite physical capacities.

There is a distinction between, on the one hand, the development and exploitation of talents and abilities and, on the other hand, the sheer enjoyment and exploration of experiences for their own sake. A talent or ability may be exhausted, but the ability to take pleasure in familiar experiences may be inexhaustible. As I observed in Chapter 5, under certain circumstances some persons are capable of enjoying the same sorts of intellectual, aesthetic, or recreational activities over and over again, provided that the activities are themselves somewhat varied and one has the choice of moving from one activity to another. Philosophers of immortality disagree as to whether this enjoyment is possible for all eternity. While Williams insists that stultifying boredom would inevitably result, Momeyer denies it.

From Momeyer's perspective, one might reach the limits of what it is possible for one's body to do and to experience without thereby necessarily wanting to go beyond those limits. One might become as good as one could be at an activity without inevitably finding that the activity was no longer worth pursuing. One might choose to enjoy the potentially endless variations in doing and experiencing that are possible even within the limitations set by one's finite material nature: "There is always another historical moment to discover, or poem to write. It's true that one might not be able to keep developing into a better poet, or a better historian. But if the original impetus was just to do it, not to figure out how to keep doing it better, then I think the problem of exhaustion disappears" (Sue Donaldson, personal communication, 2000). According to this view, although a person might reach the limits of her capacity as a violin player, for example, she still would have indefinitely varied possibilities for violin-related experiences—such as enjoying listening to violin music and playing the violin alone and with others.

Sue Donaldson argues that the potential value, to the individual, of living a life that is given meaning through mere variations of experience—as contrasted with developments and improvements in experience—would depend on fundamental choices by the individual of what kind of life to live, what gives meaning to life, and what kind of self to be. She suggests two different possible perspectives on what gives life meaning:

> Does meaning come from striving, from engaging in project- or goal-oriented activity? Or is it through repetition (with variation) of certain kinds of activities (e.g. cooking, planting a garden, honoring religious or other types of rituals)? Is it from being the active subject of a life, or from the more vicarious pleasures of standing on the sidelines and observing others? Is the primary source of meaning

problem-solving, or creativity, or contemplation? . . . I think those who are more accomplishment or problem-solving oriented are going to have far greater concerns about the prospect of becoming bored with immortality, or of reaching the physical limits of their talent and abilities. Eventually you will do the best you can do, and be the best you can be. But if you're the kind of person who revels in ritual, or the inexhaustible pleasure of learning about other people's lives in other times and places—if your orientation is not so much on self-development but rather on the intrinsic fascinations of the external world—then I don't think the problem of exhaustion of one's personal resources arises in the same way. (personal communication, 2000)

Philosopher Margaret Urban Walker makes a comparable distinction between two fundamentally different ways of being in the world. She writes, first, about a unifying theme within the ethically diverse theories of several twentieth-century philosophers, which she describes as "the idea of an individual's life as a self-consciously controlled career[, which] binds a whole life or lifetime together in a unified way for which the individual is accountable" (1999, 102–103). According to this normative view of a good human life, the individual is expected to create, follow through on, and control the course of a narrative plot or project that governs the unfolding of the life and is the expression of the individual's individual autonomy (103). The ideal person is a "fit, energetic, and productive individual who sets himself a course of progressive achievement within the boundaries of society's rules and institutions, and whose orderly life testifies to his self-discipline and individual effort" (102). Walker calls this vision the "career self."

By contrast, Walker describes, second, a normative view of the self according to which the stages of life feature "central lessons, tasks, pleasures, experiences, or bonds." The individual appreciates and "savors" them for their distinctiveness rather than for their continuity as part of an ongoing life project. Some of the lessons and tasks may involve loss or pain, which might nonetheless take on a positive meaning. "Our lives on this view are more like journeys than careers: our physical trajectories are continuous, but where we stop to visit and what affects us may not follow a linear path. Some of what affects us may transform us into discontinuity with who or what we were before" (1999, 108). Most significantly for my discussion of the desirability of immortality, Walker remarks that "there is no reason for us to cease *living* this life, even in very late years, short of grave incapacitation. It embodies no eventually unfulfillable demand for achievement or progress; it requires only normal awareness, capacities for feeling, and opportunities to belong to or with something other than or larger than oneself. The meanings in such a life are many, and we do not wholly control much less create them" (108, her emphasis).

James Lindemann Nelson introduces the phrase *living life seriatim*, which he derives from Hilde Lindemann Nelson, as a means of describing this alternative normative vision of the self. For the seriatim self, life is "less an overall unified project and more . . . a set of fits and starts" (1999, 122). "The seriatim self may see her life as made up of many jobs, lots of them quite big enough, thank you, but none necessarily life-defining, nor especially valued for the particular role they play in contributing to the achievement of a 'rational plan' for the whole" (123). This self might derive value from "the goods of relationship" rather than achievement. "But the seriatim self has escaped, more or less, the ideological pressures, as well as the ideological material rewards that encourage people to identify themselves with their careers, and hence may live a life both more shaped by contingencies than by the expression of personal agency and more involved in relationships prized intrinsically, not because they are instrumental to achieving the agent's quest" (123–124).

The argument with which I concluded the previous section, that immortality could be undesirable because one eventually comes to the limits of what is possibly achievable in a material human body, appears to apply most clearly to the life of the career self. I suspect that the implicit assumption of the normativeness of the career self may in part drive Hardwig's urgent advocacy of a duty to die. In listing the conditions under which he thinks people would "rather be dead than continue to live" he includes quadriplegia and AIDS. He lists loss of independence and loss of control among the conditions that make life no longer worth living (2000, 83). This is, I suggest, the career self speaking, the self that recognizes meaning in the achievement of new goals and the attainment of additional accomplishments. The career self values self-control, independence, and high autonomy, is unwilling or unable to imagine reinventing its life in ways that might infuse meaning or value in disability or suffering (Wendell 1996, 104, 109), and hence is unable to discern a reason for living when some significant aspects of living become a "burden."

Similarly, when Nuland advocates that each of us accept our death at its appointed time, he adds a career-self spin to his vision of the life that will make that death acceptable: "Life must be useful and rewarding. If by our work and pleasure, our triumphs and our failures, each of us is contributing to an evolving process of continuity not only of our species but of the entire balance of nature, the dignity we create in the time allotted to us becomes a continuum with the dignity we achieve by the altruism of accepting the necessity of death" (1994, 267). According to Nuland, then, dignity and value in life must be acquired at what would seem to be a huge cost: we must contribute not only to others in our immediate environment but to our entire species and to all of nature. When these contributions are no longer possible, then death becomes acceptable. When usefulness ends and triumphs become inaccessible, life is no longer worth living. For the career self, arriving at the limits of one's abilities and being unable to progress beyond them is a reason to accept death.

The argument that immortality is undesirable because one eventually comes to the limits of what is possibly achievable in a material human body does not as obviously apply in the case of the seriatim self. In the absence of overriding goals or commitments to development, growth, accomplishment, and the exploitation of talents and abilities, the seriatim self could value an unending existence filled with individual pleasures, experiences, tasks, relationships, observations, and learnings. As Robert

Nozick points out, "We may desire to do things; our desire need not be merely to have done them" (Nozick 1981, 580). Such a self would find nothing important or terminal about reaching the limits of personal competence and self-development. Nor is it implausible that such a self might continue to want to live, to enjoy living, even when some capacities have diminished or disappeared or even when the self also experiences some suffering. The seriatim self exists contentedly within its limits.

Or so argues Donaldson. By contrast, Nelson, who endorses the seriatim self as an admirable way of being that offers possible advantages over life as a career self, suggests that a seriatim self would be less likely to cling to life than the career self may be. Whereas the career self seeks opportunities for ongoing agency and achievement of goals, the seriatim self, valuing the well-being of others, whose existence and perpetuation may be independent of her own continued existence, is less committed to personal survival (Nelson 1999, 126). Nelson seeks to show that the harm of death may vary depending on what people value and that what people value may be related to their gender. He develops an account according to which the harm of death varies in relation to the degree to which one values "the goods of experience and action vis-à-vis unexperienced goods" (119), such as the well-being of others. Nelson believes that women are more likely than men to value such unexperienced goods—to care, for example, about the future flourishing of their children and grandchildren, even if they will not be alive to witness that flourishing. His conclusion—and, despite Nelson's intentions, it may not be one that feminists would welcome—is that death may be a greater harm for men, to whom death means the loss of the goods of experience and action, than for women, for whom it need not mean the loss of unexperienced goods (124–125).

I agree with Nelson's general point that "death's harm can be, at least in part, a function of what and how a person values" (1999, 126) and that death's harm is not, therefore, merely a function of accumulated years. The truth of this claim is also demonstrated when individuals choose to die for the preservation of an ideal, a cause, or another person and when individuals die believing that they will join God in a life everlasting. Such persons do, or at least ought to, value death differently from those who do not interpret their death as being for someone or something else or those who do not interpret their demise in religious terms.

I also agree with Nelson that the badness of death is gendered, for as I have argued in earlier chapters, by virtue of their gender older women may have lacked some of the life opportunities from which older men have benefited. But the attribution to women of a preference for unexperienced goods over the goods of experience and action may or may not be correct. It is an empirical claim for which there is little clear empirical evidence. The danger of Nelson's claim about death's gender is that it could be used to endorse a gendered distinction between a self-sacrificing, acquiescent feminine life perspective, with which one accepts death and seeks little for oneself, and an assertive, self-aggrandizing masculine life perspective, with which one desires to go on living and is not happy without fully experiencing and doing. I reject a position that might imply that women were less interested in or needful of a prolonged life just because they valued the flourishing of others over their own. The prolongation of human life potentially provides the opportunity for everyone to flourish, and we should not make a priori assumptions about which individuals will want it or what their reasons might be.

Without making unverified presumptions about gender preferences and tendencies, I suggest that the seriatim self is, generally, a person who is less oriented to the future, to movement toward goals, than the career self is, and hence the seriatim self may be open to and accepting of both the possibility of personal annihilation and the possibility of personal survival, although the content of such personal survival would be quite different from that sought by the career self. The perceived value of endless life could well be closely related to the general type of person one is and the sort of life one chooses to live. Conversely, examination of the possibilities and problems that immortality holds out may also influence our assessment of the life orientation we have chosen. If immortality lived as a human person entails an eventual end to goal seeking and striving, new accomplishments and fresh achievements, does this prospect suggest anything about the nature of a finite life devoted to deriving meaning from striving toward goals? Sue Donaldson (personal communication, 2000) points to "people whose lives are built around more purely creative pursuits (in which the doing is the point, not the outcome) or spiritual pursuits (contemplation, and other kinds of self-obliterating activity) or certain kinds of scholarly pursuits (losing oneself in the minutia[e] of different times or places, or biographical subjects)." Such persons, she says, are in fact exploiting their talents and abilities, but such exploitation is not the point or goal of the activity, which is "intrinsically motivated." Interestingly, the effect, if not the goal, of many such activities is self-forgetting, self-submersion, or even self-obliteration, states quite different from the self-conscious, even self-aggrandizing, condition of the career self.

Yet the advantages of life as it is lived by a career self should not be underestimated, and its relationship to prolongevitism and immortality is not so straightforward as Donaldson's arguments suggest. Although Kamm does not use the concept of career self, she makes several remarks about achievements that are relevant to an understanding of the career self and to its relationship to longevity and immortality. The dread of death that comes from the thought that at death everything is "all over" should be obviated, according to Kamm, with respect to what she calls the "goods of achievement," which death cannot harm or destroy (1993, 36). "It seems to be true of some of the most important goods [of life], including having a good character and knowing important truths, that, once one has them, they are complete in themselves. The more we can appreciate our lives as achievement, the less we depend on future life" (66). This argument suggests that the career self need not necessarily long for immortality or even a greatly extended life once it has achieved certain goals that are not harmed by death. Interestingly, then, the argument derived from Kamm converges with the argument derived from Nelson: just as the seriatim self need not cling to life because it values the good of others, a good that is usually independent of one's continuing existence, so also the career self need not cling to life because it values the goods of achievement, goods that are usually independent of one's continuing existence.

I shall make no attempt to adjudicate between the desirability of the career self and the desirability of the seriatim self. The strengths and vulnerabilities of each are sufficiently complex that it seems to me these two approaches to living a human life represent genuinely valuable alternatives and not mere moral obverses of each other.[15] Although I do not endorse one form of selfhood over the other, I wish to emphasize that the kind of individual that one is and that one has chosen to make oneself could well make a legitimate difference to one's assessment of the desirability of immortality. Yet the relationship between each of these selves and the potential desirability of immortality is complex.[16] Because my own life choice could be described as being a career self, I find longer life attractive in that it offers the opportunity for more mountains to climb, more rivers to cross. But mountains already climbed and rivers crossed are achievements that might make it easier to face death with equanimity, and worries about the exhaustion of physical potential and the threat of "using things up" constitute a real impediment to the desirability of immortality. Yet the attractions of the seriatim self have also convinced me that immortality may not inevitably be stultifying even once one's material limits are reached. The seriatim self might choose either to enjoy a life lived without further conquests or to accept death, content in the knowledge that her relationships and experiences have been enough to give meaning to her life and that others whom she values will survive her.

CONCLUSION

I like to hope that a serious examination of the putative value of immortality can bring us out of what Clark (1995, 23) calls "the merely feeble 'mortalism' that passes for maturity" when we adopt the apologist view of longevity and death. This examination of whether earthly immortality is desirable suggests that human beings may not yet have fully engaged in the imaginative project of exploring what immortality is and involves. I believe that ordinarily when human beings have discussed and desired immortality, they have had in mind merely the indefinite postponement of death. The longing for immortality, the "death of death" (Momeyer 1988, 29), is a vivid representation of the prolongevist tendencies in many human beings. In our current reality, I'm in no way convinced that contemporary human beings have yet reached the point at which the human life is long enough. In fact, I think my arguments in this book show that, given a minimal level of health and well-being, a much longer life would almost certainly be desirable for large numbers of people.

On a collective level, however, there appear to be insuperable global barriers to the desirability of prolonging human life indefinitely. A time could easily come when the disparity between the resources devoted to life-lengthening and preservation and the resources devoted to other goals would be so great that the resources would have to be pulled away from lengthening and preserving life. Collectively, if not individually, as the conditions that would enable an indefinitely long life to be enjoyable and productive become harder and harder to create, the prolongation of human life would become proportionately less desirable. In material terms, human immortality is too much for this planet to sustain, and for many people it may also be individually undesirable because of the finite physical capacities of the human body. This is not to say that our temporal limits are what make us human. But it is to emphasize that our material embodiment makes us what we are and what we ultimately can become.

SEVEN

Personal and Policy Implications
"Rage against the Dying of the Light"?

It is not easy to enter into the imaginative depiction of a life of immortality. But doing so is no mere academic speculation or exercise in creative dreaming. Thinking seriously about immortality has much to tell us about the prospects and problems of prolongevitism both as a moral choice and as a social policy. As I acknowledged in the two preceding chapters, prolongevitism generates extraordinary obstacles when it is taken to its limit, the advocacy of unending life. The resource costs alone would make immortality untenable for all but a select few. Moreover, a life without end would generate enormous demands on the immortal individual's capacity to live a meaningful life within the limits of a material body.

However, the imaginative exploration of the strengths and weaknesses of an immortal life offers significant insights into what makes a human life worth living and, specifically, into why a longer life than human beings now enjoy is worth seeking. Perrett argues that most human beings do not have the chance during their lives to realize their potential. He thinks that for most of them the only possibility of realizing their potential would be to have some form of life after death. "In denying the reality of an afterlife, humanism is committed to the view that for the vast majority existence is in the end irredeemably tragic" (1986, 219). I contend that the tragedy of human life would be mitigated if not vitiated if people had the opportunity to live full human lives—"full" both in the sense of being long and in the sense of being rich with opportunities. It is my hope that the preceding chapters succeed in making a strong case for at least a limited form of prolongevitism, one that takes account of the cultural context, including ageism, ableism, racism, classism, and sexism, in which long life and the nature of aging are discussed and evaluated. As Chapter 4 showed, the case for prolongevitism cannot be based on the alleged intrinsic value of longevity, of life itself, or of human lives. Instead, it is founded on a genuine appreciation of human potential, of what people want within their lives and are capable of doing and experiencing when their opportunities are increased. It is rational to want a longer life because life itself is the precondition for all else that we might want.

At its most fundamental level, prolonged life offers the opportunity for additional and varied experiences. Human beings do not inevitably tire of experiences based on fundamental human biological drives such as eating, physical movement, and sexual activity. Nor do we cease to enjoy relationships with persons of all ages, both those relationships that we already have, which we seek to cultivate and develop, and those that are new to us. In addition, to at least some degree, human beings are capable of enjoying some types of intellectual, aesthetic, or recreational activities over and over again, provided that the activities are varied and there is a choice of moving from one activity to another. At the same time, a prolonged life provides the opportunity for the pursuit of open-ended projects involving artistic, scientific, or intellectual inquiry and development, moral improvement and growth, or the search for wisdom and enlightenment.

Indeed, a prolonged life creates prospects for self-transformation, for re-creating one's identity by adopting innovative life plans, different values, and new goals. Many human beings, perhaps the vast majority, never have the chance fully to explore and express all their potential as physical/emotional/moral/intellectual beings. A more prolonged life would provide at least some of that missed opportunity. Given the resources and the opportunities, human beings are capable of changing their lives, often even in the face of oppressive or debilitating circumstances. Contrary to stereotypes about disadvantaged or aging people (or those who are both), the potential for this versatility and flexibility is a fundamental characteristic of all human beings at all ages.

If, as I argue, it is important to remember that human beings are capable of self-transformation, it is also essential to recognize that the kind of self that one is and that one may (choose to) become can have implications for one's attitude toward the value of a prolonged life and one's beliefs about what purposes such a prolonged life may serve. In Chapter 6 I outlined a broad contrast between an identity as a "career self" and an identity as a "seriatim self." According to the perspective of the career self, life is a teleological narrative, with challenges to be conquered, plans to be realized, and goals to be achieved. Life is a trajectory along which setbacks can be encountered and progress, more or less, may be made. By contrast, from the perspective of the seriatim self, life is a journey undertaken not for its outcomes but for the sake of the lessons, tasks, pleasures, and relationships that may be savored along the way. For the seriatim self much that can be enjoyed and experienced is not contained within the context of striving and achievement and is not defined, constrained, or measured by progress toward a goal.

Yet even though the contrast between the career self and the seriatim self has a certain intuitive plausibility, a plausibility borne out, I think, in our ordinary observations of the differences among people's lived lives and felt values, the implications of this contrast for perspectives on human longevity are not so clear. As I argued in the previous chapter, one might anticipate that the seriatim self would want to go on living just for the sake of continued enjoyment of the seriatim pleasures and challenges of everyday life, independent of any long-term ambitions or plans. Unlike the career self, who may no longer want to go on living once all plans have been achieved and whose "immortality" is constituted by the achievements that she leaves behind her, the seriatim self need not fear or even anticipate an anomic condition in which all goals have been achieved or all capacities exhausted, for she is able to live within the context of limited tasks and activities, content to experience and reexperience the joys of the present time. She continues to value her life and her way of living, even if and when some of her capacities have diminished or disappeared or even when she suffers. According to this interpretation, the seriatim self exists contentedly within its limits.

But another interpretation is possible, according to which it is the career self that will value continued survival, for the career self sees human existence as an open-ended set of challenges. Unlike the seriatim self, who rests content with what she is doing and who values connections with others who may outlive her, the career self will continue to seek opportunities for activity, striving, self-development, and the achievement of goals. Within any foreseeable possibilities of extending the human life span, the career self will always want more life, for the current limits on human existence probably do not provide for the expression of the full range of potential and capacity of the human body and mind.

I believe we cannot assume that one kind of self is more likely than the other to value longevity and to seek to extend its life span. We can assume, however, that the kind of self that one is may very well affect, and legitimately so, one's attitudes toward the value of long life and the nature of the threat that our eventual and inevitable death constitutes.

THE CONTEXT FOR
PROLONGEVIST SOCIAL POLICY

In Chapter 2 I showed that the four main arguments in favor of apologism—arguments purporting to show why death should not be dreaded, arguments based on the "rhythm of life," arguments about why the human life span is long enough, and arguments founded on the supposed social costs of prolonging human life—are unsuccessful. In light of this demonstration of the weaknesses of apologism, it is striking and significant that apologism appears to win the approval of many contemporary scientists, biomedical ethicists, historians, and cultural commentators. As Richard Sprott (1991, 121) says, approvingly, "The search for the means to greatly extend human life span is generally viewed with great skepticism by most competent gerontologists."

Admittedly, with respect to what might be called "catastrophic care," Western health-care systems, especially in the United States and perhaps especially for those with wealth and white-skin privilege, have been pro-longevist, in the sense that drastic steps are often taken to keep alive people who are in mortal danger from conditions such as heart attack, stroke, and cancer. More generally, however, it is fair to say that in both historical and contemporary times, and despite protestations to the contrary (e.g., Callahan 1995, 24), there have been more suspicion and criticism of prolongevitism than attempts to argue in its support. Contemporary biomedical ethicists are inclined to castigate both the desire of some people to cling to life and the desperate attempts by some of the relatives of dying people to prolong their lives. Lawyers, sometimes unintentionally abetted by members of the Roman Catholic clergy, urge people to make living wills in which they reject "heroic measures" when seriously ill. There is a growing discussion of the alleged value, importance, and justification of doctor-assisted suicide (e.g., Prado and Taylor 1999; Prado 2000). And as Momeyer points out, there is a pervasive accompanying tendency to romanticize death through concepts such as "death with dignity," "natural death" (1988, 15), and "meaningful death" (Hardwig 1997a, 40–42). Given the apparently defeatist, even fatalistic, nature of much writing in favor of apologism, it is puzzling, and perhaps even a reason for cultural suspicion, to find apologism so popular and prolongevitism nearly universally rejected by ethicists, physicians, and intellectuals who speak out in public on end-of-life issues.

Moreover, as Chapters 2, 3, and 4 showed, the debate about the value of longevity and the postponement of death occurs within a context of endemic ageism. Ample evidence indicates that within Western culture living a long life is interpreted to mean living a life of illness, disability, poverty, and lack of opportunity. Long-lived people are perceived as inevitably constituting a debilitating psychological and socioeconomic burden for the hard-working members of younger cohorts. As a result of this perception, some biomedical ethicists go so far as to say that aging, ill people have a duty to die.

However, as I have argued, it is an egregious error to assume that all elderly people are in a state of poor physical health and mental decline or are fixed, inflexible, and without any meaningful capacity for enjoying life. People who are fortunate to live long lives are not all in a state of personal debility or dependence; many are leading autonomous, active, and valuable lives without making any special demands for individual or state support. They are as capable of learning, developing, and transforming their lives as younger people are. So it is therefore just false to claim that all elderly people constitute nothing but a "burden." Indeed, such a generalization is ageist in the extreme.

And long-living people who do have an illness or disability are not thereby prevented from leading rich, full lives; to the extent that they are dependent, their dependence should not be interpreted as evidence that increased longevity is bad. There are varying patterns of dependence throughout the life span. Although an individual of any age may have significant needs that generate heavy demands on others, that person is not usually only a burden. Even when in need, people are capable of giving back to others. Moreover, some of the needs and dependencies that long-lived people experience can be ameliorated or even avoided with the right sorts of health care and social support. Certainly some health problems and some disabilities are not yet open either to cure or to prevention. But it is false to assume either that only elderly and long-lived people experience ill health and disability or that a life with chronic health problems or disabilities is not worth living. To assume that prolonging life is a mistake because old age involves pain and misery is both a gross overgeneralization and an unwarranted expression of ableist prejudices.

The debate about human longevity also has racial and class dimensions. Poor people (Mirowsky and Ross 2000, 134–135), native people (Newbold 1998), and black people (U.S. Bureau of the Census 1999) have lower life expectancies than do middle- and owning-class white people. For example, a white boy born in the United States in 1997 could expect to live 74.3 years, whereas the life expectancy of a black boy born the same year was only 67.3. It could be said, with considerable truth, that insofar as prolongevitism has acquired any purchase whatsoever in modern times, it is a prolongevitism for the privileged, who have benefited most from increased life expectancy. In rejecting prolongevitism, apologists are disproportionately disadvantaging those who, in youth and middle age, have not had the benefits enjoyed by those with material privilege and white skin, for absent the conditions necessary for a longer life marginalized people will never have the opportunities that their more fortunate fellow citizens have automatically received. But poverty and oppression are not inevitable, and, to the extent that a shorter life span and liabilities in old age are created by deprivation and injustice, they can be remedied or, better still, prevented.

The unthinking rejection of prolongevitism on the basis of the alleged burden of elderly people also has a gendered dimension, partly because women live longer than men and constitute the majority of elderly people. In other words, the significance of life-span extension is, at present, largely although not exclusively a women's issue. In addition, individual and institutional sexism means that women's lives are accorded a lower value than men's. The existence of gendered expectations about women's biological and cultural roles makes it less likely that women will have had as full a life as men and more likely that the quality of women's lives will be lower than that of men. Women are often valued primarily as caregivers and may not be valued if they give up that role or if they become, themselves, the subjects of care.

I therefore reject the arguments for apologism that are based on classist, racist, sexist, ableist assumptions about the alleged burdens constituted by elderly people, and I reject apologism itself because it disproportionately disadvantages members of groups who have had less access to social goods such as health, education, meaningful work, and comfortable living conditions.

In Chapter 3 I also showed that if we reexamine unthinking notions of what constitutes a burden, we see that aging people do not have a "duty to die." Nonetheless, prolongevitism is in no way committed to forcing people to go on living if they no longer wish to and have good reasons not to. My rejection of apologism does not mean that human life should be preserved at all costs or that it is never good for a human life to come to an end. I am not saying that individual human lives must be extended or that all persons ought, on pain of irrationality, to desire to extend their lives. I am saying that, at least as a normative issue, the prolongation of life should be a matter of individual human choice. As Brennan (2001, 734–735) remarks, it seems unlikely that "one perfect life span . . . would work well for everyone. Some people may well have had a full and complete life by age ninety, others may have tired of it by forty, and still others might be enjoying life at the ripe old age of three hundred. . . . The best of all worlds would be one which involved choice—the freedom to continue one's life or not as one saw fit." Old age, even great old age, by itself, is not an adequate criterion for withholding medical care.[1] At best, the decision not to prolong human lives should be made on a case-by-case basis, with the understanding that such choices cannot be made in a social or moral vacuum and that reasonable decisions to prolong life cannot be made in the absence of the relevant resources to do so. Given the assessment I have offered in previous chapters, it is unjustified, indeed impossible, to make a case for unconditional prolongevitism.

If I am correct, medical treatments that prolong mere organic survival or that extend an end-state of suffering, extreme dementia, or relentless deterioration must be recognized as pointless or even, at worst, as harmful.[2] As Raanan Gillon (1996, 200) expresses it, "It would be morally undesirable to have a moral norm that required people to keep others alive as much as possible, or even a norm that required doctors to provide life-prolonging treatment . . . to all who could be kept alive." Nor is it necessarily wrong to choose assisted suicide or voluntary euthanasia. Indi-

viduals may have compelling reasons to choose to die.[3] People may legitimately want to have the opportunity to make free, uncoerced, informed decisions about when and how they die, including having access,
where appropriate, to euthanasia and physician-assisted suicide.

So, in arguing against apologism, I am not seeking to undermine the
legitimate goals of citizens and ethicists who are concerned about developing and preserving a right to die.[4] As an advocate of prolongevitism,
I am not arguing for the creation of an environment in which human life
is prolonged at all costs and people live out their last months or years in
misery, desperately wishing they could die. Nor do I want to substitute
social pressure to go on living for current pressures to accept the end of
one's life. Prolongevitism advocates the extension of human life lived in
at least a minimum of health, comfort, and well-being. Apologistic cultural tendencies should not be allowed to prevent people from recognizing the value of living longer. My goal has been to demonstrate that
there is a good case for wanting a longer life and that it can be highly
reasonable both for individuals to seek longer lives and for societies to
put resources into the improvement of life expectancy and the extension of individual life spans. The compelling case against apologism implies both that we should question the standard disparagement of efforts
by individuals to stay alive, as well as of efforts by their families to maintain and sustain them, and that it is worthwhile to employ social and
medical means to lengthen the lives of human beings whose capacities
for emotion, perception, thought, and action are to at least some degree
intact.

There are genuine debates about the relevance and the prospective
benefits and harms of particular technologies and medications for extending life as well as about the proportion and extent of financial and
social resources that should be devoted to the prolongation of human existence. There are also genuine debates about the degree of physical, psychological, and cognitive disability that finally makes human life not
worth preserving and about the minimum conditions of quality of life
that make existence worth sustaining. An apologist critic might complain

that throughout my discussion I have avoided specifying what that minimum might be. I have done so for two reasons. First, assessing the minimum may be a highly individual decision: different people may reasonably assess various conditions of life in different ways, depending on what kind of self they are and seek to be and depending also on the social and personal circumstances in which they find themselves. Gillon (1996, 200) states, "Keeping people alive by life-prolonging treatment . . . is only morally desirable if it has an acceptable chance of fulfilling the medico-moral objective of producing net benefit over harm for the patient." But assuming, as I do, that we are talking about competent persons, individuals themselves, not their families and not their health-care providers, are best placed to assess the net benefit over harm within their personal and social context, provided they are given all relevant information for making the decision. So it is inappropriate for me to attempt to specify for individuals the minimum level of health, comfort, and well-being that justifies the prolongation of their lives.

The second reason for not specifying a minimum quality of life is that the issue inevitably leads to a consideration of the conditions under which one is justified in seeking the end of life. As I emphasized in Chapter 1, this book is not about euthanasia, suicide, or physician-assisted suicide; so I have not discussed here the criteria for making these choices. Conditions of illness and disability can vary enormously, and evaluating the range of different health conditions below which further existence is untenable would require a book of its own. Although I think that apologists such as Callahan err on the side of advocating a too-premature death, I do not want to err on the side of advocating a life that is unjustifiably prolonged. To argue for the extension of life beyond what a well-informed, competent individual wants would be contrary to all the values on which my arguments are based. But individuals, whatever their age, are entitled to live within an environment in which regarding life as worth continuing is as much respected as acquiescing in or actively seeking death. Given the apologist tenor of our times, it may behoove us to be cautious about public attitudes toward euthanasia and physician-assisted suicide[5] and to avoid suggesting that they are always reasonable or constitute a norm for ending one's life. As I argued in Chapter 3, the prevailing social climate may well have a significant influence on the extent to which people believe that life is or is not worth continuing. We should think seriously about whether apologist tendencies within the culture are playing an inappropriate role in encouraging people to regard euthanasia and assisted suicide as desirable and even inevitable. Some evidence indicates that the desire to die can change, sometimes greatly, in dying patients, depending on the person's symptoms (including depression and pain) (Foss 1999, A8). In general, we need to create and maintain a social climate in which people can make uncoerced, informed, considered decisions, supported as much as possible by family and friends and by health-care workers, both about whether to allow their lives to end and about prolonging their lives.

AFFIRMATIVE PROLONGEVITISM

Necessarily, a prolongevist must advocate increased longevity within a context both of realism with respect to the biological potential of the species and of pragmatism with respect to the material limits on health care and other resources within a given society. Just as important, the prolongevist must be sensitive to the equity implications of the fact that longevity now varies along class, race, and gender lines.

As I noted in Chapter 4, human beings have a right to life in the negative or liberty sense—that is, a right not to be killed. But, within the context of prolongevitism, any claim to an additional right to life in the positive or welfare sense is more problematic, for it seems to imply the entitlement to all possible assistance to preserve, enhance, and extend life. It therefore raises complex moral and social-policy questions with respect to the employment of social resources and the kinds, amounts, and distribution of human health care. In the rest of this chapter I examine the scope of and limitations on recognizing and acting on such a strong right to life, and I explore its general implications for the formation and enactment of social policy with respect to the distribution of health-care resources and the treatment of elderly persons.

I want to make it clear from the outset that I am not saying (as Hardwig accuses the opponents of a duty to die of doing) that prolonging life as long as it is desired is the "ultimate value around which to orient a health care system" (Hardwig 2000, 169). As I indicated in Chapter 4, I do not claim that longevity has intrinsic value. Other values, such as the promotion and enhancement of health, the prevention of disease, and the palliation of suffering through care and comfort for the sick and dying, are as important or even more important. Nelson (1996, 60) argues that health-care resources should be allocated in ways that not only promote health but also contribute to justice. I agree, and I would add that creating just policies may also contribute to health promotion. I therefore advocate a perspective that I call "affirmative prolongevitism."

Affirmative prolongevitism entails:

· directing resources, research, and services toward boosting life expectancy, ultimately so that it approaches that of the maximum human life span, and compressing morbidity—that is, enabling people to remain healthy right up to the end of life by eliminating or ameliorating negative symptoms of aging and confining illness to the last few years or even months of life (Moody 1995, 11)

· recognizing that because not every person has enjoyed fair and equal opportunities, it is false to assume that all elderly persons—and especially those who are female, who have disabilities, who are poor, who are racially identified—have already experienced all of life's goods and should be ready to die, and therefore placing a special emphasis on improving the life expectancy of members of disadvantaged groups with current low life expectancy

· adopting a life-course approach to the support of elderly people, which recognizes that young people have interests in supporting elderly people rather than regarding them as a "burden" both because elderly people are not some "other" group but one's own parents, grandparents, friends, and co-workers and because one will oneself some day likely be elderly and in need of support

I shall now outline what I take to be the necessary components of each of these proposals. I do not attempt to describe them in detail, for I hope that the case for prolongevitism made in this book establishes at least the initial plausibility of each. Working out and justifying the details would require a book of its own.

Boosting Life Expectancy and Compressing Morbidity

Given the value of human life to individual human beings and the empirical possibilities of increasing average life expectancies, I advocate that health-care and social-welfare resources continue to be directed toward increasing average life expectancy. Average life expectancy continues to grow, and we do not yet have sufficient evidence to know what would constitute a maximum. I therefore see no sufficient reason to put an artificial end to this process, as apologists like Callahan recommend, by arbitrarily setting the late seventies or early eighties as the maximum desirable life expectancy.

Increasing the average life expectancy involves focusing on the entire population rather than on just a few individuals who are near death. It also means focusing on the entire life span, with a special concern for infant and child health within the context of the family, rather than just on the deployment of heroic technological measures directed, near the very end of life, at individuals who would otherwise die. A commitment to increasing average life expectancy does not entail recognizing and promoting a full right to life in the welfare sense, at least not if recognizing such a right necessitates affording all possible assistance to preserving, enhancing, and extending life. It may mean hard decisions about the deployment of health-care resources, the uses of medical technology, and the allocation of human organs for transplantation. Affirmative pro-longevitism provides no easy answers to these problems, and it would be dishonest to promise that it does.

However, clearly, progress toward increasing average life expectancy can be readily supported and enhanced by health-promotion measures, such as improved nutrition and health care throughout the life span, as well as by improved care for those with chronic conditions or disabilities. Indeed, elderly persons may benefit at least as much from research into chronic and debilitating illnesses as from research into life-threatening diseases (Posner 1995, 280). We also need an increased emphasis on preventive measures. Some of these, such as smoking prevention and cessation programs, education about the effects of alcohol and drug use (both legal and illegal), promotion of exercise and activity, information about nutrition and exposure to the sun, defensive-driving courses, use of vaccination protocols, and safer sex education, must be targeted at individuals with the aim of educating them and promoting personal responsibility. Without blaming the victims—whether of material scarcity, of the propaganda of the tobacco companies, or of direct-to-consumer marketing of pharmaceuticals—it makes sense to encourage people to have a sense of autonomy and responsibility with respect to their health and to help them understand that if they want to have a long and healthy life, they must be committed to promoting and preserving their health during youth and middle age. If people want to live longer, they have to be willing to take steps to make it happen and not rely on medical engineering to ensure their longevity. They also have to question and possibly reject key features of dominant Western culture. These include its love affair with meat—and the concomitant deprecation of vegetarianism (Fox 1999)—its reliance on prescription and nonprescription drugs, its emphasis on passive forms of entertainment such as television, and its demands for immediate convenience and comfort above all else—demands that make cars the transportation form of choice rather than more health-enhancing means of travel such as walking, bicycling, and using public transit.

The hope of living a longer life appears to require the sacrifice of immediate gratification from smoking, excessive alcohol consumption, dangerous driving, and inactivity. Not everyone may want to make this sacrifice, if that's what it is, but people need to know that genuine choices have to be made and what their outcomes are likely to be. Young people, in particular, have difficulty taking a long view of their lives and understanding the consequences of activities engaged in during their teens and twenties for their prospects of longevity decades down the road. If they choose smoking or unsafe sexual activities, they also need to be fully educated about the possibly enormous negative impact of such activities on their health.

But the goal of prolongevitism is to increase the length of people's lives not by removing all comfort and convenience or by abolishing all challenges and risks, whose absence would be undesirable, but rather by increasing the conditions for good living. There are multiple ways to create meaning in life. Informed individuals may still reasonably choose to engage, at times, in high-risk activities such as travel to dangerous places, high-injury sporting activities, or demanding ascetic and spiritual practices, all of which have the potential to enhance human life at the risk of diminishing life span.

In addition to encouraging individual responsibility for long life, society must undertake collective measures, including such community policies as boosting employment rates, promoting safety and reducing dangers and stress in the workplace, providing adequate vacation time, ensuring the safety of the water supply, reducing or better still eliminating chemical contamination of the soil and air, protecting food sources and production, investigating psychological and mental disorders, supporting reproductive and sexual health, and promoting social-welfare programs that give everyone a minimum income to provide a safe, healthy, and secure quality of life. A sine qua non of such programs is a system of universal health-care insurance.

I reject the views of those, like Callahan, who are complaisant about the possibility that wealthy individuals could buy the care that the poor could not access and who believe that such a system is not bad. Callahan

(1987, 157) writes that many people "are willing to pay personally for private care. That possibility does favor the wealthy and . . . may do harm to the general health-care system. Yet a rigorous effort to enforce egalitarian solutions is a good prescription for an authoritarian society." Callahan says he does not believe that "a society would be made morally intolerable" (157) by the unfairness of such a system. He does not explain why a prescription for fairness is authoritarian, why a system of resource allocation that harms health care is tolerable, or to whom such a system of selective unfairness might seem tolerable.

In my view, measures such as a publicly funded health-care system enhance health and quality of life for persons at every life stage, and they ensure that increasing numbers of people reach old age and are able to live comfortably and healthily through that stage. A concomitant of efforts to extend life expectancy is the compression of morbidity; people can thus remain as healthy as possible right up to the end of life through the elimination or amelioration of negative symptoms of aging and the limitation of illness, as much as possible, to the last few years or even months of life. Achieving the compression of morbidity means working toward the extension of "active life expectancy," the period of life free of disabilities that would prevent an individual from performing personal maintenance tasks such as eating, bathing, and dressing without the assistance of another person or of special equipment and from engaging in household maintenance tasks (Manton and Land 2000, 253). The aim of the prolongevist, it will be recalled, is to extend as much as possible life lived in a state of health and well-being.

Although I advocate affirmative prolongevitism, in the short term I am not ready to argue that it is either effective or desirable to direct resources toward increasing the maximum human life span. The existing evidence suggests that, in contrast with life expectancy, which can certainly be increased especially in populations that have been disadvantaged, the maximum life span of 120 years is highly resistant to change. Moreover, this resistance strongly suggests that advancing the maximum life span would require major interventions by means of medical technology

and manipulation. Recall from Chapter 1 that possible approaches to extending human longevity include the prevention of and cures for age-
old deadly diseases such as cancer, heart disease, and Alzheimer's, and
for newer diseases, such as AIDS; nutritional regimens, including calorie restriction and the use of antioxidant supplements; the use of hormones; interventions in or modifications of the human genome; therapies for regenerating or replacing damaged body parts; and the cloning
of body parts.

The first of these measures, preventing and curing deadly diseases, remains a viable short- and long-term goal and one that can potentially
benefit human beings at every stage of life without unnecessarily threat-
ening human health. The second, which requires additional research into
the relationship between nutrition, health, and aging, is a potentially valuable and productive focus for funding.

However, the possible risks and benefits attendant on the remaining
four measures are less obvious. There are two serious disadvantages to
such interventions. First, they are likely to be dangerous to the individuals on whom they are practiced. Second, even if successful, the deployment of such interventions is likely to be inequitable, at least in the short
run. On an individual level, their cost would mean they would not be supported under any public health-insurance scheme, and hence they would
be available, if at all, only to those whose wealth enabled them to buy
the services. Some would argue that the question of the distribution of
scarce medical resources and technologies is distinct from the question
of the value of the resources themselves. They warn against confusing
questions of access with questions of value (Pence 2001, B20). But the
value of a technology or service cannot be separated entirely from the
context in which it is offered. It makes little sense to ask whether a particular resource is good in itself. We have to ask, good for whom? Who
will be able to benefit? Who will be excluded? Moreover, on a collective
level, the development and application of measures such as the cloning
of body parts and the reconfiguration of our genetic constitution are likely
to demand the expenditure of huge social resources that are better de-

voted to the health-promotion and disease-prevention measures mentioned above.[6] As I propose below, because resources are finite, the main emphasis in longevity programs ought to be placed on those who have been disadvantaged rather than on expensive and risky technologies available only to those who already enjoy life-expectancy advantages.

Placing Special Emphasis on Members of Disadvantaged Groups

I am advocating a qualified prolongevitism—one that will genuinely be for all. Affirmative prolongevitism requires ensuring that people from all social groupings have the chance to live out their life span, as opposed to merely prolonging the lives of a privileged few. We know that average life expectancy varies enormously among different social groupings. The nature of these variations may differ from one nation to another. But, as a general principle, support for increased longevity should not be limited by gender, socioeconomic class, sexual orientation, race, or ability. So the particular focus, at least in the short run, of measures to increase average life expectancy must be on members of groups that historically have been disadvantaged and that currently have low life expectancy.

As Susan Sherwin notes, members of groups that are oppressed on the basis of gender, race, and sexual orientation are more likely to be poor, and poverty makes a significant difference in a person's health prospects:

> Being poor often means living without access to adequate nutrition, housing, heat, clean water, clothing, and sanitation, and each of these factors may have a negative impact on health. Further, the poor are more likely than others to work in industries that pose serious health risks, and to do without adequate health insurance. And the poor suffer higher rates of mental illness and addiction than do other segments of the population. Financial barriers also often force the poor to let diseases reach an advanced state before they seek professional help. (Sherwin 1992, 222)[7]

Therefore, a specific prolongevist focus on persons who have been disadvantaged would mandate both the promotion of increased research into conditions and diseases that affect women and the deliberate inclusion of women in investigations of medications and treatments that have previously been confined to men (Nelson and Nelson 1996, 359). It would also include the direction of research, enhanced health care, and health promotion to populations of native people, people of color, queer people (including sex workers), and poor people of any race or sexual orientation. These research targets would help to compensate for the history of disparities between the provision of treatments and research that benefit middle-class white men and both the medical treatment of members of oppressed groups and the research into conditions that affect them, and it would ensure that disadvantaged persons begin to receive the medical care they need.

It is essential to detach prolongevitism from any ideas about "earning" longer life. As I argued in Chapter 4, having already lived a longer life than others does not necessarily make one less entitled to the prolongation of one's existence, and neither does the apparent failure to "make something" of one's life. We must be sensitive to the privileges that may have been denied, the opportunities that may have been unwillingly or inadvertently missed in some people's lives. If by virtue of membership in an oppressed group people have been disadvantaged, then they must not be further deprived through society's failure to recognize their special need for a longer life. Nor, in addition, must one "earn" an entitlement to an extended life through care of and service to others, the provision of "wisdom" and support, or the willingness to enact any other social stereotype of the "good" old person. As I argued in Chapter 4, affirmative prolongevitism is not predicated on individual merit.

This policy prescription for special attention to disadvantaged groups raises the interesting question of whether the lower life expectancy of men should be regarded as a problem and hence as a potential focus for affirmative prolongevitism. In Chapter 4 I argued that apologist social policies disproportionately disadvantage women because women have longer life expectancies than men. Callahan proposes social engineering that would deliberately deny women increased years of life that they could otherwise enjoy. Contra Callahan, I suggested that men's life expectancy should not be taken as a norm and thus be considered adequate for women.

Some of women's life-expectancy advantage over men is the result of women's high estrogen levels throughout much of their lives. Estrogen has good effects on cardiovascular health and lowers cholesterol levels. It works as an antioxidant, cleaning up "free radicals," the byproducts of cellular metabolism that contribute to neural and vascular diseases of aging (Perls and Silver 1999, 92). Although women's estrogen levels decline at menopause, women's risk of heart disease does not approach that of men until they are in their eighties or nineties (92–93). In addition, it's possible that women's two X chromosomes help them. An abnormal gene on one X chromosome may be compensated for by a normal gene on the other; thus a woman avoids a disease that a man with a comparably damaged X chromosome cannot avoid (104).

Posner (1995, 274) writes that a possible argument against directing resources to efforts to increase men's longevity is that governments should not attempt to "offset natural differences between the sexes." Posner also says, "To the extent that men are inherently more vulnerable than women, expenditures on fighting the diseases of men may have a lower payoff in years of life saved because 'competition' between diseases to kill men is more intense" (274). If men do indeed suffer an "inherent" disadvantage, it is morally objectionable to disadvantage them further by refusing to compensate for it. But men's relatively low life expectancy is not just "natural," for it is substantially shaped by social practices. Consider my father, Alexander Kenzie Overall, who died in 1997 in his seventy-sixth year. Was he simply fated, by his own inherent constitution and his relative physiological disadvantage as a man, to die earlier than his own mother, who lived until her early nineties? Or is it possible that some of his life experiences—especially going off to war as a teenager, along with the physical and psychological sequelae of that experience (he suffered the lifelong consequences of tropical diseases that he contracted during his war years; became addicted to cigarettes, alcohol, and sugar; became an alcoholic and a diabetic; and developed cancer in his seventies) and the ensuing stresses of supporting a family of five as his capacities waned and his skills became irrelevant—contributed to lowering his life expectancy from what it would otherwise have been?

Perls and Silver (1999) cite many reasons for men's lower life expectancy. These include a greater vulnerability at birth: boys are less developed and more susceptible to infection. Boys are more likely to have cognitive disorders, some of which are associated with risk-related behaviors such as alcoholism, smoking, having unprotected sex, and drug abuse (90). Because of what Perls and Silver coyly call "testosterone toxicity," men are more prone to risk-taking, which is manifested in alcoholism, car and motorcycle accidents, and higher HIV infection rates. Men's greater rates of smoking mean more heart disease and cancer; their greater rates of alcoholism mean they develop cirrhosis at a higher rate than women. "The increasing gap [in life expectancy between men and women from 1900 to 1975] is attributed to increases in male mortality due to ischemic heart disease and lung cancer, both of which increased largely as the result of men's early and widespread adoption of cigarette smoking" (Anderson 1999, 3). Men have higher rates of suicide. They have higher cholesterol levels, higher blood pressure, and more hypertension. Women tend to eat lower-fat diets, use sunscreen more regularly, and seek treatment for health problems sooner than men (Perls and Silver 1999, 96).[8]

The list of causes for men's lower life expectancy appears to include a mix of what might roughly be called physical and social factors, most of which are closely intertwined. Their physical liabilities, such as the greater tendency to heart disease, are exacerbated by cultural conditions that promote and support smoking and alcohol consumption. Moreover, some of men's social vulnerabilities, such as the tendency to take risks, may be influenced by their physiological constitution. A fair prolongevist health-care policy should target the social contexts and reinforcements that increase men's susceptibility to early death.

In rejecting the targeting of research toward efforts to increase men's longevity, Posner (1995, 274) claims that women's greater life expectancy may be "illusory" because as women enter the occupations dominated by men, they will acquire the same "self-destructive" habits and their longevity advantage will decline. He therefore worries that directing research toward diseases (of either sex) that are avoidable by behavioral changes could reduce the incentive to change one's habits. I do not accept Posner's conclusion that avoidable diseases ought not to be studied because it seems to punish inappropriately those who have acquired "lifestyle" illnesses, some of which may be encouraged, overtly or covertly, by social pressures. However, Posner's prediction, if it is well-grounded, shows the general importance of public health efforts to diminish dangerous behavior. Health-promotion campaigns that encourage non-smoking, the modest consumption of alcohol, no use of illegal substances, safe driving, safe-sex practices, good nutrition, and awareness of cancer-prevention methods such as the use of sunscreen will benefit all members of the population, women as well as men, and encourage longer life expectancy.

But I believe that we also need to look more deeply into the causes of men's lower life expectancy. We need to examine the role that gender socialization plays in creating male human beings who regard certain kinds of risky behaviors and health-compromising "life-style" activities as part of being a man. We also need to call into question the still-prevailing values that say that men's lives are expendable for purposes of dangerous labor or waging war. So on the one hand I am critical of health-care policies that favor men's physical needs and men's diseases to the exclusion or neglect of women's physical needs and diseases. But on the other hand I argue that by investigating the influence of gender prescriptions and deliberately altering them, where appropriate, through education and changing parenting practices, a social policy of affirmative prolongevitism can legitimately encompass increases to men's life expectancy.[9]

I wish to stress one final aspect of promoting longevity for disadvantaged groups, and it may seem paradoxical: I advocate a prolongevitism that is not limited by age. As my arguments in Chapters 2, 3, and 4 have showed, chronological age is not a good basis, by itself, on which to assume that people have lived long enough or are not entitled to live longer. The meaning of death is gendered. It is also inflected by race, by socioeconomic status, and by health status. We cannot assume that two people of equally advanced age have both necessarily experienced all of life's goods and should be ready to die. Not everyone has had fair and equal access to life opportunities. There may be big differences between, for example, a poor seventy-five-year-old native woman and a wealthy seventy-five-year-old white woman in the experiences they have had, the education and work to which they have had access, the nutrition and health care they have received, the sexual and reproductive services they have been offered, and the respect and support they have been accorded. Given these facts, we must be skeptical about proposals such as those of Hardwig and Battin to withhold resources from elderly people. In every society resources are not unlimited, although obviously the limitations are much less severe in the so-called developed nations. But, in considering where best to place limited resources, it is an error to regard all elderly people as constituting a homogeneous group. It is equally an error, of the most presumptuous and high-handed sort, to assume that changed or reduced abilities necessarily constitute a good reason for refusing to prolong life.

Adopting a Life-Course Approach

Jeffrey Simpson (2000, A17) writes, "A wildly disproportionate amount of [Canada's] health-care budget is spent caring for people in their last year of life and dealing with the inevitable health problems associated with old age. For those worried about the costs of health care, here are the knotty issues such as cutting off treatment for the incurable." The crucial question, however, is whether these health-care costs should be described as "wildly disproportionate." They would be genuinely disproportionate only if we made an a priori assumption that every decade, or even every year, of human life should receive approximately the same share of health-care resources. But such an assumption takes for granted precisely the point that is at issue, namely, whether people at different ages legitimately need and should be able to access different kinds and amounts of health-care resources.

Elderly people are the heaviest users of outpatient and inpatient services (Hanson 1995, 3). In the United States, the average annual expenditures for health care per person from 1985 to 1997 ranged from $425 for those under twenty-five to $2,900 for those aged sixty-five to seventy-four. But the statistics do not suggest that those who are elderly receive all the benefits to the utter neglect of the young. The average annual health-care costs of those who were aged twenty-five to thirty-four were more than twice those of the under-twenty-fives, at $1,236. And the average annual health-care costs of persons seventy-five years of age or older were, at $2,799, lower than the costs of the next younger group (U.S. Bureau of the Census 1999). Nonetheless, even if the goal of compressing morbidity into the last years or months of life is achieved, so that the most concentrated use of medical care is required only at the very end of life, we should still expect that, over the course of their aging, elderly people will have different health-care needs than younger ones and hence that it is appropriate, in both practical and moral terms, to allocate resources differentially to that stage of life.

The implicit error of politicians, journalists, ethicists, and policy analysts who engage in hand wringing about the costs of caring for elderly people is their assumption that health-care needs should be the same, or at least cost the same, at all stages of life. Interpreting elderly people as a "burden" relies, I suggest, on this key assumption. The costs of sustaining elderly people's lives and health can be understood as burdensome only if it is assumed that such people are demanding more than their fair share and if "fair" is implicitly construed as meaning "approximately equal." But there are real differences between being forty years old and being eighty years old, just as there are real differences between being forty years old and being four years old. If we would not expect the four-year-old's health-care needs to be the same and cost the same as those of the forty-year-old, so also we should not expect the eighty-year-old's health-care needs to be the same and cost the same as those of the forty-year-old.

It is simply ageism to suppose that the eighty-year-old must be like the forty-year-old in order for his needs to be considered legitimate or that the typical (if there is one) forty-year-old—or thirty-year-old or twenty-year-old—provides the standard by which health-care expectations, needs, and demands should be evaluated. We should not play into stereotypes that depict the old as adversaries or competitors of the young; nor should we condone a situation in which old people must fear the bitterness of younger people who are "forced" to support them. We cannot continue to sustain or even tolerate what Jean-Nesmy calls our culture's "lopsided glorification of youth." Human life is valuable to its possessors because it affords the ongoing opportunity for activities and experiences, and, in the absence of debilitating pain or total loss of consciousness, that opportunity exists at every age. Hence, as Jean-Nesmy (1991, 148–149) points out, there is a contradiction between extending human lives, "which means *ex hypothesi* additional years during the last third of life, and the belief that only the first third is worth living." Of course the last third is worth living, and those in the first third and second third must recognize that fact.

Many commentators have registered their anxiety that, because of demographic unevenness, a smaller proportion of people will be in the workforce by 2010 than are working now. Callahan (1999, 191), for example, is worried about "an excessive tax burden on the young to pay for the health care of the elderly." And Simpson (2000, A17) writes, "If we think the costs of health care are large today, just wait for 10 or 15 years, unless there are miracle cures around the corner for such diseases as cancer. The ratio of those working to those over 65 could fall as low as 2 to 1, compared with more than 3 to 1 today."

But the prospect is highly exaggerated. First, the technologies (including "better treatment of hip fractures, degenerative joints, osteoporosis, circulatory diseases, cataracts and other visual disorders, and diabetes") that enable people to live longer lives also permit them to remain in a healthy condition, with reduced incidence of disability, for a longer period (Posner 1995, 46). It is ironic, as Susan McDaniel points out, that growing successes in promoting healthy aging and extending people's lives are taken to challenge the health-care system and are used by so-called reformers to justify the reduction of funds for health care. In this fashion, the very successes of modern health care are claimed to undermine the viability of modern health care. Yet without good health care in a fair and supportive society, people are likely to be sicker, more vulnerable, more dependent, and in need of even more health care (McDaniel 2000, 144).

Second, the dependency ratio—that is, the ratio of nonworkers to workers—has fallen steeply since the mid-1960s in the United States, mostly because women have entered the labor force in greater numbers than before. The dependency ratio is predicted to rise after 2005 but not return to the level of the mid-sixties (Posner 1995, 40). In Canada, current projections indicate that even when the members of the baby boom are old, the dependency ratio will not be as high as it was when the members of the baby boom were children—that is, Canada has already experienced a high dependency ratio, handled it successfully, and is not likely to return to it (Gee 2000, 11).[10] In addition, the baby-boom generation will not all hit old age simultaneously. There is at least a fifteen-year difference between the youngest and the oldest boomers, so although the generation is large, its size does not pose the unmanageable challenge predicted by apocalyptic demographers. Moreover, although the children of the boomers, the so-called echo boomers, do not constitute as large a cohort as their parents do, nonetheless they are a substantial group and they will still be in the labor force when the boomers are elderly.

Third, we should not assume that old people, most of whom have already worked and paid taxes all their adult lives,[11] do not want to and will not continue to work and pay taxes. When postretirement employment is included, and comparisons are made with the recent past, the labor-force participation of old people is growing rather than declining (Posner 1995, 41). Even though the average age of retirement is falling, 25 percent of workers take up part-time or full-time jobs after their retirement (Posner 1995, 44). Posner suggests also that the average age of retirement may not continue to fall and may even rise, partly because of the future demographic decline in the number of young workers and the resulting costs to employers of replacing older with younger workers and partly because, with the prospect of living a longer life, workers will choose to retire later in order to maximize their retirement income (Posner 1995, 48–49). In addition, as workers stay healthy for longer, their productivity will decline more slowly, and mid-life career changes will become more frequent (Posner 1995, 56).

Perls and Silver (1999, 215) cite examples of corporations in which employees over seventy make significant contributions. According to the U.S. Bureau of the Census (1999), in 1998 2,200,000 men and 1,600,000 women over the age of sixty-five were in the labor force. That number may increase. The Bureau predicts that in 2006, the numbers will be 2,600,000 men and 1,700,000 women. In Canada, 10.6 percent of men sixty-five and over and 3.4 percent of women sixty-five and over are in the labor force. In Japan, which has the world's highest life expectancy, the figures are much higher: 35.9 percent of elderly men and 15.2 percent of elderly women participate in the workforce (Statistics Canada 1998). Perls and Silver (1999, 215–216) describe policies in place in Japan that encourage the hiring and retention of older workers and the retraining and reemployment of workers nearing retirement age.

In addition there is a huge national value, less easily calculated, of unpaid labor contributed by older people (Posner 1995, 45; Gee 2000, 11–12), both formally to organizations that employ them as volunteers and informally, especially in the case of old women, through domestic work such as childcare, care of those who are sick or disabled, and care of other aging relatives in the homes of their families.[12] For example, in the 1996 Canadian census, 18.7 percent of men and 22.8 percent of women sixty-five and over reported engaging in fifteen to twenty-nine hours of housework per week (Statistics Canada 1996). Moreover, in 1998, 23 percent of Canadians over sixty-five participated in formal volunteer activities (Statistics Canada 1999). By assuming that old people are not working and not willing or able to work, apologists make a direct inference that such people are a burden. On the contrary, the U.S. Bureau of the Census (1999) estimates that the "mortality cost" (financial loss) to the nation of each death of a person sixty-five or older in 1996 was $38,153, calculated on the basis of individuals' age, sex, life expectancy at time of death, labor-force participation, annual earnings, and homemaking services. The total mortality cost of the deaths of these persons was $29,836,000. We can anticipate that as medical research enables people to live longer in a healthy state, the economic value of the lives of elderly people, as producers and consumers, will increase.

Still, many elderly people do not engage in paid or unpaid labor because they choose not to do so or are unable to do so. Although, on the one hand, we should appreciate the real work that elderly people contribute, on the other hand, we ought not to expect that all elderly people can, will, or must work, and it is illegitimate and unfair to draw conclusions about the moral entitlements of those who do not. As I argued in Chapter 4, their not working does not make them undeserving of longer life. Most elderly people have already contributed two-thirds of a lifetime or more of labor to the well-being of their families and their employers. A life-course approach to aging acknowledges that people are not all alike and are different at different stages of their lives. Social policy and medical services must take into account the varying health-care and other needs that people in old age have regardless of whether they are currently working.

So I argue both that the costs of supporting elderly people are not likely to be as great as the hand wringers suppose and that younger people— by which I mean those under the age of sixty-five—should be prepared to support old people, those over sixty-five, simply because it is in the nature of human life, at least as we have lived it so far, that different stages involve different contributions and different needs. Contributing toward the collective support of elderly people reduces the demands on individuals to carry the sole responsibility for their elderly relatives. Aging is a human fate that most of us will share; hence, it is fair to expect younger people to contribute to the support of those in a group that they will one day join, just as they were supported when they were very young. When resources are not needed for the relatively healthy stages of life, they can and should be devoted to the support of the more vulnerable stages, both at the beginning and at the end of life. In taking account of human needs, societies must recognize the full spectrum of the human condition from prenatal development to death and understand that every individual will go through these stages in one way or another. Hence, there can be no genuine conflict between young and old, healthy and ill, because the young become the old and the healthy do get sick.

So far my view is not much different from that of Battin, who, drawing on the work of Norman Daniels, suggests that "the elderly should be viewed as the same persons at a later stage of their lives. . . . [Distributive problems] are more correctly understood as problems of allocating resources throughout the duration of lives" (1987, 322). In her life-course approach, however, Battin argues that a Rawlsian "veil-of-ignorance" approach would induce people to direct health-care funding to stages early in life, but, as we saw in Chapter 3, "not to underwrite treatment which would prolong life beyond its normal span. By freeing resources which might otherwise have been devoted to prolonging the lives of the elderly for use instead in the treatment of diseases which cause death or opportunity-restricting disability earlier in life, such a policy would maximize one's chances of getting a reasonable amount of life within the normal species-typical, age-relative opportunity range" (322).[13]

There are several problems with Battin's interpretation of the life-course approach to health-care funding. First, as I argued in Chapter 3 in criticizing the claim that there is a duty to die, the deliberate and substantial reallotment of social support from old people to young people generates serious problems. Most relevant to the current discussion is the fact that the first cohort of midlife and elderly people would literally sacrifice a portion of their lives for the sake of this reallotment, without profiting personally from it. The members of this cohort would be too old to have benefited from the redistribution of savings to younger people and so would not have received improved care in their youth and middle age. Then, they would be expected to give up their lives prematurely for the sake of those who would receive both better health care earlier in life and improved life expectancy as a result.

A second problem in Battin's interpretation of the life-course approach is that self-interest ordinarily has a wider purview than merely one's own survival. As social beings, we have interests in the survival of our parents, grandparents, siblings, friends, and co-workers. Hence, even from a Rawlsian veil-of-ignorance perspective, it would be unreasonable to assume that there are no elderly people or potential elderly people who might play key roles in our life. Even in a culture that countenances a duty to die, social engineering is unlikely to induce us to look on the deaths of elderly loved ones and colleagues with equanimity. So when choosing the allocation of health-care funds, we have a strong motivation not to deprive elderly people, our relatives, friends, and co-workers, of crucial treatments and services.

My third criticism of Battin's life-course approach is more general. Although I agree that resources should be devoted to the treatment of serious diseases in early life and that, over the long run, persons at all life stages will thereby benefit, the arguments in this book have demonstrated that seeking to prolong one's life is justified and that policies devoted to the extension of life expectancy are warranted. If the prolongevist perspective defended here is correct, then persons behind the Rawlsian veil of ignorance would have objective reasons for wanting to live longer. Hence, they would not rationally choose to reject resources for and methods of prolonging human life, at least provided that that life could be lived in an acceptable minimum state of health.

Battin's sights are lower. She refers only to a goal of promoting "a reasonable amount of life within the *normal* species-typical, age-relative opportunity range" (1987, 322, my emphasis). Similarly, Daniels says that in the context of distributive justice the function of health care is "the maintenance or restoration of species-typical *normal* functioning." He believes that the normal opportunity range for an individual is relative to his or her stage of life and that the health-care budget must be allocated across all stages of life (1996, 211, my emphasis). His idea is that people would opt for a distribution that favors good health care at the beginning of life to set the stage for a longer life and then a lower allocation of resources for later stages. But the arguments in this book call into question the unexamined concepts of normality that underlie most discussions of human longevity. It is not evident that we must settle for the maintenance or restoration of what is currently considered "normal" functioning in old age. At the very least, the concept of typical species functioning in elderly people should be up for discussion. Given the enormous extensions, in the previous two centuries, in average life expectancy, the improved health of the North American population, the growing achievements of elderly people in education[14] and their increasing participation in physical activities,[15] and the improvements in health-care treatments and support for persons with disabilities, it is at least premature to suppose that what is "normal" now for some statistically average old person should constitute the norm for determining the allocation of health-care resources.

Suppose, for example, as Jecker suggests, that a means could be found that is both inexpensive and virtually unlimited to sustain memory functioning in extreme old age.

> On Daniels' analysis, such treatment is not important, because
> normal species functioning in extreme old age does not include
> clear and vivid recall. Moreover, memory loss does not diminish
> the age-relative normal opportunities of someone who is, say, ninety
> years old, since the opportunities a sound memory affords are not
> normally available to the very old. Consequently, government would
> not be under a strict obligation to make such treatment available

to the elderly, for example, by reimbursing it under Medicaid and Medicare programs. This is so, even if the treatment in question were extremely cheap and abundant. (Jecker 1989, 667–668)

As Jecker (1989, 668) points out, such an approach seems unjustified "because normal functioning can be sorely inadequate," and hence altering what is currently considered to be normal species functioning could be a requirement of justice. Societies already accept this principle when they devote research time and money to developing improved hearing aids and eyeglasses, as well as surgical alterations of the eyes and ears, all of which mitigate the "normal" age-related decline in hearing and sight (672). Because existing social practices reflect skepticism about the normative force of species-typical functioning and have the power to alter it, we ought not to settle for unexamined definitions of the acceptable and "normal" capacities in elderly people.

Thus, the life-course approach suggests not that there must be a distributive competition among the different age groups—a competition that young people would win and old people would lose—but rather that adequate funds should be allocated for the last stages of life. When younger people become old, they too, in their turn, will be supported. This perspective acknowledges that it is in one's interest to support elderly people and not regard them as a "burden" because one will likely some day be elderly and in need of support oneself. So, even from a self-absorbed perspective, it is irrational to regard old people as nothing but "burdens" who have a "duty to die." Younger people should not see elderly people as some "other" group whose interests are contrary to their own but as a concrete presentation of their own future. From the perspective of younger people, elderly people are also their own parents, aunts and uncles, grandparents, friends, and co-workers. The question then is, What kind of relationships with old people do young people want? And what sort of future do they want for themselves?

Undeniably, the availability of social resources, including health care, social security, and family support, can be a constraint on achieving the goal of enabling people to live longer. Thus, Gillon (1996, 200) argues that even when life-prolonging technologies (LPTs) "can be expected to produce net benefit for the patient, and the patient or proper proxy desire[s] the LPT, justice in the allocation of scarce resources may require rationing of the available LPTs and some patients may thus morally justifiably (though regrettably) be denied LPTs." But the scarcity or availability of resources is not a fixed, divinely ordained feature of human societies. Collectively we do have choices about where to put our money, our educational efforts, and our research. Collectively we can also choose whether to foster life-enhancing attitudes such as the willingness to donate blood or the commitment to make one's body parts available after death for donation and transplantation. This book is, in part, a plea for a reconsideration of how social resources are allocated and is an attempt to call into question the knee-jerk impugnment of elderly and disabled people who refuse to accept death with meek acquiescence.

A strong public policy of affirmative prolongevitism requires a social-democratic approach to human well-being, not an approach based only on what can be provided by market forces, for which cost containment and the maximization of profit are the ruling values. A social-democratic perspective rejects the assumption that good health care and abundant social resources are only for the wealthy. Gillon (1996, 205) claims that "respect for the autonomy of those who provide the resources for health care"—that is, taxpayers—could override the provision of life-prolonging technologies for those who need them. He believes that if taxpayers collectively do not want their money to support longer life for aging persons, then it ought not to be used in that way. But many elderly people, including those who now need or may eventually need life-prolonging technologies, are also taxpayers, and, as such, they may well want some resources to be directed toward measures to prolong their lives. Taxpayers do not speak with one voice.

But even if they did, it would be both dangerous and immoral in the extreme to allow the fiat of taxpayers to determine directly who lives and who dies, for such a fiat would provide no protection for members of disadvantaged groups. They are the ones without the means to purchase alternative care and services. What role would ignorance, lack of foresight, or failure to identify with elderly people, especially those from minority populations, play in such decisions? How might some taxpayer attitudes play out in deciding the fate of vulnerable populations—native people, ex-inmates, single mothers, and those who are poor? A social-democratic perspective does not support the health of the wealthy at the expense of that of the poor. Instead, it commits us to support all members of society, whether or not they have the wherewithal to pay for medical care and social support at the ends of their lives.

In addition, a social-democratic perspective is skeptical of unthinking consumption and the elevation of spending and acquiring as ultimate social values, skeptical of the idea that having money means one should be able to purchase whatever one wants and that buying things is the main source of happiness.[16] The alternative for which I've argued here is a life—whatever kind of self, career or seriatim, one is or chooses to be—that is built primarily on experiences and relationships and not so much on the acquisition of material things. The justification for this alternative is that such a life is likely to be healthier and more fulfilling, both individually and collectively, than a life that requires the consumption of indefinitely large amounts of resources. Granted, a life that is founded on experiences rather than on the acquisition of things can also be costly and can deplete natural and social assets in ways that are morally unjustified. To take one example, a skier who insists on being transported in comfort into backcountry, difficult-to-access ski areas and on being provided there with every luxury while he indulges in his sport might contribute to the degradation of the environment and the exhaustion of resources almost as much as someone who owns a couple of cars and replaces them every year or two. Obviously the mere substitution of experiences for things is not an inevitable source of greater health and satisfaction; it does not automatically reduce resource depletion and environmental contamination. But it can, depending on the experiences sought. Backpacking into a wilderness area is preferable to going in by helicopter, plane, or car; taking the kids to the playground is preferable to buying them yet another set of expensive toys; living in solar-powered, well-insulated houses of modest size is preferable to choosing "monster homes" that require huge amounts of nonrenewable energy to heat and light.

Choices can be made, and some choices may involve the accumulation of things—a beautiful sweater, a useful kitchen tool, a hockey stick, a clarinet. I do not propose that there is just one way of having a meaningful life, although I do think that some are better than others, and I believe that some life activities can be shown to have more value and meaning than others. But, in general, if we choose to manufacture and to buy things based on their capacity to provide positive and interesting experiences at low cost, we are less likely to be pursuing a life-style that is incompatible with a social policy of affirmative prolongevitism. Such a policy requires genuine concern for truly long-range planning and the stewardship of resources so that there is a sustainable environment for future people (as well as nonhuman animals). As my suggestions indicate, the genuine application of prolongevitism requires a rethinking of the kind of society that the Western world created and tolerated over the previous century. A prolongevist social policy requires, I believe, a deep commitment to social change, change that would probably have to be fundamental. If the vast majority of people can count on living a long life, and if thereby they experience their grandchildren and other people's grandchildren growing to maturity and having children of their own, they will come to have an increased awareness of the connections among different age cohorts and of the implications of actions in the present for the well-being of members of future generations.

LAST WORDS

Because of my genetic connection to long-lived grandparents (three of whom lived into their nineties), my citizenship in a Western nation that provides good health care and a safe environment, and the life choices that I have the opportunity to make now, I am fortunate to be able to anticipate a future where I shall probably not die prematurely. I am grateful. I believe that everyone should have the prospect of extended life if they want it.

My investigation of the reasons for and against prolonging human life arose out of my lifelong preoccupation with the inevitability of death and a sense of its injustice for all human beings who continue to want to live. My examination of apologism and prolongevitism has not much mitigated my sense of the injustice of death, and my assessment of the arguments has convinced me that there are good reasons to want to prolong one's life. At the same time, for the reasons that I explored in Chapters 5 and 6, I am no longer as sure as I once was that immortality is a desirable state. I think a time will come in my own existence when I feel that I have lived long enough.

For years I have been haunted by a famous poem by Dylan Thomas, which is addressed to the poet's chronically ill father (Cyr 1998, 208). Resisting his father's growing acceptance of death, Thomas (1952, 116) presents what may be interpreted as a forthright rejection of apologism and a declaration of the significance of life, even into old age, right up until death:

> Do not go gentle into that good night,
> Old age should burn and rave at close of day;
> Rage, rage against the dying of the light

In this book I have not argued, and would not want to argue, that rage is always a desirable reaction to "the dying of the light." But I hope I have shown instead that resistance to "the dying of the light" is not difficult to understand. Other things being equal, a long life is a better life, and a social policy that promotes the extension of human life is amply justified.

I last saw my grandmother, Hazel Irene Bayes, in a Toronto hospital two days before her death in January 1994.[17] In the previous seven years she had had several illnesses, but with her characteristic resolve and joie de vivre she had always resisted them. Even after a serious stroke at the age of eighty-six she had regained the full use of her left arm and had taught herself how to walk again.

Now her body was failing her for the last time. Yet she did not want to talk about her ill health. Instead she talked about her grandchildren. She told me she was proud of me. She knew that her long, eventful, and happy life was very close to its end. She said, "Sometimes I ask myself why I struggle to stay alive, and don't just give up."

I tried to respond cheerfully. "And what answer do you get?"

Her face had an enigmatic look. "I don't know. You tell me; you're the philosopher."

I tried to reply. I thought of her zest for life and how contented she had been in the "seniors'" home where she lived after recovering from her stroke. I said, "I think you go on living because you enjoy life so much, and you're glad to be at a stage when you don't have to work, and people can take care of you." But my grandmother did not comment on my response. Near the end of her ninety-third year, I think Hazel Bayes accepted the closing of her life's story.

Almost a decade after her death, this book is my attempt to answer her last question to me.

NOTES

CHAPTER ONE

1. I am grateful to my daughter, Narnia Worth, for drawing this quotation to my attention.

2. Thank you to Samantha Brennan for informing me of Mothersill's article.

3. Thank you to Steve Leighton for drawing this section of Nussbaum's *The Therapy of Desire* to my attention.

4. See Amélie Oksenberg Rorty's interesting discussion of possible reasons for fearing death (1994, 104–105).

5. I am setting aside the question of whether any specific individuals ever deserve to die by reason, for example, of having committed egregious moral wrongdoings such as murder.

6. Thank you to Bunny Singer for recommending the Dychtwald and Flower book.

7. Retardation of natural aging might be achieved by influencing the process whereby telomeres shorten. Telomeres are like caps on the ends of chromosomes. They get shorter each time a cell divides. Gradually, as a cell ages, the telomere wears down to a nub and the cell stops dividing and dies (Abraham 2000, A6). The maximum number of times a cell can divide before reaching "cell senescence" and dying is called the "Hayflick limit," which is regulated by DNA in the cell's nucleus. The higher the Hayflick limit, the longer the average life span of the species to which the cell belongs (Perls and Silver 1999, 120–121).

8. In April 2000 it was reported that six calves created through a cloning process possessed cells biologically younger than their biological age because their telomeres were longer than normal. A cellular biologist working on the cloning project predicted that these findings could result in the production of cloned human organs and tissue (Abraham 2000, A1).

9. I do not have the space here to explore the evidence against the possibility of life after death, but I regard it as substantial.

10. I am grateful to the audience at the annual meeting of the Royal Society Kingston Seminar, April 10, 1999, for insisting on the importance of this distinction.

11. For example, according to Statistics Canada, the mean age at first marriage in Canada has been rising steadily since 1986 for both sexes. On average, first-time brides were 27.3 years old in 1996, compared with 24.8 a decade earlier. First-time grooms were 29.3 years old on average in 1996, up from 27.0 in 1986 (Statistics Canada 1999).

12. Of course, increased life expectancy does not directly obviate another problem generated by the postponement of procreation: women's fertility rate declines with age. There are genuine questions about whether deliberate medical efforts should be made to extend women's reproductive years. Several methods are possible, including the use of hormones and in vitro fertilization with prefrozen eggs to create so-called postmenopausal pregnancies (Parks 1999) and the use of transplantation of ovarian tissue (the woman's own or that of another woman), a process that not only renews the reproductive capacity but also postpones or possibly even cancels menopause. A woman might well want to prolong her young adulthood as a way of mitigating the double or triple demands of simultaneously doing paid work outside the home, gestating and raising children, and taking care of domestic work. It is difficult for a woman to acquire education and training (a necessarily lifelong process), find a mate, establish a home, develop a career, and have children if she wants them, all before the age of forty. I do not have the space here to explore this issue, but many factors generate concern about the prospect of extending women's reproductive years. These include the potential deleterious effects on women's health, the possible reinforcement of the idea that old age in women is bad, and the exacerbation of the stereotype that the purpose of women is sexual and reproductive and that consequently menopause is a horror.

13. Although individuals may accurately be described as being elderly, I think

it unfair to refer to old people in the nominative as "the elderly," an objectifying and collectivizing term that is widely used in texts discussing the alleged "burden" of aging persons (see, for example, Callahan, ter Meulen, and Topinková 1995). *The elderly* shares with comparable terms such as *the poor* and *the disabled* a distancing, dehumanizing connotation that treats its objects as if their identity is subsumed by their being elderly, poor, or disabled, and represses the fact that they are persons with full and complete human lives.

14. I have been told of elderly people who prefer being called "senior" to being called "old." But the silliness of the euphemism *senior citizen* is revealed by the fact that we would not contemplate calling people younger than sixty-five "junior citizens," a term that suggests, at best, childhood, and at worst a kind of civic immaturity that cannot reasonably be attributed to anyone who is an adult.

15. Young people, even those in their twenties, are encouraged to become anxious about whether they will be able to support themselves after retirement. Such anxiety clearly benefits financial institutions, which profit from people's desire to buy financial services that will protect them from the alleged vicissitudes and potential poverty of old age after sixty-five. The overt message is that the state is unlikely, unable, or unwilling to provide adequate financial support to individuals once they are no longer engaged in paid work. I return to this issue in Chapter 7.

CHAPTER TWO

1. See Kamm 1993 for an exhaustive discussion of the strengths and weaknesses of Lucretius's argument.

2. The only exception to this preference that I can see would be if I could know that X was an empty, dull, unfulfilled life, and also know that Y, though shorter, would be rich with the fulfillment of potential.

3. See Brueckner and Fischer 1998 for a discussion of the implications of this possibility.

4. See Feldman 1992, pp. 143–156, for a discussion of and solution to some puzzles associated with the claim that death is bad because it deprives the individual of what he would otherwise have experienced.

5. Callahan adds that one of the characteristics of "sustainable medicine" is that it will provide "a level of medical and public health care sufficient to give . . .

a good chance of making it through the [present] life cycle" (1998, 35, italics removed from original).

6. This approach may be not just a scholarly convention but also a cultural trend. Gerald Nachman (1999, A7) remarks:

> Death is suddenly fashionable, like some kind of ultimate weight-loss program. . . . An affirmative attitude toward dying is self-esteem's final triumph. . . . They [recent books and movies] all portray dying as an experience not to be missed, where a good time is had by all. . . . Dying, insist death's new public relations people, is just "a part of life," a transition, like graduation day, and shouldn't be feared but graciously welcomed. . . . The premise seems to be that, since death gets us all sooner or later, let's make death our little friend, so as to demystify it.

7. Dixon's article provides a superb critique of many of Callahan's assumptions about the nature of old age and the obligations and social role of elderly people.

8. See the discussion in Chapter 3.

9. It is startling that Callahan does not regard such stereotyping as morally questionable. He writes:

> Old age combines a biological stage in life and a social status in society, and it is not inappropriate that they be understood as intertwined. . . . For policy purposes, the group characteristics of the elderly are as important as their individual variations. Those characteristics legitimate age-based entitlement and welfare programs as well as social policies designed to help the elderly maintain social respect. They could also be used to sanction a limit to those entitlements in the face of resource scarcity. (Callahan 1995, 24)

10. Perls and Silver (1999, 148) also acknowledge that physicians may be less likely to refer elderly patients to medical-school-affiliated teaching hospitals and tertiary-care centers, where treatment costs are high, and they may be less willing to offer expensive treatments such as coronary-artery bypass surgery and organ transplantation. Whether such decisions are justified is open to debate.

11. For an egregious example, see ter Meulen, Topinková, and Callahan 1995, 149–150. They insist that even if a majority of elderly people are healthy, many are not; even if more are able to continue working past retirement, economic ob-

stacles make it difficult; and even if many are able to stay in their homes, few family members are available to assist them.

12. Jackie Davies suggested this perspective to me.

13. I am grateful to Cindy Price, who prompted me to think this idea through.

14. I am grateful to Jennifer Parks for drawing Bell's article to my attention.

15. Another possible way in which long-living elders might deprive their youthful relatives has been suggested. If the elderly routinely live until 120, then young people will be deprived of any experience of death in the family until much later in life and hence will miss out on opportunities for maturation and growth (Cindy Price, private communication, May 3, 2000). But this is not a real problem. First, if people routinely lived until 120, they would at least experience the deaths of their great-grandparents, or even their great-great-grandparents, during their youth. Second, increasing longevity would probably not eliminate accidental deaths (car accidents, etc.), with which people would still have to deal. Finally, I wonder whether experiencing a family death early in one's life is necessary for growth and maturation or whether, on the contrary, it is a source of suffering and limitation from which one must recover, especially if the deceased is a close relative such as a parent.

16. However, Nielsen (1994, 255) acknowledges that "the inevitability, and at least seemingly evident finality, of death" is much harder for him to accept when he thinks of "the suffering, ignorant and degraded millions, living in hellish conditions, . . . who have unremittingly, through no fault of their own, lived blighted lives."

17. In a note Callahan adds, without criticism, "In their study of the 'global burden of disease', the public health physicians Christopher [J. L.] Murray and Alan [D.] Lopez noted that 'a range of studies confirms [a] broad social preference to "weight" the value of a year lived by a young adult more heavily than one lived by a very young child or an older adult'" (Callahan 1998, 314, n. 9).

18. Kathleen Marie Dixon (1994, 616) suggests that there is a noteworthy similarity between this expectation of sacrifice on the part of elderly people and the traditional normative expectation of sacrifice on the part of women of any age. The idea of ignoring one's personal needs and goals in the interests of younger people "is remarkable for its resemblance to ideologies used to segregate the sexes and limit the social, political, and economic power of women." She also suggests that apologists such as Callahan promote a separate-spheres approach for elderly

people, which is comparable to the ideas of sexual segregation and complementarity traditionally associated with gender stereotypes (629–630).

19. For example, with regard to supporting "burdensome" old people, Henry Fairlie writes, "Something is wrong with a society that is willing to drain itself to foster such an unproductive section of its population, one that does not even promise (as children do) one day to be productive" (quoted in Sprott 1991, 129). In Chapter 7 I discuss in more detail the real social contributions made by elderly people through paid and unpaid labor.

20. Copper (1988, 95) also argues that professional self-interests lie behind the current cultural association of long life with misery. She suggests that it is in the interests of "the social workers, therapists and gerontologists who earn their livings working for agencies that study or serve the old" to convince the politicians, foundations, and individuals who fund them that their elderly clients are "terribly needy—unable to take care of themselves, isolated, pitiful, helpless."

CHAPTER THREE

1. For a science-fiction depiction of a world in which individuals have a socially engineered duty to die at an early age, see *Logan's Run* (1967), by William Nolan and George Clayton Johnson. Thanks to Cindy Price and Sue Donaldson for drawing this book to my attention.

2. Susan Wolf (1996), Diane Raymond (1999), and Jennifer Parks (2000) have argued (though from different perspectives) that gender biases significantly affect how women and men are differentially treated when they request euthanasia and assisted suicide.

3. Younger people can be intolerant of the frailty of elderly people, expressing impatience with an old woman's difficulty in hearing or an old man's failing eyesight. So some of the most ordinary sequelae of aging may be interpreted as burdensome by the temporarily quick and able-bodied. Moreover, if impatience leads to avoidance, then elderly people's difficulties can be exacerbated: isolation, for example, can lead to depression and lowered attentiveness in people whose abilities are already changing and declining. Thus the aging person comes to appear even more burdensome—as a result, to at least some extent, of behavior on the part of the caregivers themselves. Thanks to Lisa McNee for pointing this consequence out.

4. Interestingly, although Callahan is, as we have seen, a determined apologist, he categorically rejects the existence of a duty to die.

5. In 1998 the Canadian Council on Social Development estimated the costs of raising a boy from birth to age eighteen at $159,927, and the costs of raising a girl from birth to age eighteen at $158,826 (both figures in Canadian dollars). These figures do not include the opportunity costs for the parents. The slight difference in costs is explained by the higher estimated food costs for boys (although clothes are claimed to cost more for girls).

6. However, at a conference where I discussed this material, one member of the audience, who talked of caring for her elderly mother, expressed fear about the implications of denying that old people can be burdens. She was worried that any apparent downplaying of the demands of caring for dependent old people could be used as an excuse by governments to withdraw what little support they now provide for elderly persons.

7. I am grateful to Carlos Prado and David Bakhurst for clarifying this idea.

8. Thanks to Ted Worth for this analogy.

9. Some of Hardwig's examples of cases where there might be a duty to die are gendered—but gendered in a peculiar way. He is, for example, quick to point out cases in which elderly women constitute the burden a family must face (e.g., Hardwig 2000, 3). And he is fond of giving examples of women with Alzheimer's disease who are cared for by their husbands (e.g., 45–48), even though in statistical terms the caregiver for an aging person with dementia is likely to be female. He also, inexplicably, expresses great empathy for a man who tries to have sex with his wife who has Alzheimer's and who resists him with fear and bewilderment (87). Hardwig does not ask why any man would be entitled to sex with a woman who is severely mentally disabled and who rejects him—even if that woman is his wife.

10. Jennifer Parks suggests that Hardwig's thesis, with its emphasis on human relationships, gives the appearance of being the expression of a feminist ethic of care (personal communication). I agree that his arguments are, at times, couched in those terms, although I also think that a genuinely caring feminist approach to end-of-life issues would preclude the existence of any general duty to die.

11. Compare the ways in which women in the labor force are criticized for their alleged failure to care for their children.

12. Wolf argues that the strong cultural expectation of self-sacrifice by women may have a literally deadly impact on the likelihood that women will be provided with physician-assisted suicide in order to cease being a "burden." "A woman requesting assisted suicide or euthanasia is likely to be seen as doing the 'right' thing. . . . She may even be valorized for appropriate feminine self-sacrificing behavior, such as sparing her family further burden or the sight of an unaesthetic deterioration. Thus she may be subtly encouraged to seek death" (1996, 306). If Wolf is right, the inculcation of a duty to die could possibly contribute to an increase in women's tendency to seek physician-assisted suicide and an increase in the likelihood that it would be offered and granted. This is an empirical issue, but the potential is troubling.

13. Hardwig's views on the unlikelihood of changing one's life in old age echo those of Callahan (1987, 67): "Many people, sadly, fail to have all the opportunities they might have: they may never have found love, may not have had the income to travel, may not have gained much knowledge through lack of education, and so on. More old age is not likely to make up for those deficiencies, however; the pattern of such lives, including their deprivations, is unlikely to change significantly in old age, much less open radically new opportunities hitherto missing."

14. But Hardwig (2000, 95) claims, without citing any evidence, that "there is really very little legal risk in physician-assisted suicide, especially if the family is in agreement."

15. Al Fell pointed out this connection to me.

16. I am reminded of a society imagined by Robert Heinlein in his science-fiction novel *Time Enough for Love*. In that society, "if a man is seventy-five years old there now, he becomes officially dead. His heirs inherit, he can't own property, his ration books are canceled—anybody can kill him just for the hell of it" (1973, 274). This imaginary society is, I suggest, engaging in generational cleansing.

17. Similarly, in a commentary on Hardwig's work, Callahan endorses the idea that deliberately choosing to die to avoid burdening others is "above and beyond the call of duty." At the same time, he advocates a "duty to accept a limitation of resources which will increase the risk of death, even significantly." Hence, he says, there is no duty to die, but there is a duty to run the risk of death by disease, rather than by one's own hand (2000, 140).

18. Beloff (1988, 7), writing on the situation in Great Britain, worries that

even if he were able to enter a "state-run geriatric institution," his wife would "still have to endure the anguish of having to watch [him] as [he] became progressively more helpless and debilitated." Hence Beloff believes that even socialized health care fails to alleviate the burden imposed by elderly ill relatives. Yet surely such care would constitute a better alternative for those who would otherwise have to be responsible for the provision of twenty-four-hour care or would have to watch their loved one deteriorate and die for lack of care.

19. Hardwig later states emphatically that he does not agree with these policy implications of the emphasis in the United States on individual responsibility. However, he adds that because these are the conditions that prevail, we must cope with them. Moreover, even if social-policy improvements were enacted, he thinks that a duty to die would still inevitably reemerge because of the ongoing successes of medicine in enabling human beings to live longer and because of the resulting increased likelihood that more people would spend longer periods of time with chronic illness, debility, and dementia (Hardwig 2000, 179–180).

20. Thank you to Alistair Macleod for helping me with this idea.

CHAPTER FOUR

1. I am grateful to David Ritter for reminding me of this quotation.

2. But see Parks's "Respect for Life, Respect for Women, and the Treatment of Spare Human Embryos" (1992) for a discussion of the ways in which the concept of respect has been used without genuine regard for the interests of women.

3. As a vegetarian I believe that the killing of nonhuman animals for food or for other products is in most cases unjustified. So I think that vegetarianism implies a commitment to greater longevity for animals that are otherwise used for these purposes. But I do not have the space here to defend this argument.

4. We could interpret apologists like Callahan and Hardwig as accepting the existence of a liberty right to life but denying the existence of a welfare right to life, especially after midlife.

5. Similarly, feminists Hilde Lindemann Nelson and James Lindemann Nelson explicitly call for gender-based distinctions in health-care interventions near the end of life, partly in order to compensate women for "the sexism that has trammeled their opportunities for self-development" (1996, 362).

6. Apologists such as Callahan and Battin seem to think that extending the

lives of elderly persons is justifiable only as a side effect of the generation of medical knowledge to help the young and middle-aged and to reduce premature death.

7. For example, Claude Jean-Nesmy (1991, 150) writes, "The renunciations of old age simplify, purify, permit one to rediscover not another youth, but something more valuable: the clarity and accessibility of childhood. . . . To see all, to learn to keep silent, not to multiply absolutes[,] . . . to draw from one's long experience a kind of benevolent and sympathetic indulgence, this seems to me [a] possible 'gift' of old age."

CHAPTER FIVE

1. Woody Allen is supposed to have said, "I don't want to achieve immortality in my work, I want to achieve it by not dying" (quoted in Pogrebin 1996, 300).

2. Nakae Chomin's physician gave him one and a half years to live. Chomin wrote: "Some of you may say that one year and a half is very short; I say it is an eternity. But if you wish to say it is short, then ten years is also short, and fifty years is short, and so, too, is one hundred years. If this life is limited in time and that after death is unlimited, then the limited compared to the unlimited period is not even short: it's nothing" (quoted in Enright 1983, 78).

3. Cf. Momeyer (1988, 35), who describes what he calls the paradox that neither dying nor indefinitely continuous living is a desirable state for human beings.

4. Sylvia Burkinshaw has suggested to me that one possible drawback of immortality here on earth would be that one would never find out what happens after death—whether, that is, there is life after death. But I am assuming that if eternal life before death is worthwhile, it would obviate any value to or interest in life after death. I also think that the prospect of life after death is even more implausible than eternal life before death.

5. Evidence from the demise of other species, as well as the application of the Copernican principle (that there is nothing special about our own location in time), suggests that the human species itself will have a finite existence (Gott 1999), and therefore no one human being could possibly be immortal. However, at least for the sake of argument, we need to entertain the possibility that human beings could evolve into another sort of entity, a possibility that I consider in Chapter 6. Millard Schumaker has suggested to me that the question of whether

immortality is humanly attainable is inevitably otiose because not only the world but also the galaxy and even the universe will not last forever. However, I'm not sure we know this to be true. Although our immediate astronomical neighborhood will likely change drastically over eons of time, it may be that the universe itself is eternal.

6. Many thanks to Sue Donaldson for making this point to me. I return to this theme in Chapter 6.

7. I also have to set aside epistemological questions about how one could know that the ostensible immortality-producing mechanism was what it was claimed to be.

8. This book was the inspiration for the science-fiction film *The Bicentennial Man.*

9. Karel Čapek's play *The Makropulos Secret*, which is discussed further below, canvasses both possibilities: immortality "for all humanity" and immortality for the few, "only the leaders, only productive, efficient men [*sic*], . . . [the] ten or twenty thousand men who are irreplaceable" (Čapek [1922] 1990, 170, 171).

10. "What if we think of a new concept of immortality? Need it even rule out death by disease? Maybe all that you (conceptually) want to rule out is death as the natural and inevitable result of aging" (Samantha Brennan, personal communication, 1999). My thanks to Samantha Brennan for helping me see this implication.

11. Compare the distinction at the cellular level between accidental cell death and cellular death through senescence (Clark 1996, 63).

12. I am grateful to Alistair Macleod for making this point.

13. In addition to these needs, Deborah Knight has pointed out to me the additional challenge of how to balance the needs of the immortals against the needs of the mortal population.

14. I owe this argument to Ted Worth. Will Kymlicka has suggested to me that because this argument is concerned with the individual rationality of immortality (rather than its effects on collective well-being), my original stipulation that immortality is potentially open to everyone is at this point no longer useful or relevant, for it is not in the interests of the individual that everyone could choose to be immortal. A particular individual would be better off if, for example, only she had the power to decide who got to be immortal. In this way she could ensure that her treasured friends and family members lived on with her forever, whereas her enemies, and anyone else who might curtail her plea-

sures as an immortal, did not. However, I am not convinced that this sort of power would genuinely further the individual's interests. Certainly it could make her the target of the wrath and vengeful impulses of everyone else. Moreover, knowing that she has that power, her associates would be likely to treat her differently than they would an ordinary mortal or even an immortal without the power to confer immortality on others. Could they be trusted? Would they be honest? Would they be pleased to be made immortal by someone else's fiat, regardless of their own wishes?

15. Thanks to Deborah Knight and Sylvia Burkinshaw for pointing this problem out.

16. Thanks to Jackie Davies for this suggestion.

17. I am grateful to Stella Carney for drawing this book to my attention.

18. In Čapek's original play, Elina is 337 when the play opens and took the elixir at the age of 16.

19. "But the threat of monotony in eternal activities could not be dealt with . . . by regarding immortal boredom as an unavoidable ache derived from standing ceaselessly at one's post. (This is one reason why I said that boredom in eternity would have to be *unthinkable*.) For the question would be unavoidable, in what campaign one was supposed to be serving, what one's ceaseless sentry-watch was for" (Williams 1975, 424, his emphasis).

20. Thank you to Sylvat Aziz for suggesting this approach.

21. I owe this example to Sue Donaldson.

22. I am grateful to Steve Leighton and Alistair Macleod for developing crucial parts of this argument.

23. The central character in Chapter 10 of Julian Barnes's *A History of the World in 10½ Chapters* (1989) becomes immortal in heaven and after many millennia starts to face the problem that there is nothing left that he wants to do. Because he gets whatever he wants in heaven, he contemplates dealing with his problem by "'wanting to be[come] someone who never gets tired of eternity'" (306). In the context of the story, such a desire seems to be an aspiration to achieve a state of deliberate intellectual impoverishment and mental impairment.

24. If we invoke science-fiction possibilities, the prospects grow even wider. For example, Will Kymlicka has suggested to me that if time travel were possible, it would afford an endless series of possibilities for new experiences. Sue Donaldson has suggested that another way around the problem of boredom would be to imagine a life of consciousness interspersed with long "timeouts," during

which one would rest and recover, and then one would reawake to a world different from the past and hence sufficiently stimulating as to obviate boredom. Cf. Heinlein 1973, 106.

25. Leslie Elliott has suggested the following argument to me. A person possessing a certain sort of moral vision might remain committed to doing good for people, and hence have a life purpose, even if all her other capacities for experience and enjoyment were completely exhausted. In other words, the moral ideal would make her life worthwhile regardless of the boredom she might otherwise feel. In cases such as this, even boredom would fail to make life not worth living. I don't know whether such a state is possible. But if it were, it would help to show that Williams's pessimism about the horror of eternal life is mistaken.

CHAPTER SIX

1. In early 2000 a collection of jokes was circulating on the Internet with the title "Can't Believe They Said This." One item in the collection claimed that in the 1994 Miss USA contest, Miss Alabama replied to the question "If you could live forever, would you and why?" as follows: "I would not live forever, because we should not live forever, because if we were supposed to live forever, then we would live forever, but we cannot live forever, which is why I would not live forever." Setting aside its possible theological assumptions, this response is not as confused as its placement in "Can't Believe They Said This" might suggest. Miss Alabama could be interpreted as arguing that the empirical evidence that human beings do not live forever supports the normative claim that, as human beings, we ought not to live forever. This claim is not so very different from Macquarrie's.

2. Or as Sylvia Burkinshaw put it to me, such a person would just get "sick of herself." In Barnes's *A History of the World in 10½ Chapters*, the central character is told that immortals eventually choose to die because they realize that "they're stuck with being themselves. Millennium after millennium of being themselves" (1989, 304).

3. According to Williams, for those seeking endless life, the only possible alternative to the fixity of character he alleges is necessary for the persistence of personal identity and to the resulting overpowering boredom would be reincarnation. Yet even reincarnation, in his view, if it did not necessarily fail the requirement of identity of character, would probably fail the requirement that "log-

ically disjoint lives could be an object of hope to one who did not want to die" (Williams 1975, 420). Kaufman agrees. He writes that theories of reincarnation remain "unsatisfying" because "without my experiencing another life as my life, it is hard to see why I should care one way or another" (1996, 307).

4. Indeed, Richard Posner suggests that because aging brings about large changes in an individual, it makes sense to think of him or her as becoming a different person. He says that we should think of the change as meaning that two persons "time-share" the same identity (1995, 86ff.).

5. Sue Donaldson has pointed out that a reliance on personal transformation as a way to give content and meaning to an immortal life has, potentially, a morally problematic implication: the possibility that endless personal transformations could eventually lead individuals to their "dark side." In the previous chapter, when I suggested that moral improvement offers an apparently limitless and challenging project, I also acknowledged that for individuals for whom the moral life held few or no attractions the goal of becoming a better person would be nugatory. But Donaldson (personal communication, 2000) anticipates a more sinister problem: "As I try out all the different ways of being me, and gradually exhaust the ways of being a relatively decent me, won't I be tempted to cross the line? To explore what evils and perversions I am capable of?" On the level of community, such a possibility would indeed be dangerous. On a personal level, to a decent person trying to live by his or her moral standards, such a prospect would be horrifying—though by the very nature of the hypothesis it might cease to be so and might even become attractive through eons of time. The only response I can make is that personal transformation is a matter of moral orientation, personal choice, and perhaps also some good fortune. I find nothing inevitable about a good person's "going bad," and I do not see evidence that morally good or morally neutral life projects are inherently exhaustible in such a way that one must necessarily choose the bad in order to avoid terminal boredom or because all other possible transformations have already been experienced. This is not to say that exploring one's "dark side" would not be possible, or even likely, for some individuals. I just do not see it as an irresistible concomitant of immortality. As I argued in Chapter 5, the commitment to integrity, to moral growth and understanding, could provide a project sufficiently open-ended as to obviate any serious temptation toward evil doing as a life's project.

6. I owe this argument to Sue Donaldson.

7. This condition would be comparable to Donnelly's explication of the state of heavenly immortality, in which, as noted above, an individual could be thirty-three going on a thousand-plus years (1994, 316).

8. In a letter to William Strahan, Adam Smith described David Hume's thoughts on impending death: "I have done everything of consequence which I ever meant to do, and I could at no time expect to leave my relations and friends in a better situation than that in which I am now likely to leave them: I therefore have all reason to die contented." Hume was a fortunate man; yet still he imagined himself giving various excuses to Charon, god of the underworld, to try to delay his death a little longer (quoted in Enright 1983, 60).

9. The more that the replacement of body parts becomes possible, the less the immortal is vulnerable to sudden death. In Chapter 5 I stipulated that immortals would not be bullet-proof. They could still experience accidental death or death by murder. To the extent that otherwise fatally damaged body parts can be replaced, this stipulation is gradually obviated.

10. Interestingly, the robot hero in both *The Positronic Man* and its cinematic spin-off, *The Bicentennial Man*, rejects mechanized immortality: "I would rather die as a man than live eternally as a robot" (Asimov and Silverberg 1995, 284).

11. Parfit imagines that the teleporter is further developed so that one day a new Scanner records the individual's blueprint without destroying his original brain and body. But because of defects in the new Scanner, the original individual on earth dies of cardiac failure, while his duplicate on Mars is perfectly healthy and continues his life there (1984, 199ff.).

12. See Clark 1995 for other possible ways of sustaining the physical self for eternity.

13. I am grateful to Henry Laycock for this suggestion.

14. Religious persons who long for eternal life spent with God may not fully understand the implications of what they want. The religious believer might take refuge in stipulating that eternal life in heaven does not require a physical body and that because God himself is an infinite being, the immortal person could never tire of contemplation of God's greatness. However, it is difficult to attach much, if any, meaning to the idea of existence without physical embodiment or to understand what it would mean to be in a nonmaterial relationship with an infinite spirit. Hence, these stipulative answers are not helpful in explicating the meaning and value of an eternal life lived in heaven.

15. Perhaps, by speaking of two kinds of self, I am incorrectly implying that

these two different perspectives cannot be accommodated in one person. The project of raising children, to take just one example, appears to combine both career-self and seriatim-self perspectives. A conscientious parent prepares her child for independence and adulthood; so, in that respect, child rearing has a serious and important goal toward which the parent is aiming. However, many of the greatest pleasures of being a parent are seriatim pleasures: spending time with the child just for the sake of the relationship itself, without any sense that the interactions must be directed toward a goal or that the relationship must accomplish some purpose.

16. Perhaps, too, given what I have said about the potential for self-transformation, it would be possible for a person to choose to be a career self for one part of her life and a seriatim self for another part.

CHAPTER SEVEN

1. As Bell (1992, 86) emphasizes, the willingness of some old people to forego resources, experiences, or interventions in favor of giving them to younger people does not in any way justify the imposition of an age-related standard for allocating resources.

2. The descriptions in Nuland 1994 of painful, futile, debilitating misery at the end of life make it evident that such conditions are in no way worth prolonging.

3. See C. G. Prado and S. J. Taylor's nuanced discussion of criteria for the justification of assisted suicide (1999). But see also Tania Salem's skeptical perspective, which situates assisted suicide as simply another form of the medicalization of death (1999).

4. Thanks to Steve Leighton for pointing out this issue to me.

5. Just as we are about suicide. We do not encourage suicide, and indeed we make every effort to prevent it and to revive individuals who attempt it.

6. Although I remain skeptical about the costs and risks of genetic modifications, I have some sympathy for the argument by Nancy Jecker that genetic manipulation, if available, should be devoted not just to sustaining life itself and not just to maintaining age-relative functioning. She proposes that because people usually experience declines in age-relative functioning, at least as it normally is, we should consider the possibility of actively improving that functioning (1989, 668). I discuss this proposal later in the chapter.

7. See Sherwin 1992, 223 ff., for a discussion of the ways in which gender, race, and socioeconomic status have influenced patients' medical care, including diagnosis and treatment, and the direction of medical research.

8. From their studies of centenarians, Perls and Silver learned the following:

> While women were healthier than men from their fifties through to their eighties, during the tenth lap [decade] there was a "gender cross-over." Now the remaining men, although significantly smaller in number, were much healthier than women, because all the unhealthy men had been culled out.
>
> Men who "get over the hump" are aging stars, gifted with a much lower risk of heart disease, dementia, cancer, or other chronic diseases. They reach extreme age because they effortlessly vault over the obstacles that force other men out of the longevity marathon. Women . . . do not need to age quite as well as men in order to live to 100. They can survive with some illnesses. But for men to remain in the longevity marathon, they have to be all-star aging athletes. (Perls and Silver 1999, 94)

9. Nonetheless, not all arguments in favor of increasing men's longevity are equally convincing. For example, Posner's main argument in favor of redirecting research away from women's diseases and toward men's diseases is that doing so would benefit women "because it would give elderly women a greater prospect of male companionship, something many of them greatly value" (1995, 277). This suggestion appears to presuppose that having a man in her life is what gives meaning to an elderly woman's existence and that without a man she would rather be dead.

10. Some evidence suggests that in Canada eliminating all aggressive treatments, hospice care, and advance directives for persons sixty-five and over would save only 1 percent of total national health-care costs (Gee 2000, 20).

11. Posner (1995, 295) argues not only that elderly people receiving social security payments have already contributed to social security throughout their lifetimes but also that they "paid in the form of school taxes for a large part of the taxpaying generation's human capital that in turn generates the tax revenues that defray the cost of social security retirement benefits."

12. For example, my grandmother, Hazel Irene Bayes, cared for both my grandfather and my mentally disabled uncle in their home right up until she had

a stroke at the age of eighty-six. At that point, my grandfather was ninety-one and my uncle fifty-nine.

13. In a real-world context, the impetus to direct health-care funding to the first parts of life might be exacerbated if, as I suggested in Chapter 6, people underwent transformations throughout their lives. The self that I am now might fail to anticipate the needs and aspirations of the self that I will be in old age. As Posner (1995, 266–267) remarks, "To allow the young to make life and death decisions for the old is to give one person, the younger self, undue control over a resource (a body) shared with another, the individual's older self. . . . The young self may scant his future self's interest in extending life not because the young self is short-sighted or lacks self-control but simply because it has different preferences." If so, there will be urgent reasons for young selves to develop a better awareness of the moral entitlements both of their own future old selves and of present-day old selves.

14. According to the U.S. Bureau of the Census (1999), whereas, in 1980, 8,200,000 persons over sixty-five had one to three years of college, and 8,600,000 had four or more years of college, by 1998 the comparable figures were 17,200,000 and 14,800,000.

15. Statistics from the U.S. Bureau of the Census (1999) indicate that elderly people are more active than many who are younger. To take just a few examples, while 24.3 percent of males eighteen to twenty-nine years old participate in regular sustained activity (defined as any activity that occurs five times or more per week and lasts for thirty minutes or more per occasion), 25.5 percent of males sixty-five to seventy-four participate in such activity. And whereas 10.8 percent of females aged eighteen to twenty-nine participate in regular vigorous activity (defined as rhythmic contraction of the large muscle groups performed at 50 percent or more of estimated age- and sex-specific maximum cardiorespiratory capacity three times per week or more for at least twenty minutes per occasion), 15.4 percent of women aged sixty-five to seventy-four participate in such activities.

16. If, as Malcolm Cowley suggests (1980, 37), elderly people are less avid consumers than young people because their wants are fewer, then elderly people are thereby contributing, at least indirectly, to the betterment of society. I'm grateful to Carlos Prado for giving me Cowley's book.

17. I tell a longer version of this story in my book *Thinking Like a Woman: Personal Life and Political Ideas* (Overall 2001, 28–31).

REFERENCES

Abraham, Carolyn.
    2000. "Cloned Cells Turn Back Aging Process." *Globe and Mail* (Toronto), 28 April, A1, A6.

Ackerman, Felicia.
    1999. Letter. *Lingua Franca* 9, no. 1 (February):7.

Anderson, Robert N.
    1999. "United States Life Tables, 1997." *National Vital Statistics Reports from the Centers for Disease Control and Prevention,* 47, no. 28 (December 13):1–37.

Ariès, Philippe.
    1974. *Western Attitudes toward Death: From the Middle Ages to the Present.* Translated by Patricia M. Ranum. Baltimore: Johns Hopkins University Press.

Aristotle.
    1941. "Nicomachean Ethics." Edited by Richard McKeon. In *The Basic Works of Aristotle.* New York: Random House.

    1984. "On Length and Shortness of Life." Translated by G.R.T. Ross. In *The Complete Works of Aristotle,* vol. 1, edited by Jonathan Barnes. Princeton, N.J.: Princeton University Press, pp. 740–744.

Asimov, Isaac, and Robert Silverberg.
    1995. *The Positronic Man.* New York: Bantam Books.

Babbitt, Natalie.
   1975. *Tuck Everlasting*. New York: Farrar, Straus & Giroux.
Barnes, Julian.
   1989. *A History of the World in 10½ Chapters*. New York: Vintage Books.
Bartlett, John.
   1968. *Bartlett's Familiar Quotations*. 14th ed. Boston: Little, Brown.
Battin, Margaret Pabst
   1987. "Age Rationing and the Just Distribution of Health Care: Is There a
      Duty to Die?" *Ethics* 97 (January):317–340.
Beauchesne, Eric.
   1999. "Canadians Living Longer and Better." *Kingston (Ontario) Whig-
      Standard*, 23 December, 12.
Bell, Nora Kizer.
   1992. "If Age Becomes a Standard for Rationing Health Care . . ." In *Femi-
      nist Perspectives in Medical Ethics*, edited by Helen Bequaert Holmes and
      Laura M. Purdy. Bloomington: Indiana University Press, pp. 82–90.
Beloff, John.
   1988. "Do We Have a Duty to Die?" *Euthanasia Review* 3 (spring/sum-
      mer):3–9.
Ben-Porath, Yoram.
   1991. "Economic Implications of Human Life Span Extension." In *Life Span
      Extension: Consequences and Open Questions*, edited by Frédéric C. Ludwig.
      New York: Springer, pp. 93–101.
Blasszauer, Bela.
   1995. "Institutional Care of the Elderly: Lessons From Hungary." In *A
      World Growing Old: The Coming Health Care Challenges*, edited by Daniel
      Callahan, Ruud H. J. ter Meulen, and Eva Topinková. Washington, D.C.:
      Georgetown University Press, pp. 127–136.
Brennan, Samantha.
   2001. "The Badness of Death, the Wrongness of Killing, and the Moral Im-
      portance of Autonomy."*Dialogue* 40 (fall):723–737.
Brueckner, Anthony, and John Martin Fischer.
   1998. "Being Born Earlier." *Australasian Journal of Philosophy* 76 (March):
      110–114.

Callahan, Daniel.

1987. *Setting Limits: Medical Goals in an Aging Society.* New York: Simon & Schuster.

1990. *What Kind of Life: The Limits of Medical Progress.* New York: Simon & Schuster.

1995. "Aging and the Life Cycle: A Moral Norm?" In *A World Growing Old: The Coming Health Care Challenges,* edited by Daniel Callahan, Ruud H. J. ter Meulen, and Eva Topinková. Washington, D.C.: Georgetown University Press, pp. 20–27.

1996. "Limiting Health Care for the Old." In *Ethical Issues in Death and Dying,* 2d ed., edited by Tom L. Beauchamp and Robert M. Veatch. Upper Saddle River, N.J.: Prentice-Hall, pp. 441–443.

1998. *False Hopes: Why America's Quest for Perfect Health Is a Recipe for Failure.* New York: Simon & Schuster.

1999. "Age, Sex, and Resource Allocation." In *Mother Time: Women, Aging, and Ethics,* edited by Margaret Urban Walker. Lanham, Md.: Rowman & Littlefield, pp. 189–199.

2000. "Our Burden upon Others: A Response to John Hardwig." In John Hardwig, with Nat Hentoff, Dan Callahan, Larry Churchill, Felicia Cohn, and Joanne Lynn, *Is There a Duty to Die? And Other Essays in Medical Ethics.* New York: Routledge, pp. 139–145.

Callahan, Daniel, Ruud H. J. ter Meulen, and Eva Topinková, eds.

1995. *A World Growing Old: The Coming Health Care Challenges.* Washington, D.C.: Georgetown University Press.

Canadian Council on Social Development.

1998. "The Cost of Raising Children, 1998." Retrieved January 16, 2001, from http://www.ccsd.ca/factsheets/fsrzch98.htm.

Čapek, Karel. [1922]

1990. "The Makropulos Secret." Translated by Yveta Synek Graff and Robert T. Jones. In *Toward the Radical Center: A Karel Čapek Reader,* edited by Peter Kussi. Highland Park, N.J.: Catbird Press, pp. 110–177.

Capron, Alexander Morgan.

1987. "The Right to Die: Progress and Peril." *Euthanasia Review* 2 (spring/ summer):41–59.

Clark, Stephen R. L.

1995. *How to Live Forever: Science Fiction and Philosophy.* London: Routledge.

Clark, William R.

1996. *Sex and the Origins of Death.* New York: Oxford University Press.

Cohn, Felicia, and Joanne Lynn.

2000. "A Duty to Care." In John Hardwig, with Nat Hentoff, Dan Callahan, Larry Churchill, Felicia Cohn, and Joanne Lynn, *Is There a Duty to Die? And Other Essays in Medical Ethics.* New York: Routledge, pp. 145–154.

Copper, Baba.

1988. *Over the Hill: Reflections on Ageism between Women.* Freedom, Calif.: Crossing Press.

Cowley, Malcolm.

1980. *The View from 80.* New York: Penguin Books.

Cyr, Marc D.

1998. "Dylan Thomas's 'Do Not Go Gentle into That Good Night': Through 'Lapis Lazuli' to *King Lear.*" *Papers on Language and Literature* 34 no. 2:207–217.

Daniels, Norman.

1996. "On Permitting Death in Order to Conserve Resources." In *Intending Death: The Ethics of Assisted Suicide and Euthanasia,* edited by Tom L. Beauchamp. Upper Saddle River, N.J.: Prentice-Hall, pp. 208–216.

Dixon, Kathleen Marie.

1994. "Oppressive Limits: Callahan's Foundation Myth." *Journal of Medicine and Philosophy* 19:613–637.

Donnelly, John.

1994. "Eschatological Enquiry." In *Language, Metaphysics, and Death,* 2d ed., edited by John Donnelly. New York: Fordham University Press, pp. 302–319.

Dychtwald, Ken, and Joe Flower.

1989. *Age Wave: The Challenges and Opportunities of an Aging North America.* Los Angeles: Tarcher.

Enright, D. J.

1983. *The Oxford Book of Death.* Oxford: Oxford University Press.

Feldman, Fred.

    1992. *Confrontations with the Reaper: A Philosophical Study of the Nature and Value of Death.* New York: Oxford University Press.

Flew, Antony.

    1967. "Immortality." *The Encyclopedia of Philosophy*, vol. 4, edited by Paul Edwards. New York: Macmillan, pp. 139–150.

Foss, Krista.

    1999. "Will to Live Ebbs and Flows: Study." *Globe and Mail* (Toronto), 3 September, A8.

Fox, Michael Allen.

    1999. *Deep Vegetarianism.* Philadelphia: Temple University Press.

Gee, Ellen M.

    2000. "Population and Politics: Voodoo Demography, Population Aging, and Canadian Social Policy." In *The Overselling of Population Aging: Apocalyptic Demography, Intergenerational Challenges, and Social Policy*, edited by Ellen M. Gee and Gloria M. Gutman. Toronto: Oxford University Press, pp. 5–25.

Gendron, Louise.

    1999. "Vivre jusqu'à 130 ans." *L'Actualité* (July):31–42.

Gillon, Raanan.

    1996. "Intending or Permitting Death in Order to Conserve Resources." In *Intending Death: The Ethics of Assisted Suicide and Euthanasia*, edited by Tom L. Beauchamp. Upper Saddle River, N.J.: Prentice-Hall, pp. 199–207.

Gott, J. Richard, III.

    1999. "The Copernican Principle and Human Survivability." In *Human Survivability in the 21st Century.* Transactions of the Royal Society of Canada, ser. 6, vol. 9. Toronto: University of Toronto Press, pp. 131–147.

Gruman, Gerald J.

    1977. *A History of Ideas about the Prolongation of Life: The Evolution of Prolongevity Theses to 1800.* Reprint of vol. 56, pt. 9, of the *Transactions of the American Philosophical Society*, 1966. New York: Arno Press.

Gullette, Margaret Morganroth.

    1997a. *Declining to Decline: Cultural Combat and the Politics of the Midlife.* Charlottesville: University Press of Virginia.

1997b. "Menopause as Magic Marker: Discursive Consolidation in the United States and Strategies for Cultural Combat." In *Reinterpreting Menopause: Cultural and Philosophical Issues*, edited by Paul Komesaroff, Philipa Rothfield, and Jeanne Daly. New York: Routledge, pp. 176–199.

Hall, Carl.

1999. "Fabled Fountain of Youth Firming Up." *Globe and Mail* (Toronto), 9 January, D8.

Hanson, Mark J.

1995. "How We Care for the Elderly." In *A World Growing Old: The Coming Health Care Challenges*, edited by Daniel Callahan, Ruud H. J. ter Meulen, and Eva Topinková. Washington, D.C.: Georgetown University Press, pp. 1–8.

Hardwig, John.

1997a. "Is There a Duty to Die?" *Hastings Center Report* 27 no. 2:34–42.

1997b. Letter. *Hastings Center Report* 27 no. 6:6–7.

Hardwig, John, with Nat Hentoff, Dan Callahan, Larry Churchill, Felicia Cohn, and Joanne Lynn.

2000. *Is There a Duty to Die? And Other Essays in Medical Ethics*. New York: Routledge.

Harris, George W.

1997. *Dignity and Vulnerability: Strength and Quality of Character*. Berkeley: University of California Press.

Harris, John.

1996. "The Value of Life." In *Ethical Issues in Death and Dying*, 2d ed., edited by Tom L. Beauchamp and Robert M. Veatch. Upper Saddle River, N.J.: Prentice-Hall, pp. 435–440.

2000. "Intimations of Immortality." *Science* 288 (April 7):59.

Heilbrun, Carolyn G.

1997. *The Last Gift of Time: Life beyond Sixty*. New York: Dial Press.

Heinlein, Robert H.

1973. *Time Enough for Love: The Lives of Lazarus Long*. New York: Berkley.

Hentoff, Nat.

2000. "Duty to Die?" In John Hardwig, with Nat Hentoff, Dan Callahan,

Larry Churchill, Felicia Cohn, and Joanne Lynn, *Is There a Duty to Die? And Other Essays in Medical Ethics.* New York: Routledge, pp. 137–139.

Holstein, Martha.

1999. "Home Care, Women, and Aging: A Case Study of Injustice." In *Mother Time: Women, Aging, and Ethics*, edited by Margaret Urban Walker. Lanham, Md.: Rowman & Littlefield, pp. 227–244.

Holt, Jim.

1999. "Staying Alive." *Lingua Franca* 8, no. 9 (December/January):76.

Honderich, Ted, ed.

1995. *The Oxford Companion to Philosophy.* Oxford: Oxford University Press.

Jantzen, Grace.

1994. "Do We Need Immortality?" In *Language, Metaphysics, and Death*, 2d ed., edited by John Donnelly. New York: Fordham University Press, pp. 265–277.

Jean-Nesmy, Claude.

1991. "The Perspective of Senescence and Death: An Opportunity for Man to Mature." In *Life Span Extension: Consequences and Open Questions*, edited by Frédéric C. Ludwig. New York: Springer, pp. 146–153.

Jecker, Nancy S.

1989. "Towards a Theory of Age-Group Justice." *Journal of Medicine and Philosophy* 14: 655–676.

Kamm, F. M.

1993. *Morality, Mortality.* Vol. 1, *Death and Whom to Save from It.* New York: Oxford University Press.

Kaufman, Frederik.

1996. "Death and Deprivation: Or, Why Lucretius' Symmetry Argument Fails." *Australasian Journal of Philosophy* 74 no. 2:305–312.

Linehan, Elizabeth A.

1997. Letter. *Hastings Center Report* 27 no. 6:4–5.

Lock, Margaret.

1998. "Anomalous Women and Political Strategies for Aging Societies." In *The Politics of Women's Health: Exploring Agency and Autonomy*, coordinated by Susan Sherwin. Philadelphia: Temple University Press, pp. 178–204.

Lucretius.

 1997. *On the Nature of Things.* Translated by John Selby Watson. Amherst, N.Y.: Prometheus Books.

Macdonald, Barbara, with Cynthia Rich.

 1991. *Look Me in the Eye: Old Women, Aging and Ageism.* Expanded edition. Minneapolis: Spinsters Ink.

Macquarrie, John.

 1972. *Existentialism: An Introduction, Guide and Assessment.* London: Penguin Books.

Maggio, Rosalie.

 1996. *The New Beacon Book of Quotations by Women.* Boston: Beacon Press.

Manton, Kenneth G., and Kenneth C. Land.

 2000. "Active Life Expectancy Estimates for the U.S. Elderly Population: A Multidimensional Continuous-Mixture Model of Functional Change Applied to Completed Cohorts, 1982–1996." *Demography* 37, no. 3 (August):253–265.

Martin, Raymond.

 1994. "Survival of Bodily Death: A Question of Values." In *Language, Metaphysics, and Death,* 2d ed., edited by John Donnelly. New York: Fordham University Press, pp. 344–366.

Martin-Matthews, Anne.

 2000. "Intergenerational Caregiving: How Apocalyptic and Dominant Demographies Frame the Questions and Shape the Answers." In *The Overselling of Population Aging: Apocalyptic Demography, Intergenerational Challenges, and Social Policy,* edited by Ellen M. Gee and Gloria M. Gutman. Toronto: Oxford University Press, pp. 64–79.

Marvell, Andrew.

 1964. "To His Coy Mistress." In *An Anthology of Verse,* edited by Roberta A. Charlesworth and Dennis Lee. Toronto: Oxford University Press, pp. 243–244.

McDaniel, Susan A.

 2000. "What Did You Ever Do for Me? Intergenerational Linkages in a Restructuring Canada." In *The Overselling of Population Aging: Apocalyptic Demography, Intergenerational Challenges, and Social Policy,* edited by Ellen M.

Gee and Gloria M. Gutman. Toronto: Oxford University Press, pp. 129–152.

McLaren, Arlene T.

    1982. "The Myth of Dependency." *Resources for Feminist Research/Documentation sur la recherche féministe* 11:213–214.

Mirowsky, John, and Catherine E. Ross.

    2000. "Socioeconomic Status and Subjective Life Expectancy." *Social Psychology Quarterly* 63 no. 2:133–151.

Momeyer, Richard W.

    1988. *Confronting Death*. Bloomington: Indiana University Press.

Moody, Harry R.

    1995. "The Meaning of Old Age: Scenarios for the Future." In *A World Growing Old: The Coming Health Care Challenges*, edited by Daniel Callahan, Ruud H. J. ter Meulen, and Eva Topinková. Washington, D.C.: Georgetown University Press, pp. 9–19.

Moore, Eric G., and Mark W. Rosenberg, with Donald McGuinness.

    1997. *Growing Old in Canada: Demographic and Geographic Perspectives*. Scarborough, Ontario: FTP Nelson.

Mothersill, Mary.

    1999. "Old Age." *Proceedings and Addresses of the American Philosophical Association* 73:9–23.

Nachman, Gerald.

    1999. "I'll Take Life, Thanks." *Globe and Mail* (Toronto), 16 July, A7.

Nagel, Thomas.

    1975. "Death." In *Moral Problems: A Collection of Philosophical Essays*, 2d ed., edited by James Rachels. New York: Harper & Row, pp. 401–409.

Nelson, Hilde Lindemann, and James Lindemann Nelson.

    1996. "Justice in the Allocation of Health Care Resources: A Feminist Account." In *Feminism and Bioethics: Beyond Reproduction*, edited by Susan M. Wolf. New York: Oxford University Press, pp. 351–370.

Nelson, James Lindemann.

    1996. "Measured Fairness, Situated Justice: Feminist Reflections on Health Care Rationing." *Kennedy Institute of Ethics Journal* 6 no. 1:53–68.

1999. "Death's Gender." In *Mother Time: Women, Aging, and Ethics*, edited by Margaret Urban Walker. Lanham, Md.: Rowman & Littlefield, pp. 113–129.

Nett, Emily M.
1982. "A Call for Feminist Correctives to Research on Elders." *Resources for Feminist Research/Documentation sur la recherche féministe* 11:225–226.

Newbold, K. Bruce.
1998. "Problems in Search of Solutions: Health and Canadian Aboriginals." *Journal of Community Health* 23, no. 1 (February):59–73.

Nielsen, Kai.
1994. "The Faces of Immortality." In *Language, Metaphysics, and Death*, 2d ed., edited by John Donnelly. New York: Fordham University Press, pp. 237–264.

Nolan, William F., and George Clayton Johnson.
1967. *Logan's Run*. New York: Dial Press.

Nozick, Robert.
1981. *Philosophical Explanations*. Cambridge, Mass.: Belknap Press.

Nuland, Sherwin B.
1994. *How We Die: Reflections on Life's Final Chapter*. New York: Knopf.

Nussbaum, Martha.
1994. *The Therapy of Desire*. Princeton, N.J.: Princeton University Press.

Overall, Christine.
2001. *Thinking Like a Woman: Personal Life and Political Ideas*. Toronto: Sumach Press.

Parfit, Derek.
1984. *Reasons and Persons*. Oxford: Clarendon Press.

Parker, Brant, and Johnny Hart.
1999. "The Wizard of Id." *Kingston (Ontario) Whig-Standard*, 8 January.

Parks, Jennifer A.
1992. "Respect for Life, Respect for Women, and the Treatment of Spare Human Embryos." Master's thesis, Department of Philosophy, Queen's University, Kingston, Ontario.

1999. "On the Use of IVF by Post-Menopausal Women." *Hypatia: A Journal of Feminist Philosophy* 14 no. 1:77–96.

2000. "Why Gender Matters to the Euthanasia Debate: On Decisional Capacity and the Rejection of Women's Death Requests." *Hastings Center Report* 30 no. 1:30–36.

Pearson, Ian.
2000. "The Future of Death." Retrieved March 15, 2002, from http://www
.groupbt.com/innovation%20and%20technology/old/Insights/Ian%20
Pearson/d/Death.htm.

Pence, Gregory E.
2001. "Setting a Common, Careful Policy for Bioethics." *Chronicle of Higher Education* 47, no. 18 (January 12):B20.

Penelhum, Terence.
1982. "Survival and Identity: Some Recent Discussions." In *Analytical Philosophy of Religion in Canada*, edited by Mostafa Faghfoury. Ottawa: University of Ottawa Press, pp. 35–53.

Perls, Thomas T., and Margery Hutter Silver.
1999. *Living to 100: Lessons in Living to Your Maximum Potential at Any Age.* New York: Basic Books.

Perrett, Roy W.
1986. "Regarding Immortality." *Religious Studies* 22:219–233.

The Philosopher's Index.
1940–2001. Computerized database.

Pogrebin, Letty Cottin.
1996. *Getting Over Getting Older: An Intimate Journey.* New York: Berkley.

Posner, Richard A.
1995. *Aging and Old Age.* Chicago: University of Chicago Press.

Post, Stephen G.
1990. "Women and Elderly Parents: Moral Controversy in an Aging Society." *Hypatia: A Journal of Feminist Philosophy* 5 no. 1:83–89.

Prado, C. G., ed.
2000. *Assisted Suicide: Canadian Perspectives.* Ottawa: University of Ottawa Press.

Prado, C. G., and S. J. Taylor.
1999. *Assisted Suicide: Theory and Practice in Effective Death.* Amherst, N.Y.: Prometheus Books.

Priest, Lisa.

    2000. "The Rich Get More Special Medicine." *Globe and Mail* (Toronto), 25 April, A1, A4.

Raymond, Diane.

    1999. "'Fatal Practices': A Feminist Analysis of Physician-Assisted Suicide and Euthanasia." *Hypatia: A Journal of Feminist Philosophy* 14 no. 2:1–25.

Robinson, Spider.

    2000. "When We Will Be Like Gods." *Globe and Mail* (Toronto), 1 January, M9.

Rorty, Amélie Oksenberg.

    1994. "Fearing Death." In *Language, Metaphysics, and Death*, 2d ed., edited by John Donnelly. New York: Fordham University Press, pp. 102–116.

Rosenberg, Jay F.

    1983. *Thinking Clearly about Death*. Englewood Cliffs, N.J.: Prentice-Hall.

Rosenthal, Carolyn J.

    2000. "Aging Families: Have Current Changes and Challenges Been 'Oversold'?" In *The Overselling of Population Aging: Apocalyptic Demography, Intergenerational Challenges, and Social Policy*, edited by Ellen M. Gee and Gloria M. Gutman. Toronto: Oxford University Press, pp. 45–63.

Ross, Valerie.

    1998. "We Don't Wanna Grow Up." *Globe and Mail* (Toronto), 31 October, C1, C8.

Ruddick, Sara.

    1999. "Virtues and Age." In *Mother Time: Women, Aging, and Ethics*, edited by Margaret Urban Walker. Lanham, Md.: Rowman & Littlefield, pp. 45–60.

Salem, Tania.

    1999. "Physician-Assisted Suicide: Promoting Autonomy—or Medicalizing Suicide?" *Hastings Center Report* 29 no. 3: 30–36.

Sherwin, Susan.

    1992. *No Longer Patient: Feminist Ethics and Health Care*. Philadelphia: Temple University Press.

Silvers, Anita.

1999. "Aging Fairly: Feminist and Disability Perspectives on Intergenerational Justice." In *Mother Time: Women, Aging, and Ethics,* edited by Margaret Urban Walker. Lanham, Md.: Rowman & Littlefield, pp. 203–226.

Simpson, Jeffrey.

2000. "Touting 'Wellness' Is Laudable, but Not Enough." *Globe and Mail* (Toronto), 5 April, A17.

Singer, Peter.

1991. "Research into Aging: Should It Be Guided by the Interests of Present Individuals, Future Individuals, or the Species?" In *Life Span Extension: Consequences and Open Questions,* edited by Frédéric C. Ludwig. New York: Springer, pp. 132–145.

Smith, David W. E.

1993. *Human Longevity.* New York: Oxford University Press.

Spark, Muriel.

1959. *Memento Mori.* Harmondsworth, England: Penguin Books.

Spayde, Jon.

1998. "Death Takes a Holiday." *Utne Reader,* July-August, 18–21.

Sprott, Richard L.

1991. "Policy Implications and Ethical Dilemmas Posed by an Aging Population." In *Life Span Extension: Consequences and Open Questions,* edited by Frédéric C. Ludwig. New York: Springer, pp. 120–131.

Statistics Canada.

1991. "Health Expectancy in Canada." Retrieved February 7, 2001, from http://www.statcan.ca/english/Pgdb/People/Health/health38.htm.

1996. *Population 15 Years and Over by Sex, Age Groups, and Hours of Unpaid Housework, for Canada, Provinces, Territories and Census Metropolitan Areas, 1996 Census.* Ottawa: Government of Canada.

1997. *The Daily* (July 29). Retrieved April 3, 1999, from http://www.statcan.ca/Daily/English/970729/d970729.htm#ART3.

1998. "Participation Rates and Unemployment Rates by Age and Sex, Canada and Selected Countries." Retrieved January 11, 2001, from http://www.statcan.ca/english/Pgdb/People/Labour/labor23a.htm.

1999. *The Daily* (October 1). Retrieved January 31, 2001, from http://www
.statcan.ca/Daily/English/991001/d991001a.htm.

Steele, Hunter.
1976. "Could Body-Bound Immortality Be Liveable?" *Mind* 85:424–427.

ter Meulen, Ruud H. J.
1995. "Solidarity with the Elderly and the Allocation of Resources." In *A
World Growing Old: The Coming Health Care Challenges*, edited by Daniel
Callahan, Ruud H. J. ter Meulen, and Eva Topinková. Washington, D.C.:
Georgetown University Press, pp. 73–84.

ter Meulen, Ruud H. J., Eva Topinková, and Daniel Callahan.
1995. "What Do We Owe the Elderly? Allocating Social and Health Care
Resources." In *A World Growing Old: The Coming Health Care Challenges*,
edited by Daniel Callahan, Ruud H. J. ter Meulen, and Eva Topinková.
Washington, D.C.: Georgetown University Press, pp. 148–168.

Thomas, Dylan.
1952. "Do Not Go Gentle into That Good Night." *Collected Poems 1934–
1952*. London: Dent, p. 116.

U.S. Bureau of the Census.
1999. *Statistical Abstract of the United States: 1999.* 119th ed. No. 127: Expectation of Life at Birth, 1970 to 1997, and Projections, 1995 to 2010; no.
154: Deaths—Life Years Lost and Mortality Costs, by Age, Sex, and Cause:
1996; no. 184: Average Annual Expenditure per Consumer Unit for Health
Care: 1985 to 1997; no. 222: Days of Disability, by Type and Selected Characteristics: 1980 to 1996; no. 248: Percentage of Adults Engaging in
Leisure-Time Physical Activity: 1996; no. 650: Civilian Labor Force and
Participation Rates, with Projections: 1970–2006; no. 1421, Expectation
of Life at Birth, by Race and Sex: 1900 to 1997. Washington, D.C.

Van Tongeren, Paul.
1995. "Life Extension and the Meaning of Life." In *A World Growing Old:
The Coming Health Care Challenges*, edited by Daniel Callahan, Ruud H. J.
ter Meulen, and Eva Topinková. Washington, D.C.: Georgetown University Press, pp. 28–38.

Walker, Margaret Urban.
1999. "Getting Out of Line: Alternatives to Life as a Career." In *Mother*

Time: Women, Aging, and Ethics, edited by Margaret Urban Walker. Lanham, Md.: Rowman & Littlefield, pp. 97–111.

Wendell, Susan.
   1996.   *The Rejected Body: Feminist Philosophical Reflections on Disability.* New York: Routledge.

Wiggins, David.
   1967.   *Identity and Spatio-temporal Continuity.* Oxford: Blackwell.

Williams, Bernard.
   1975.   "The Makropulos Case: Reflections on the Tedium of Immortality." In *Moral Problems: A Collection of Philosophical Essays*, 2d ed., edited by James Rachels. New York: Harper & Row, pp. 410–428.

Wolf, Susan M.
   1996.   "Gender, Feminism, and Death: Physician-Assisted Suicide and Euthanasia." In *Feminism and Bioethics: Beyond Reproduction*, edited by Susan M. Wolf. New York: Oxford University Press, pp. 282–317.

Woods, John.
   1978.   *Engineered Death: Abortion, Suicide, Euthanasia and Senecide.* Ottawa: University of Ottawa Press.

World Health Organization.
   2000.   "WHO Issues New Healthy Life Expectancy Rankings." Press release (June 4).

Yu, Byung Pal.
   1999.   "Approaches to Anti-Aging Intervention: The Promises and the Uncertainties." *Mechanisms of Ageing and Development* 111:73–87.

INDEX

Ackerman, Felicia, 16

affirmative prolongevitism, 193–217; boosting life expectancy component of, 194, 195–200; compressing morbidity component of, 194, 198; emphasis on disadvantaged people component of, 194, 200–205; life-course approach component of, 194–195, 205–217; social-democratic approach to well-being required for, 215–217

afterlife: belief in, 32–33, 125, 183–184; immortality as negating, 230n4; lack of evidence of, 14, 222n9; and physical limitations of body, 235n14

age: appropriate, for interest in death and mortality, 6; of death, relationship between tragedy of death and, 48–49, 109, 110; of fifty, and view of death, 3; and health-care expenditures, 42, 55, 206–207; of immortals, 161–164, 235n7; and increased duty to die, 79, 82; of "last stages of life," 20; of maximum life span, 9–10; of "natural life span," 39, 43; of one hundred or more, 9, 12–13; prolongevitism not limited by, 205; relation-

ship between apologist beliefs and, 40–41; and right to life, 109–111; of sixty-five, 20–21; and value of year of life, 225n17. *See also* old age

ageism, 42, 43, 59, 187–188, 207

age rationing of health care: and duty to die, 85–90, 228n17; gender bias in, 112–113, 202; lack of justification for, 190, 236n1; and right to life, 111–113

aging, 20, 35–36, 42, 43, 188, 234n4

Allen, Woody, 230n1

animals: nonhuman, absence of boredom in, 146–147; prolonging life of, 104–106, 229n3

apologism, 16, 23–63; author's conclusion on, 62–63, 189–190; belief in, relationship between age and, 40–41; contemporary social context characterized by, 187–193; "death as natural" argument for, 30–37; duty to die as social application of, 64, 65; "fear of death" argument for, 23–29; "high social costs of prolonging life" argument for, 52–62; "present length of life is long enough" argument for, 37–51; quality of life as issue for, 44, 224n11

old age (continued)
ishing opportunity to change class in, 82, 228n13; extension of, 17, 18–19; honored meaning of, reduced by progress in extending life, 40, 45–46; medicine's concern with diseases of, 36–37; misery believed to accompany, 40, 41, 226n20; planning for, 77
old people. See elderly people
On the Nature of Things (Lucretius), 24
organ replacement, 167–169, 235nn9,10
Overall, Alexander Kenzie, 202–203
overpopulation, 55–56, 134–135, 139, 225n18

Parfit, Derek, 169, 170, 235n11
Parks, Jennifer, 226n2, 227n10
Pearson, Ian, 168
Perls, Thomas: centenarian study by, 9; on health of men over ninety, 237n8; on health of older people, 42; on medical treatment offered elderly patients, 224n10; on number of elderly people, 7; on people over sixty-five in labor force, 209; on reasons for men's lower life expectancy, 203
Perrett, Roy, 125–126, 183–184
The Philosopher's Index, 15
philosophy: death as viewed in, 1–3; longevity as focus in, 15–16
physical limitations: on experiences in life, 165–167, 235n8; as problem with immortality, 164–173; and religious belief in afterlife, 174, 235n14; replacement of organ and body parts to overcome, 167–169, 235nn9,10; replication to overcome, 169–171, 235n11
physician-assisted suicide. See assisted suicide
planning for old age, responsibility for, 77
Pogrebin, Letty Cottin, 76–77, 114, 150

The Positronic Man (Asimov and Silverberg), 129, 168, 235n10
Posner, Richard: on age of retirement in future, 209; on identity change with aging, 234n4; on reason for not attempting to increase men's longevity, 202; on reason for researching men's diseases, 237n9; on taxes paid by elderly, 237n11; warns against funding research of "lifestyle" illnesses, 204; on young people making decisions about health care for elderly people, 238n13
Post, Stephen, 80
progress: concept of, and value seen in living longer, 38; in extending life, as contributing to devaluation of old age, 40, 45–46
prolongevitism, 95–123; author's conclusion on, 122–123; "beneficial social consequences" argument for, 117–121; contemporary social context not supportive of, 187–193; defined, 16–17; and desire for immortality, 125–126, 230nn2,3; "intrinsic value of life" argument for, 98–106; "intrinsic value of longevity" argument for, 96–98; postponement vs. denial of death as goal of, 34; quality of life as issue for, 44; "right to life" argument for, 106–117. See also affirmative prolongevitism; extending human life

quality of life: apologists and prolongevists in agreement on, 44, 224n11; average, lowered by extending life, 44; importance of, with extended life span, 40–41; length of life vs., 22, 103–104; minimum conditions of, for prolonging life, 191–192; responsibility for protecting, of loved ones, 77
quietism. See apologism

Compositor: Integrated Composition Systems
Text: 10/15 Janson
Display: Janson
Printer and Binder: Sheridan Books, Inc.
Index: Jean Mann

RETURN TO: FONG

LC